“打开经济学之门”
原版注释基础读本

金融学基础——原理篇

FINANCE：THE BASICS

（注释版）

（英）埃里克·班克斯　著
刘清江　孙　偲　译注

经济科学出版社

图书在版编目（CIP）数据

金融学基础——原理篇（注释版）/（英）班克斯著；刘清江，孙偲译注 .—北京：经济科学出版社，2011. 12
（“打开经济学之门”原版注释基础读本）
ISBN 978 - 7 - 5141 - 0919 - 1

Ⅰ. ①金…　Ⅱ. ①班…②刘…③孙…　Ⅲ. ①金融学 - 英文
Ⅳ. ①F830

中国版本图书馆 CIP 数据核字（2011）第 158860 号

责任编辑：龚　勋　孙　偲
责任校对：刘　昕
版式设计：代小卫
技术编辑：王世伟

金融学基础——原理篇
（注释版）
（英）埃里克·班克斯　著
刘清江　孙　偲　译注
经济科学出版社出版、发行　新华书店经销
社址：北京市海淀区阜成路甲 28 号　邮编：100142
总编部电话：88191217　发行部电话：88191540
网址：www. esp. com. cn
电子邮件：esp@ esp. com. cn
北京中科印刷有限公司印装
787 × 1092　16 开　17.75 印张　310000 字
2011 年 12 月第 1 版　2011 年 12 月第 1 次印刷
ISBN 978 - 7 - 5141 - 0919 - 1　定价：32.00 元

策划人语

《“打开经济学之门”原版注释基础读本》系列丛书是经济科学出版社适应新形势下高校双语教学需求的精心策划之作。

秉承经济科学出版社“繁荣经济科学，宣传服务财政”的办社宗旨，丛书的策划者从中国读者的英文阅读实际水平出发，从海量的国外教材和教辅书中挑选了广义经济学的八本入门读本，内容涵盖经济学、管理学、金融学、营销学等门类，编写体例分为原理篇、概念篇和人物篇三大类，原理篇旨在介绍该学科最基础的理论框架；概念篇则一一介绍该学科最核心的概念；同时，丛书的另外一大创新是：还尝试着加入了人物篇，例如，《管理学基础——人物篇》介绍了自文艺复兴时期以来的50位著名的管理学大师的生平和思想。丛书力图通过原理、概念、人物的多角度、多层面呈现，为初涉经济学领域的青年学子和所有非经济学专业的读者们立体地勾画出一副完整的学术图景，而且是原汁原味的呈现。

《“打开经济学之门”原版注释基础读本》系列丛书被设计成开放式结构：我们将根据读者的反馈逐渐地出版更多的切合中国读者需求的好作品。丛书知识性和趣味性并重，英文通俗易懂，适合大学本科低年级学生、高职高专学生阅读。

丛书的初衷是出版中文翻译版本，然而在漫长的试译、翻译、校译过程中，一方面是深感语言传达的艰难，另一方面是考虑到时至21世纪，中国读者的英文阅读水平早已经超越了出版者的预期，读者对译文标准性的挑剔也成为出版者的新高度，从而逐渐萌发了出版注释版的想法：为读者提供全英文的读本，只加上少量的中文注解。通过与国外出版者艰难的谈判，最终成功地说服了外方，获得了在中国出版英文注释版的独家授权。为此，我们付出了超出预期好几倍的辛劳。

然而，这仅仅只是开始，读者的接受和喜欢才是我们最终的目标。希望读者喜欢我们的创意，为我们提供更多的创意！

2011 年 11 月

目　录

致谢 …… 1

第一部分
概念和方法 …… 1
金融世界 …… 3
财务报表 …… 23
财务概念及方法 …… 52

第二部分
工具和交易 …… 83
普通股和优先股 …… 85
贷款和债券 …… 112
投资基金 …… 145
衍生品与保险 …… 167
公司理财 …… 203

第三部分
参与者与市场 …… 225
金融参与者 …… 227
全球金融市场 …… 248

参考文献 …… 267
主题词索引 …… 270

致　谢

Great thanks are due to Andrea Hartill, commissioning editor at Routledge, for her support and guidance on this project. David Avital, assistant editor, deserves gratitude for his assistance on many points related to the early preparation of the book. Thanks are also due to Marianne Bulman and the production and marketing teams at Routledge for their help in preparing and distributing the book. Several referees at Merrill Lynch, Barclays, and Citibank, who provided helpful comments during the preparation of this text, also deserve recognition.

Most of all my deepest thanks go-yet again-to Milena.

EB

第一部分

概念和方法

1

THE WORLD OF FINANCE

金融世界

CHAPTER OVERVIEW 本章概述

In this chapter we will consider the basic definitions and concepts of the financial world, the meaning and scope of finance, and how it impacts daily activities. We will then consider the goals of finance, which center on how a firm maximizes value, ensures proper liquidity and solvency, and manages risks. With this background in hand we will then discuss the financial process, a cycle based on financial reporting, planning, and decision-making, and consider how market factors can impact the cycle. We will conclude with a brief overview of the book, describing in general terms the concepts/tools, instruments/transactions, and markets/ participants discussed in subsequent chapters.

DEFINITION AND SCOPE OF FINANCE 金融的定义和范围

Finance is the study of concepts, applications, and systems that affect the value (or wealth) of individuals, companies, and countries over the short and long term. The study of finance is both qualitative and quantitative, and we shall consider both dimensions in this book. Once we understand the es-

金融是对短期和长期影响个人、公司和国家的价值(或财富)的概念、应用、程序和系统的研究。

sential elements of finance, we can identify the motivations and goals that drive specific actions and decisions.

THE WORLD OF FINANCE 金融世界

Finance affects the daily lives of people and organizations. Though financial dealings have existed for centuries, their presence and importance have become even more apparent in our modern era of technology, information, consumption, and investment. Indeed, the penetration of finance is so thorough that we needn't look far to see its impact: on any given day we are likely to be aware of economic growth and inflation estimates, stock market and interest rate quotes, oil price trends, credit and mortgage loan offers, corporate earnings announcements, and takeovers and bankruptcies. A financial transaction occurs every time we place savings into a deposit account or the stock market, or make a purchase on a credit card. A financial transaction also occurs when a company borrows money from its bankers or issues bonds to investors or acquires a competitor. And a financial transaction occurs when a government agency issues bonds to finance its budget requirements, sells state-owned assets to the private sector, or changes its interest rate policies. It's easy to imagine that, when each one of these individual transactions is multiplied by thousands or millions of similar transactions, asset prices and capital flows can change and affect the fortunes of individuals, companies, and countries.

While finance can obviously affect a whole range of participants-from countries to companies and individuals-we will focus our discussion on companies. The corporate focus is useful because companies drive much of the financial activity that impacts all other participants. For instance, companies issue stock and bonds, which individuals can purchase for their savings and investment plans. Similarly, companies generate earnings and create jobs, which together help boost a country's national output. The narrower corporate focus is also practical, as it makes the material easier to manage and focus.

THE GOALS OF FINANCE 金融目标

A company exists to produce goods and services, and doing so successfully leads to the creation of an enterprise with value. In fact, a company operating in a free market economy aims to maximize the value of its operation. Naturally, this is just one primary goal-we can easily imagine that a company may also try to achieve other goals, such as building market share, establishing competitive leadership, creating an international presence, developing brand name recognition, promoting employee/community support, and so forth. Ultimately, however, a company seeks to create a maximum level of enduring enterprise value. This, in turn, can be accomplished by maximizing profits, managing liquidity and solvency, and managing financial and operating risks.

MAXIMIZING PROFITS 利润最大化

Companies seek to maximize value (wealth) while adhering to certain social, legal, and regulatory constraints. When markets are left to their own devices-meaning government involvement is at an absolute minimum and consumers are free to choose what goods/services to buy-strong companies will expand and profit, while weaker ones will be relegated to a small market niche or even close down. How can a company become stronger and increase its wealth? The obvious answer is by increasing its profits: a company that makes more money is more valuable than one that makes less money, and if it can do so continuously, over a long period of time, it becomes stronger.

公司寻求在遵守某些社会法律和监管限制情况下的公司价值（财富）的最大化。

Let's consider a simple example to help frame the discussion. Assume that a hypothetical company, ABC Co. (which we shall revisit throughout the book), is in business to produce certain goods, which it sells to its customers. In order to produce these goods it has a staff of workers and owns a factory (which it depreciates, or reduces in value, on a regular basis as a result of normal "wear and tear"). The purchase price of the factory is paid by taking out a loan from a local bank. The rest of the company's assets (i. e. items that it owns) are kept in short-term bank deposits. The revenues earned by selling the goods are used to buy raw materials from abroad, repay the interest and principal on the loan, the salaries of the employees, the rent on the office space, and taxes to the government. The remaining balance, net income or net profit, is then reinvested in the business. This example raises a number of important questions about how the company operates and how it can maximize its profits. For instance, does the company maximize profits by:

- Buying raw materials from abroad rather than locally?
- Borrowing from the local bank, rather than issuing bonds or stock?
- Purchasing the factory instead of leasing it?
- Depreciating the factory on an accelerated basis rather than a straight-line basis?
- Renting the office space instead of buying it?
- Keeping its remaining assets in short-term bank deposits rather than long-term securities?
- Reinvesting net profits rather than paying them out to the owners?

The correct answers are not immediately apparent, mainly because we need to understand more about the company, its financial structure, its operating environment, and the competitive marketplace. And, of course, we need a proper suite of financial concepts and tools so we can evaluate the issues and alternatives; we shall consider these concepts and tools in subsequent chapters. The point to stress is that each one of these questions forms part of the financial decision-making process that every company must go through in managing its operations.

Let's now extend the example one step further, to illustrate that the scope of finance is very broad. Assume that the company wants to expand its operations and decides to buy a competing firm. To arrange the acquisition it borrows from its local bankers. Once the acquired company is fully integrated the firm invests in factories located around the world, which allows it to source raw materials in each local marketplace, produce goods in a local setting, and then sell them to the local consumer base. Any profits it earns are 50 percent reinvested in the local operations, while the remaining 50 percent is repatriated to the home office.

Once again, we ask whether ABC Co. maximizes profits by:

- Acquiring a competitor instead of growing through internal resources?
- Using loans instead of stock to buy the competitor?
- Making a series of long-term investments in local markets instead of concentrating production in the home market?
- Sourcing raw materials in each local market rather than arranging a single centralized purchase agreement for all markets?
- Retaining 50 percent of its local profits in each local operation and repatriating the other 50 percent to head office?

The correct answers are still uncertain because we again lack the necessary tools and information.

So how does a company actually create profits? Broadly speaking it can do so by investing, speculating, or restructuring. Let's consider each one.

Generating revenues and profits is accomplished primarily by investing in productive resources-plant and equipment, technology, intellectual property, human resources, and financial assets. We can define investing as the commitment of capital in a venture, project, asset, or security in order to create more value. Investment is often geared toward physical assets, like the purchase or construction of a factory, the development of a power plant, or the purchase or lease of a fleet of ships. Automobile manufacturers, airlines, energy companies, steel companies, and others regularly invest in such physical assets. In other cases investment is based on the purchase of securities, such as stocks and bonds, that are also designed to generate a return. This is an "indirect" form of investment in productive assets, as the company buying securities (perhaps for its investment or retirement benefits portfolio) is actually contributing its capital to the firm that has issued the security; that firm, in turn, is likely to be using the proceeds to invest in the hard assets and projects we have just mentioned. Some firms, like banks, insurance companies, and mutual funds/unit trusts, have a great deal of investments in securities.

Some firms try to make profits by speculating. Speculating, like investing, is a method of committing capital in order to generate a satisfactory return. Speculative activities are generally centered on a company's purchase or sale of securities, financial contracts, or select physical assets (commodities, real estate) rather than the direct purchase of productive assets used to create goods and services. In fact, specialized institutions like banks and investment funds are primarily involved in speculative activities. The intent in these situations is to balance risk and return: speculators are often willing to assume a great deal of risk if they believe the returns they can earn are adequate.

A firm can also create or expand profits by restructuring corporate operations. It may do so by altering its business through a corporate finance transaction such as a merger or acquisition, or the sale of a subsidiary no longer considered essential to the corporate process. It can also do so by restructuring its balance sheet. A company pursuing such strategies hopes to expand the revenue base, lower costs, and/or increase operating efficiencies-any, or all, of which can help generate profits.

MANAGING LIQUIDITY AND SOLVENCY
管理流动性和偿付能力

While a company may wish to maximize its profits and value, it must first be in sound financial condition. A company that has been weakened by bad decisions or market circumstances is interested primarily in surviving from month to month and is unlikely to be thinking about ways of expanding its earnings power and value. Accordingly, it must make sure that its foundation is strong. In financial terms this relates to two key areas: liquidity and solvency.

Liquidity is defined as a sufficiency of cash to pay bills and cover any surprises or emergencies. Liquidity management, a key aspect of short-term financial planning, deals with daily cash inflows and outflows. Firms that lack enough cash to cover their short-term outflows and those that rely on only a few sources of external funding, such as bank credit lines, are at a greater risk of losses if they encounter difficulties. Companies that keep a prudent amount of cash on hand and arrange external financing across a broad range of markets, instruments, investors/lenders, and maturities, stand a much better chance of weathering problems arising from an excess of unexpected payments or the loss of a particular funding source.

So, companies create liquidity by keeping some portion of assets in the form of cash or short-term securities (such as treasury bills) and establishing proper bank credit arrangements. If ABC Co. has a £10 million credit line with its bank and is presented with unexpected payments of £5 million, it can pay the charges using the credit line and continue on with its operations undisrupted. Naturally, it will have to repay the money it has borrowed to meet the emergency payment, but it will have more time to do so (perhaps up to several years). The main point is that ABC Co. has averted a cash crisis. Or, instead of using the bank facility ABC Co. may sell £5 million of short-term treasury bills that it holds in its portfolio expressly for emergencies. The objective is the same: averting a liquidity squeeze by arranging in advance the right mechanism to deal with the problem. Naturally, proper management of liquidity raises certain questions:

- What is the best type of liquidity credit facility for a company?
- Should liquidity be accessed by preserving more cash and short-term assets on the balance sheet (internal), arranging more bank credit lines (external), or both?
- If assets are to be used, is a discount to the value of those assets necessary in order to provide a better reflection of liquidation value?
- How much liquidity capacity is necessary?
- Do liquidity needs change during the season or economic cycle?
- How much enterprise value is lost by holding too much non-earning cash on the balance sheet?

The finance framework helps a company answer these questions and develop the right kind of program to ensure a liquidity crisis is avoided. While liquidity planning is an essential process for all companies, it is especially critical for small-and medium-sized companies that lack the resources and credit access that large firms enjoy.

偿付能力是指作为一个资本（或永久/半永久性基金）满足意外损失的充足程度。

Solvency is defined as a sufficiency of capital (or permanent/semi-permanent funds) to meet unexpected losses. Companies generally operate their businesses with a certain amount of equity capital and retained earnings (and certain classes of long-term debt) to protect against potentially large and unexpected losses that consume its resources. By preserving this buffer a company tries to ensure that it can remain a going concern, even under dire circumstances. For instance, if ABC Co.

has a capital base of £250 million that supports £1 billion of assets, and it generates loss of £150 million as a result of negative judgments on a lawsuit, it will deplete a portion of its capital base, i. e. the buffer falls from £250 million to £100 million. While this is clearly a dangerous situation and ABC Co. will need to rebuild its financial position as quickly as possible, it can still continue operating. If the company didn't have enough capital funds to absorb the loss it would be technically insolvent and have to file for bankruptcy. In order to manage solvency properly a company must address the following types of issues:

- How much of a capital buffer is needed to protect the firm under various scenarios?
- Should that buffer grow over time, with expansion of the balance sheet, or both?
- What is the best mix of capital?
- Do regulators demand a minimum level of capitalization?
- Can long-term debt be counted as part of the capital buffer?

Once again, the finance framework helps answer these questions in a manner that is rational and consistent.

MANAGING RISK 管理风险

Since finance is concerned with a series of fluctuating variables and dynamic decisions it is keenly focused on risk-which we define as the uncertainty or variability surrounding a future event. In fact, evaluating and managing risks are fundamental components of financial management. We will formalize our discussion of risk over the coming chapters, but note for now that in a risky world a company must weigh all of the costs and benefits arising from a short-term or long-term action designed to boost profits or value. If a firm absorbs too much risk it may suffer losses or financial distress, or even failure/bankruptcy. Conversely, if it takes too little risk a firm may miss the opportunity to create profits or accumulate market share. While tak-

评估和管理风险是财务管理的基本组成部分。

ing risk can help a company achieve its goals, at some point incremental risk-taking may not be sensible. The marginal benefit gained from each incremental risky project or investment may decline, to the point where risk and return are misbalanced.

Risk comes in many different forms, including operating risk, financial risk, legal risk, and environmental risk; each of these can be decomposed into even more granular classes. For instance, ABC Co., as a producer of goods, is exposed to operating risk, which is the risk of loss arising from the firm's inability to sell goods/ services or obtain raw material inputs, or from damage to its plant and equipment. The company is almost assuredly exposed to some degree of financial risk, which is the risk of loss coming from an adverse movement in financial markets/prices or the failure of a client/counterparty to perform on its contractual obligations. ABC Co. may also be exposed to legal risk, which is the risk of loss arising from litigation or other legal/documentary errors, and environmental risk, or the risk of loss arising from damage to the environment.

Risk can be managed by hedging, risk reduction, and risk diversification; some risks can also be mitigated by loss control, or pre-emptive behaviors that reduce the likelihood that perils will occur.

Hedging protects a company's risk exposures from adverse market movements, so that the likelihood of a loss is reduced or eliminated. For instance, assume that ABC Co. relies on natural gas to power the factory that makes its goods. As the price of natural gas rises, ABC Co.'s costs increase and its operating income declines; this assumes that the firm cannot pass on the price increase to its customers, which is probably a fair assumption. In order to protect its operating income, ABC Co. can hedge itself against rising natural gas prices by arranging a transaction that provides it with a gain, or income, as gas prices rise. The gain on the hedge can be used to offset the increased costs (which lower operating income). Conversely, if gas prices fall, ABC Co.'s costs decline and its operating income rises; this will be offset by losses on the hedge. A properly constructed hedge will therefore make ABC Co. indifferent to the level and direction of natural gas prices.

Risk can also be reduced through financial contracts such as insurance. Assume ABC Co. is exposed to losses if its factory is damaged. If fire destroys the factory, for example, the company will suffer a loss from both physical destruction of the plant and from interrupted business. In order to protect against this eventuality, it can purchase an insurance policy that provides a compensatory payment if fire damage occurs.

Before creating a risk management strategy ABC Co. must resolve various questions:

- How much risk should the company take in each category?
- Is this risk core or ancillary to the business?
- Is the company being properly compensated for taking risk?
- Should the risk be transferred, reduced or eliminated, or should it be preserved?
- Which mechanism should be used to transfer/reduce risk?
- How much does it cost the company to shift or eliminate particular classes of risk?

The definitive answers to these questions will again depend on a company and its operations, its comfort and experience with risk, and the nature of the markets/opportunities.

THE FINANCIAL PROCESS 财务流程

A company trying to maximize the value of its operations clearly faces many financial decisions. Financial decision-making depends on a process that standardizes the task and provides continuous feedback. The financial process can be viewed as a three-stage cycle that is driven by the financial goals a firm hopes to achieve. The process begins with a review of the company's financial position (financial reporting/analysis) and is followed by the development of short-and long-term plans (financial planning), which leads to the execution of certain actions (financial decisions). These decisions will yield results that affect the firm's financial position, allowing the cycle to begin anew. The process is thus continuous: a company operating in a dynamic environment must constantly evaluate its financial position and options in order to continue meeting its goals.

FINANCIAL REPORTING/ANALYSIS 财务报表/分析

财务报表/分析涉及公司财务状况的组成、结构及发展趋势。

Financial reporting/analysis relates to the composition, structure, and trend of a company's financial position, most often conveyed through three key financial statements that are prepared and distributed every quarter or year:

- Balance sheet: A point-in-time reflection of a company's assets, liabilities, and capital
- Income statement: A cumulative reflection of a company's revenues, expenses, and profits
- Cash flow statement: A cumulative reflection of the cash flowing into, and out of, a company.

These statements are supplemented by other information, including financial footnotes and detailed management discussion and analysis. All of this reporting/analysis demands established accounting rules, which inject uniformity into the process. Through the reporting mechanism internal and external stakeholders can determine how a firm, such as ABC Co., has performed over time (and versus the competition) and what its financial position is at any moment. We will review these key financial statements in more detail in Chapter 2.

FINANCIAL PLANNING 财务规划

Financial planning is the second phase of the financial

process. It helps define the actions that a firm needs to take over the short term and long term to meet its goals.

Some aspects of financial planning deal with an immediate time horizon, generally one week to one year. These issues center on the daily management and progress of corporate operations, such as:

- Working capital and liquidity management: Managing cash, short-term assets and liabilities
- Hedge management: Rebalancing financial/operating risks through the use of various types of instruments intended to protect against losses
- Funding management: Arranging financing through the loan or capital markets.

Other dimensions of financial planning are based on longer-term goals. Such strategic financial management is critical to the methodical expansion of corporate operations and enterprise value. Issues in this category relate to:

- Capital investment: Managing long-term investment projects, research and development, and capital expenditures
- Capital structure: Identifying the optimal blend of debt, equity, and off balance sheet funding
- Mergers and acquisitions: Creating expansion opportunities through corporate combinations or restructuring
- Tax planning: Optimizing operations to reduce the tax burden
- International operations: Managing operations in, and expanding into, offshore markets
- Dividend policy: Developing a proper methodology to pay dividends to investors
- Risk management: Creating a consistent, long-term, approach to the management of financial, operating, and legal risks.

While short-and long-term planning are essential to the continued success of any company, they can lead to different goals: plans (and subsequent decisions) that are based on the short term tend to focus on near-term profitability; those of a longer-term nature center on sustainable enterprise value creation over multiple reporting periods.

FINANCIAL DECISIONS 财务决率

A company can make decisions once its financial position is well understood and its tactical/strategic plans have been formulated. Decisions are made by using specific financial concepts and tools, such as the risk/return tradeoff, risk diversification, cost of capital, time value of money, net present value, and investment rules (all of which we will discuss in Chapter 3). Concepts and tools help a company objectively understand the impact of translating plans into actionable decisions.

The three dimensions of the financial process are thus part of a continuous cycle: a firm examines its financial position, develops short-term and long-term plans and makes decisions to put the plans into motion. The next set of financial statements will reflect some aspects of decisions that have been taken, and can be used as the basis for further short-term and long-term financial plans and decisions. Figure 1.1 summarizes this cycle. Naturally, a company following this process must make its short and long-term financial actions meaningful and must also be flexible enough to adapt to changing circumstances.

EXTERNAL AND INTERNAL FACTORS 外部和内部因素

External and internal forces impact the financial actions and activities of firms operating in a complex economic world. Every company is influenced, directly or indirectly, by macroeconomic factors, such as economic growth, inflation, interest

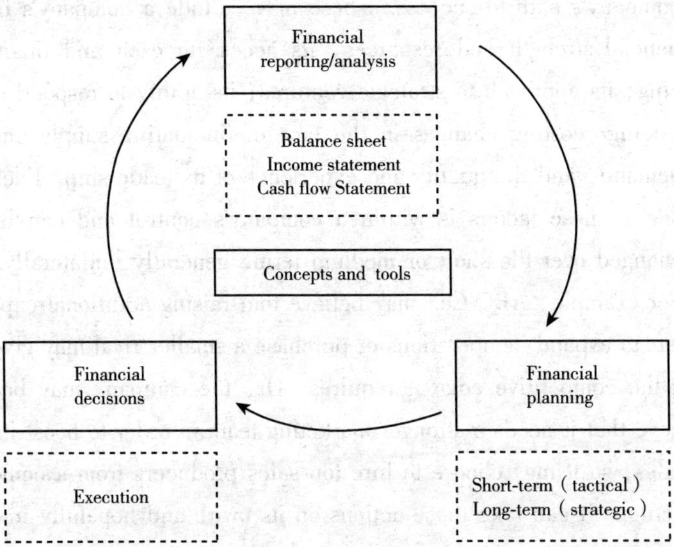

Figure 1. 1 The three-stage cycle of the financial process

rates, currency rates, commodity/input prices, consumer confidence, and debt levels. It may also be impacted by the state of the industry in which it operates, competitive pressures, availability of substitutes, and regulatory restrictions. A company must generally react or adapt to these external forces: since they are so powerful and pervasive, they are typically beyond the control or influence of any single company (or industry), and must therefore be viewed as factors that shape the base operating environment. Assume, for instance, that ABC Co. is operating in a macro environment characterized by healthy growth, strong consumer confidence, and robust demand; all other things being equal, ABC Co.'s ability to sell its products will be greater than if the economy were in recession. Similarly, if several new competitors have entered the same industry, ABC Co. may feel heightened pressures that force it to change its pricing or marketing tactics. It can react or adapt to, but not change, the competitive environment.

Internal forces are equally important in dictating a

company's path to success. These may include a company's financial strength and resources, its access to cash and financing, its approach to strategic ventures, its ability to respond to pricing/ costing changes in the face of fluctuating supply and demand, and the quality and experience of its leadership. Each one of these factors is within a company's control and can be changed over the short or medium term, generally unilaterally. For example, ABC Co. may believe that raising additional capital to expand its operations or purchase a smaller rival may give it the competitive edge it requires. Or, the company may believe that it needs a stronger marketing team in order to boost its sales, so it may choose to hire top sales producers from a competitor. It can take these actions on its own, and hopefully improve its fortunes.

THE COMPLETE FINANCIAL PICTURE 完整的财务描述

We've now introduced several elements of the financial world: definition/scope, goals, and process, along with the impact of internal/external forces. Once these are assembled, we develop a summary picture of the financial world.

To recapitulate, we know that finance is the study of how companies (and individuals and countries) can increase value or wealth. By using financial concepts and tools in a three-stage financial process, a company can achieve its financial goals. While value maximization is the ultimate goal for a firm operating in a free market economy, it is driven by maximization of profits, effective management of liquidity and solvency, and proper management of risks. But the financial process is dynamic and subject to the effects of internal and external factors. So, any process that is implemented to fulfill financial goals must take account of these factors and adapt to them through a continuous feedback process. This financial picture is summarized in Figure 1.2.

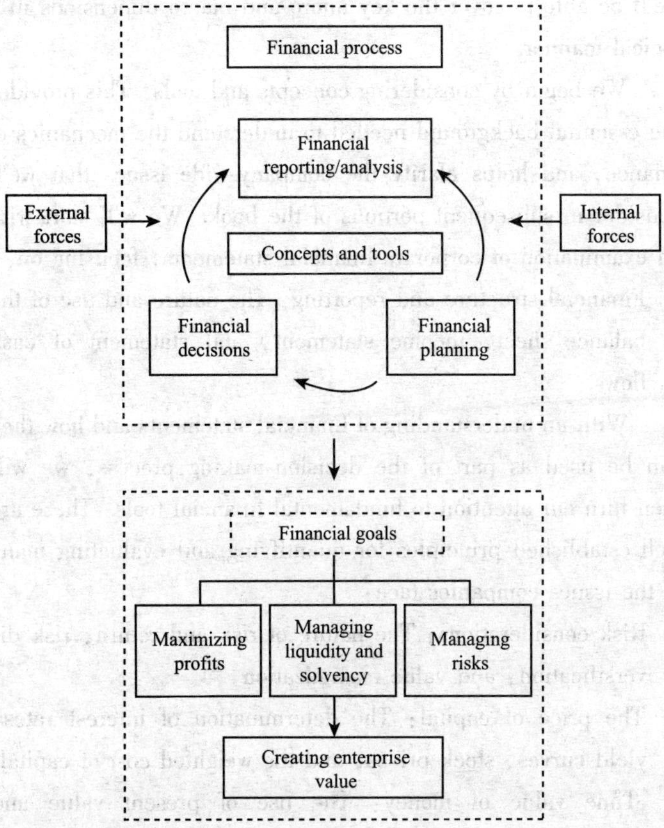

Figure 1.2 The complete financial picture

OUTLINE AND STRUCTURE OF THE BOOK 本书大纲和结构

Finance is clearly vital to the activities of companies, individuals and sovereign nations. The question is how to deal with the topic in a manner that is comprehensive-but also manageable, relevant, and interesting. To accomplish this goal we will approach the subject by focusing on three broad areas, or "pillars": concepts and tools, instruments and transactions, and participants and markets. By exploring finance in this way, we'll be able to cover the key micro and macro dimensions in a logical manner.

We begin by considering concepts and tools. This provides the essential background needed to understand the mechanics of finance, and helps clarify the company-wide issues that we'll consider in subsequent portions of the book. We will start with an examination of corporate financial statements, focusing on:

- Financial structure and reporting: The nature and use of the balance sheet, income statement, and statement of cash flows.

With an understanding of financial statements and how they can be used as part of the decision-making process, we will then turn our attention to fundamental financial tools. These are well established principles for quantifying and evaluating many of the issues companies face:

- Risk considerations: The nature of risk and return, risk diversification, and value maximization
- The price of capital: The determination of interest rates/yield curves, stock prices, and the weighted cost of capital
- Time value of money: The use of present value and future value
- Investment decisions: The use of net present value, internal rate of return, and decision rules.

Once we've assembled this financial "toolkit" we'll explore the nature of financial instruments and transactions that let companies achieve particular goals. Our intent with this second pillar is to demonstrate how specific assets, liabilities, off balance sheet contracts and restructuring transactions are used to advance the fortunes of companies and their stakeholders. Our discussion will focus on:

- Common and preferred stock: The nature and use of equity-related instruments
- Loans and bonds: The nature and use of debt-related instru-

ments

- Investment funds: The nature and use of investment mechanisms that incorporate multiple assets
- Derivatives and insurance: The nature of risk management and the use of instruments to hedge or assume risk
- Corporate finance: The nature and use of corporate restructuring transactions.

Concepts and Tools	Instruments and Transactions	Participants and Markets
Financial statement analysis and reporting	Common and preferred stock	Financial participants
Risk considerations	Loans and bonds	Global financial markets
The price of capital	Investment funds	
Time value of money	Derivatives and insurance	
Investment decisions	Corporate finance	

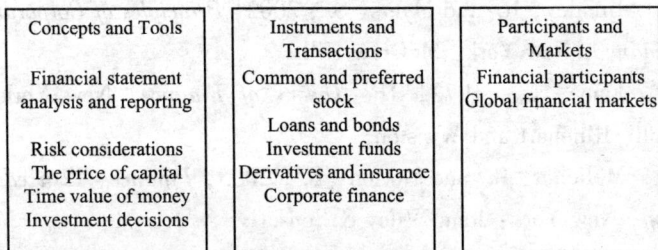

Figure 1.3 Three pillars of finance

We will then examine the third pillar of finance-the macro picture. Specifically, we will consider how key participants and markets support, and are supported by, activities at the micro level. We shall do this by describing:

- Financial participants: Intermediaries, end-users, and investors
- Global financial markets: Macro-structure of the markets, macro variables, monetary policy, and the nature of the twenty-first century marketplace.

The three pillars that comprise the world of finance are summarized in Figure 1.3.

摘要

研究参与者财富和价值的金融是商业世界中日常生活的关键组成部分。金融行为和交易广泛地存在于现代世界中，影响到个人、公司和整个国家。一家公司增加价值的顶级目标可以通过满足一系列重要的财务目标来实现，这其中就包括利润最大化、谨慎的流动性和偿付能力管理以及仔细的风险管理。标准的三阶段财务流程是基于财务报表、短期和长期财务规划和财务决策三阶段，这使得一家公司以一种系统的方式实现其目标。财务经理做出的任何决策必须考虑一系列的内部和外部市场力量；虽然公司一般需要对外部因素做出反应，但是能够更容易地影响内部因素。

FURTHER READING 延伸阅读

Brealey, R. and Myers, S., 2002, *Principles of Corporate Finance*, New York: McGraw Hill.

Fama, E., 1972, The *Theory of Finance*, New York: Holt, Rinehart and Winston.

Melicher, R. and Norton, E., 2005, *Finance*, 12*th edition*, New York: John Wiley & Sons.

Oxford University Press, 1998, *Dictionary of Finance and Banking*, 2*nd edition*, Oxford: Oxford University Press.

2

THE FINANCIAL STATEMENTS

财务报表

CHAPTER OVERVIEW 本章概述

A company attempting to maximize profits, maintain appropriate levels of liquidity and solvency, and prudently manage risks, must first understand the state and trend of its financial position. In this chapter we consider the process of standard financial reporting, analyze the structure and use of the three main financial statements (balance sheet, income statement, and statement of cash flows), and discuss how financial statement ratio analysis can be used to decipher the financial strengths and weaknesses of a firm. We will conclude by considering how financial statements are used in the decision-making process.

FINANCIAL REPORTING 财务报表

Financial reporting-the process by which a company prepares and presents its accounts-is a key element of the modern accounting framework. Modern accounting is, itself, built atop the dual entry system, meaning that every commercial transaction results in a debit (subtraction) and a credit (addition) to particular ledger accounts. For instance, when a company pur-

财务报告——由一家公司准备和呈现其账目的过程——是现代会计框架的一个关键因素。

chases a computer for cash it debits the "cash" account and credits the "computer equipment" account. Similarly, when it sells the computer to a third party it debits the "computer equipment" account and credits the "cash" account.

Financial reporting leads ultimately to the creation of financial statements that let managers, investors, and other stakeholders evaluate financial strength or weakness. Naturally, a degree of uniformity in approach and presentation must exist in order for statements to be useful. If no standards existed, then every company would simply do as it pleased, making it impossible to compare performance across companies-or, indeed, within a company, if it decided to change its standards every year.

Regulators and companies have adopted standards of financial reporting to ensure consistency. Though these can vary across some national systems, the essential process of financial reporting and presentation is the same: every company posts transactions that affect its daily operations to relevant ledger accounts according to pre-defined rules or guidelines. The major guidelines are set forth via Generally Accepted Accounting Principles (GAAP) and the International Financial Reporting Standards (IFRS); GAAP and IFRS provide guidance on how different transactions need to be treated from an accounting perspective, but provide some degree of leeway regarding interpretation. These accounts are then aggregated into unaudited trial statements over certain common reporting periods. An external auditor independently audits (examines) statements to ensure conformity to established standards. This gives those outside the company comfort that the financial picture being presented is true and accurate. The end goal is, of course, uniform production every quarter and year of the key financial statements we discuss in the sections below. Figure 2.1 summarizes the financial reporting process.

KEY FINANCIAL STATEMENTS 主要财务报表

We can capture the essence of a company's financial position through:

- The balance sheet: A uniform, "point-in-time" representation of assets, liabilities, and capital
- The income statement: A cumulative record of the firm's profits and losses
- The statement of cash flows: A cumulative record of the firm's cash inflows and outflows.

Let's consider each in greater detail.

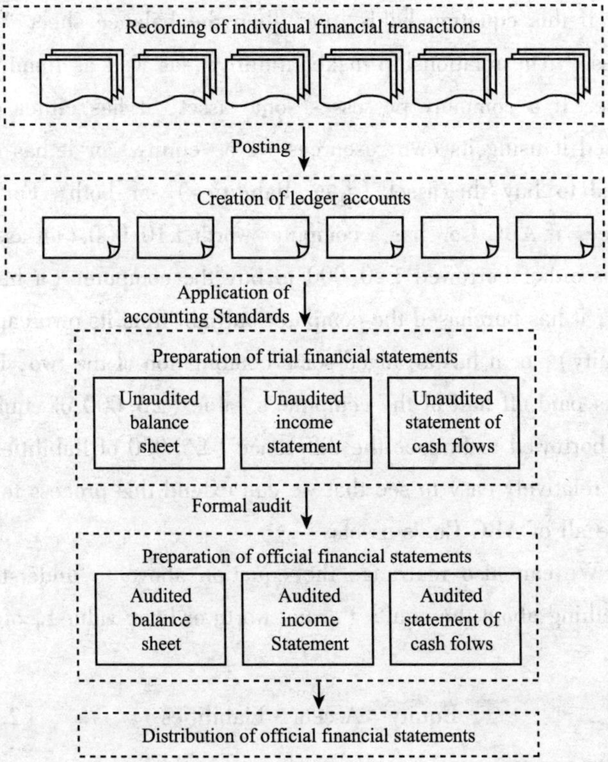

Figure 2.1 The financial reporting process

THE BALANCE SHEET 资产负债表

A company that is in business to produce goods or services requires assets (items of value that are legally owned by the company) that it funds through liabilities (amounts that are owed by the company to others) and some form of equity (amounts representing an ownership interest in the company); note that the terms equity, capital, and stock are synonymous. These three broad categories, presented in a statement known as the balance sheet, are linked together by an important accounting relationship, which says that:

$$\text{Assets} = \text{Liabilities} + \text{Equity} \qquad [2.1]$$

If this equation holds true, then the balance sheet "balances." The relationship makes intuitive, as well as financial, sense. If a company possesses some asset, it has either purchased it using its own resources (i. e. equity) or it has borrowed to buy the asset (i. e. liabilities) -or both. For instance, if ABC Co. has a computer worth £10, 000 (an asset) it has either borrowed £10, 000 to buy the computer (a liability), it has purchased the computer outright from its own capital (equity), or it has arranged some combination of the two, i. e. it has paid off half of the computer's value (£5, 000 of equity) and borrowed to finance the difference (£5, 000 of liabilities). It is relatively easy to see that we can extend this process to include all of ABC Co.'s assets.

We can also rearrange the equation above to understand something about the equity (or net worth or book value), of the firm:

$$\text{Equity} = \text{Assets} - \text{Liabilities} \qquad [2.2]$$

This tells us that the actual worth of the company is the difference between its assets and liabilities. Thus, if ABC Co.

has borrowed £5,000 to buy the £10,000 computer, its equity (or net worth) in the asset is equal to £5,000 (i.e. £10,000 £5,000). Again, we can extend this across all accounts to find the equity value of the firm. A critical point to note is that when assets are worth less than liabilities, the firm has "negative equity" and is considered insolvent. Thus, if the computer is really worth £2,000 and the company borrowed £5,000 to buy it, its equity is equal to—£3,000. Not surprisingly, financial managers are heavily focused on ensuring that the value of assets always exceeds the value of liabilities.

It's also worth pointing out that balance sheet items can be valued in historical terms or current market terms; when historical values are used (e.g. the original acquisition price of an asset), some accounts may be understated as a result of inflation pressures and changing replacement cost values.

Though the actual number of asset accounts in a large firm can number into the hundreds or thousands, we can condense them into a smaller group of key accounts:

- Cash and short-term securities: Accounts that form the company's asset-based liquidity. A company needs to keep some amount of cash and "equivalents" on hand to pay bills as they come due, or to meet unexpected payments. However, since cash doesn't generate much of a return, a company can't afford to tie up too much of its resources in such liquid accounts; it must strike a balance between sufficient cash and sufficient earnings. 现金和短期证券
- Accounts receivable: A form of credit extended by the company to its customers. For instance, customers receive goods/services from the company and may only pay the balance within 30 – 180 days; in other words, the company effectively makes short-term loans to its customers. The volume of receivables is a function of a company's business (sales volume) and its credit policies: a small base of business, and/or a more stringent credit policy will lead to a 应收账款

smaller amount of receivables, and vice-versa.

预付款

- Prepayments: Payments made by a company for goods/services to be received at a future time. For instance, a company may prepay all of its property and casualty insurance premiums, even though it receives the benefits of insurance coverage throughout the year.

存货

- Inventories: Accounts comprised of the items needed to manufacture physical goods that are ultimately sold to customers. Inventories are generally classified by their stage in the production process, including raw material, work-in-progress, and finished goods. Inventories have to be managed smoothly so that there is no disruption in the production process and enough finished goods are available for sale. In some cases it is beneficial for a company to build up its inventory of raw materials, particularly when it can do so at a good price. But accumulating too much inventory is not a good idea: a company with a great deal of unsold inventory must still finance it, which becomes a cost that detracts from profits.

房地产、工厂和设备

- Property, plant, and equipment (PP&E): All of the physical infrastructure a company needs to run its business, such as computers, office buildings, trucking fleets, assembly lines, and so forth. Since PP&E declines in value through normal "wear and tear" its value is regularly reduced through depreciation, a non-cash expense. Accumulated depreciation may be shown as a "contra account," or deduction, to the PP&E accounts.

无形资产

- Intangibles: All assets that cannot be physically seen or touched, but which add value to the firm. This includes items such as trademarks, patents, and intellectual property, as well as goodwill, which is excess value paid when acquiring another firm.

Let us note that cash, securities, receivables, prepayments, and inventories are regarded collectively as current assets and form one half of the working capital equation. We'll discuss working capital at several points later in the chapter.

Liability accounts generally include: 负债账户

- Accounts payable: A form of credit accepted by the company from its suppliers. For instance, the company may receive raw materials/services from its suppliers and can then pay its bill immediately and gain the benefit of a "cash" discount, or it can forego the discount and defer payment for 30 – 180 days; the latter is equivalent to accepting short-term loans from the suppliers. The level of payables is a function of a company's business (sales), its access to other forms of credit, and its overall creditworthiness. Thus, if a firm has a great deal of business it requires more raw material inventories, which it can finance through payables. If it has limited access to other forms of credit it may want to boost its payables, though its ability to do so will depend on the overall strength of its financial position. 应付账款
- Short-term debt: Credit extended to a company through short-term loans and securities (maturities are generally less than one year). 短期负债
- Deferred taxes and expenses: Accounts representing payments due from the company but which have been deferred until some future period. 递延税款和费用
- Medium-and long-term debt: Credit extended to a company for maturities ranging from 1 – 30 years; this may again be in the form of loans or securities. 中期和长期负债

We shall discuss some of these liability accounts in more detail in Chapter 5. Accounts payable and short-term debt comprise the general category of current liabilities, which forms the second half of the working capital equation. Total working capital is simply current assets less current liabilities and serves as a good proxy for firmwide liquidity, as we'll see below.

The capital accounts, which represent the residual balance remaining after all assets have been liquidated and all creditor 资本性账户

(liability) claims have been repaid, may include:

优先股

- Preferred stock: A form of dividend-paying ownership capital issued by the company to investors.

普通股

- Common stock: Another form of ownership capital issued by the company to investors. The common stock account may be divided into several sub-accounts including par value (the nominal amount of shares issued) and paid-in surplus (the difference between the market value of the amount raised and the par value). If a company repurchases its common stock from the market, it reduces the amount outstanding via the treasury stock contra-account.

留存收益

- Retained earnings: An account representing profits generated over time that are preserved within the company and reinvested in additional projects/investments.

We shall discuss capital instruments in greater depth in Chapter 4. The actual balance sheet mix of assets, liabilities, and capital is, of course, company-specific. Each individual firm has its own size and proportion of assets, liabilities, and capital, as we shall note in subsequent chapters.

In addition to balance sheet items, companies may also have certain "off balance sheet" accounts that represent contingencies or uncertainties that can ultimately impact the financial position. Items that are generally presented off balance sheet include undrawn/unfunded bank loans, financial guarantees, derivative contracts, and leases. However, gradual changes in accounting rules over the past few years have brought some aspects of this activity back on the balance sheet, leading to improved transparency.

The actual presentation of the balance sheet is often specific to a country or accounting regime. While most accounting systems feature the accounts listed above and adhere to the fundamental accounting equations we have noted, presentation can vary. Figures 2.2 and 2.3, for instance, show accounts in terms of US GAAP and UK GAAP.

Assets	Liabilities
Cash and securities	Accounts payable
Accounts receivable	Short-term debt
Prepayments	**Total current liabilities**
Inventories	Deferred taxes and payments
Total current assets	Medium-/long-tern debt
Property, Plant and equipment	**Total long-term liabilities**
(Accumulated depreciation)	
Intangibles	
Total fixed assets	
	Equity
	Preferred stock
	Common stock
	• par value
	• paid-in surplus
	(Treasury stock)
	Retained earnings
	Total equity

Figure 2.2 Sample US GAAP balance sheet

Property,plant and equipment
(Accumulated depreciation)
Intangibles
Long-term inverstments
Total fixed assets
Cash and securties
Accounts receivable
Prepayments
Inventories
Total current assets
Accounts payable
Short-term debt
Total current liabilities
Medium-and long-term debt
Net assets
Preferred stock
Common stock
(Treasury stock)
Retained earnings
Net capital

Figure 2.3 Sample UK GAAP balance sheet

In the US presentation current assets plus fixed assets must equal current liabilities plus long-term liabilities plus equity. In the UK presentation, fixed assets plus current assets less current liabilities less long-term liabilities yield net assets; this must then equal net capital.

To show how the accounts are constructed (and that the US and UK versions are, in fact, equivalent), let's introduce key accounts for ABC Co.. Assume that ABC Co., which manufacturers certain goods, has a factory worth £50 million (that has already been depreciated by 10 percent, or £5 million), accounts receivable of £10 million, accounts payable of £15 million, inventories of goods in various stages of completion valued at £20 million, cash on hand of £10 million, and medium-term loans of £40 million; over the past few years it has accumulated retained earnings of £150 million and has issued common stock of £150 million (comprised of £10 million of par value and £140 million of paid-in surplus).

ABC Co.'s balance sheet position under the US and UK versions is shown in Figures 2.4 and 2.5.

Assets

Cash	£100m
Accounts receivable	£100m
Inventories	£200m
Property,plant and equipment	£500m
(Accumulated depreciation)	(£50m)
Total assets	£850m

Liabilities

Accounts payable	£150m
Short-term loan	£100m
Medium-term loan	£300m
Total liabilities	£550m

Equity

Common stock	£150m
Retained earning	£150m
Total equity	£300m

Figure 2.4 ABC Co.'s US GAAP balance sheet

The presentation of the balance sheet created through the financial reporting process is, of course, important, as it provides

Property,plant and equipment	
(accumulated depreciation)	£500m
Total fixed assets	(£50m)
Cash	£450m
Accounts receivable	£100m
Invetories	£100m
Total current assets	£200m
Accounts payable	£400m
Short-term loan	£150m
Total current liabilities	£100m
Medium-term loan	£250m
Net assets	£300m
Common stock	£150m
Retained earnings	£150m
Net capital	£300m

Figure 2.5 ABC Co.'s UK GAAP balance sheet

a snapshot of the firm's position. But the balance sheet becomes even more useful when we examine how it evolves over time and how it compares with the balance sheets of competitors. We'll consider this trend/comparison analysis later in the chapter.

THE INCOME STATEMENT 收益表

The income statement, the second major statement we consider, records the revenues and expenses of the firm throughout the fiscal accounting period. Unlike the balance sheet, which reflects a company's financial position at a single point in time (e.g. each The financial statements quarter-or year-end), the income statement accumulates all of the revenue and expense information for the reporting period and is therefore cumulative-and not "point-in-time."

Though the income statement may again include a significant number of entries, we focus on the key items:

- Gross revenues, which is the total amount of goods/services sold by the company to its customers. This is often known as gross sales or turnover, and is considered the "top line" reflection of a company's ability to generate some volume of goods/ services at a particular price. 总收入

销售货物成本

- Cost of goods sold, which is the amount it costs the company to produce or convey the goods/services it sells; this generally includes raw materials and other inputs, as well as labor/ production costs.

毛利润

- Gross profit, which is the difference between the revenues earned and the cost involved in producing those revenues.
- Selling, general, and administrative expenses (SG&A), which represent the non-production costs the company incurs in creating its goods/services; this may include marketing, advertising, occupancy, employee health benefits, executive salaries, and so forth.

利息费用

- Interest expense, which is the amount the company pays its creditors in periodic interest. Interest payable relates to short- and long-term loans and bonds, as well as accounts payable.

利息收入

- Interest income, which is the amount the company earns in interest from its investments in short-or long-term securities.

其他收入/开支

- Other income/expenses, which includes other inflows and outflows that are unrelated to the firm's core business; if these are non-recurring and exceptional, they may be classified under a separate "extraordinary items" account.

经营（税前）收入

- Operating (or pre-tax) income, which is simply gross profit less SG&A, interest expense, and other income/expenses; this figure yields a taxable income equivalent

税收

- Taxes, which is the amount the firm has paid in income taxes

净收益

- Net income, which is the difference between pre-tax income and taxes paid. This is the "bottom line" result of a company's business, and reflects the true profitability of the operation. Managers and analysts often examine another income statement subtotal-earnings before interest and taxes (EBIT) -which is simply gross profit less SG&A expenses, before any interest or taxes are paid. EBIT is often used as a way of measuring a company's ability to absorb a given amount of debt.

We have again generalized this statement for simplicity-firms in different industries face somewhat different account entries that reflect the unique nature of their businesses. Similarly, different accounting regimes (e. g. US versus UK) feature slightly different entries and subtotals. Nevertheless, the structure noted above, and summarized in Figure 2. 6, depicts the logic behind income statement construction and is adaptable across industries and countries. As with the balance sheet, income statement trends and peer comparison are very important in helping interpret a company's true position.

Income Statement

Gross revenues
−Cost of goods sold
=Gross profit
−SG&A expenses
−Interest expense
+Interest income
+Other income
−Other expenses
=Operating income
−Income taxes
=Net income

Figure 2. 6 Sample income statement

Let's assume that ABC Co. has sold goods that generate revenues of £650 million and the costs associated with the production of these goods amount to £520 million. The company has also booked £50 million in SG&A expenses, £20 million in interest expenses, and £5 million in other expenses; these have been partly offset by £15 million in other income. Together, these items produce net income of £70 million. Based on a tax rate of 30 percent, ABC Co.'s net income for the year amounts to £49 million, as illustrated in Figure 2. 7

THE STATEMENT OF CASH FLOWS 现金流量表

The last of the major financial statements intended to con-

Income Statement

Gross revenues	£650m
–Cost of goods sold	£520m
=Gross profit	£130m
–SG&A expenses	£50m
–Interest expense	£20m
+Interest income	£15m
+Other income	£5m
=per–tax income	£70m
–Income taxes	£21m
=Net income	£49m

Figure 2. 7　ABC Co. 's income statement

现金流量表通过公司的财务结构和运作的状况。

vey a picture of a company's financial structure and operations is the statement of cash flows. This statement draws together items from the income statement and balance sheet in a uniform manner to reveal the nature of the firm's cash sources and uses, and its net cash position at the end of a reporting period. The basic cash flow statement is generally divided into three segments: operating cash flow, investing cash flow, and financing cash flow (though again, some subtle cross-border differences exist).

经营性现金流量

- Operating cash flow provides information on the actual cash impact (receipts and outflows) of the firm's normal operations. This section begins with the net income generated by the business, adds back depreciation (which is a non-cash operating expense) and then adjusts for changes in working capital (which, as noted above, includes cash and securities, receivables, and inventories, less payables and short-term debt). Depreciation is a particularly important item: though it's a non-cash expense, it produces cash flow by reducing taxable income. The net of the operating cash flow section provides information on a firm's ability to generate cash from its core business.

投资性现金流量

- Investing cash flow yields information on how the company uses its cash in the pursuit of productive ventures or investments. The investing cash flow section examines the purchase of other companies or PP&E (outflows of cash), the purchase of securities and other financial assets (outflow), the sale of existing subsidiaries or joint venture stakes (inflow), or the sale of securities (inflow). The net of this section provides an indication of whether a company is using its cash to expand into new or existing areas.

- Financing cash flow indicates how much external funding (if any) the firm requires in order to finance its operating and investing activities. The financing cash flow section focuses on new debt and stock issuance (which represent cash inflows), debt repayment (outflow), dividend payments (outflow), and treasury stock repurchases (outflow). The net of the financing cash flow section indicates whether the firm needs to access external financing to carry on its business activities.

筹资性现金流量

The statement of cash flows helps us understand the state of a company's health: it reveals whether sufficient cash, and access to cash, exists in order for the company to operate as a going concern, how that cash is being used, and whether external financing, such as we discuss in Chapters 4 and 5, is required. Importantly, the statement reflects cash balances at a specific point in time and whether the firm can meet its debt, financial/capital investment, and dividend obligations. This brings us back to our earlier point on liquidity management: it is essential for every company to maintain sufficient cash access from operating, investing, and financing sources to cover known obligations and any unexpected payments. Figure 2.8 summarizes the essential cash flow statement; Figure 2.9 provides the same information in slightly different form, focusing on sources of cash and uses of cash.

Let's again extend our example of ABC Co. by examining its statement of cash flows. We know from the income statement presented above that ABC Co.'s net income for the year amounted to £49 million. Let's assume that it had depreciation expen-

Statement of Cash Flows

Operating cash flow
Net income
+ Depreciation
− Increase in working capital
+ Decrease in working capital
= Net operating cash flow

Investing cast flow
Sale of securties
+ Sale of PP&E
− Purchase of securities
− Purchase of PP&E
= Net investing cash flow

Financing cash flow
Issuance of debt, stock
− Repayment of debt
− Repayment of stock
− Payment of dividends
= Net financing cash flow

=Net cash surplus/deficit

Figure 2. 8 Sample statement of cash flows

Sources of cash (inflows)
Net income
Depreciation
Medium-and long-term debt issuance
Common and preferred stock issuance
Decreases in assets (e.g., receivables, investments)
Increases in liabilities (e.g. payables, deferrals)

Uses of cash (outflows)
Net losses
Capital expenditures
Investment purchases
Medium-and long-term debt repayment
Common stock reurchase
Dividend payments
Increases in assets (e.g., receivables, inventory)
Decreases in liabilities (e.g. payables, deferrals)

Figure 2. 9 Common sources and uses of cash

ses of £10 million and decreased its payables by £15 million. From an investing perspective the company sold £25 million of securities from its portfolio and bought new plant and equipment valued at £50 million. Finally, from a financing perspective let's assume that ABC Co. repaid £10 million of debt and reissued another £50 million and that it paid £20 million in dividends to its investors. Based on these simple entries, the company's net cash position at the end of the year amounted to £69 million; the results are summarized in Figure 2. 10.

Statement of Cash Flows

Operating cash flow	
Net income	£49m
+ Depreciation	£10m
– Increase in working capital	
+ Decrease in working capital	£15m
= Net operating cash flow	**£74m**
Investing cast flow	
Sale of securities	£25m
+ Sale of PP&E	
– Purchase of securities	
– Purchase of PP&E	£50m
= Net investing cash flow	**–£25m**
Financing cash flow	
Issuance of debt, stock	£50m
– Repayment of debt	£10m
– Repayment of stock	
– Payment of dividends	£20m
= Net financing cash flow	**£20m**
=Net cash surplus/deficit	**£69m**

Figure 2. 10 ABC Co. 's statement of cash flows

Adding the £69 million cash surplus to the firm's existing cash holdings on the balance sheet reveals its net cash position at the end of the reporting period. Once again, examining ABC Co. 's cash performance over time is critical.

FINANCIAL RATIOS 财务比率

Financial ratios are used to supplement the analysis and decision-making process by allowing easy measurement and interpretation of important indicators within, and across, the key

财务比率能用来辅助分析和决策的过程，使之易于测量和解释重要的指标。

statements. Though we can compute and analyze a large number of ratios, it is helpful to focus on measures that a financial manager is most likely to be concerned about, including those related to profitability, liquidity, and solvency (leverage/capitalization).

PROFITABILITY RATIOS 盈利比率

Profitability ratios quantify how much money a firm makes based on its assets or capital, and how much of its revenues it is able to translate into net income.

资产收益率

- Return on assets describes how much profit the firm's asset base is able to produce. It is computed as:

$$\text{return on assets (ROA)} = \frac{\text{net income}}{\text{total assets}} \qquad [2.3]$$

The higher the ROA result, the more efficient the company is in using its assets to generate profits. In our example, ABC Co.'s ROA is equal to 5.76 percent (£49 million/£850 million). Naturally, in order to be meaningful this ratio needs to be compared against ABC Co.'s ROA over previous periods and against its competitors and industry peers. This will tell us whether the company is doing better or worse. For instance, if ABC Co.'s ROA over the previous two years amounts to 4.50 percent and 5.25 percent, then the measure suggests the firm's profitability is improving. However, if the average for companies in ABC Co.'s industry is 6.25 percent, then ABC Co. appears weaker and will have to focus on ways of improving its profit position to close the competitive gap.

权益收益率

- Return on equity measures how much profit the firm's equity base is able to produce. It is computed via:

$$\text{return on equity (ROE)} = \frac{\text{net income}}{\text{total equity}} \qquad [2.4]$$

In this example ABC Co.'s ROE is equal to 16.2 percent

(£49 million/£300 million). As with ROA, the higher the figure, the more effective the company is in using its equity base to generate profits. Once again, however, the result must be compared against prior periods and industry peers in order to be meaningful.

- Gross margin indicates how much of each dollar or pound of revenue (from sales of goods/services) remains after removing the costs of producing the goods/services, and is calculated as:

毛利润率

$$\text{gross margin} = \frac{\text{gross profit}}{\text{revenues}} \qquad [2.5]$$

In ABC Co.'s case the gross margin is 20 percent (£130 million/ £650 million), meaning that for every pound of sales it generates, 80 pence is used to cover the cost of producing the goods/services. It is easy to see that if the gross margin rose to 30 percent, only 70 pence of every pound would be used to cover production costs; accordingly, the result becomes more favorable as the margin increases. The same is true of all profit margin computations.

- Operating margin is similar to the gross margin computation, except that it focuses on profitability after deducting all expenses except taxes. It is computed as:

经营利润率

$$\text{operating margin} = \frac{\text{operating profit}}{\text{revenues}} \qquad [2.6]$$

ABC Co.'s operating margin amounts to 10.76 percent (£70 million/£650 million), meaning that costs of production and associated expenses consume more than 90 pence of each pound of sales.

- Net margin is again similar to the gross and operating margins, except that it is based on a firm's "bottom line" profitability-after all expenses, including income taxes, have been met. It is computed as:

净利润率

$$\text{net margin} = \frac{\text{net income}}{\text{revenues}} \qquad [2.7]$$

Not surprisingly, the higher the net margin, the more efficient the firm is in managing its total costs. In ABC Co.'s case its net margin is 7.54 percent (£49 million/£650 million). That is, for every £1 of sales, 7.5 pence flows to the bottom line for onward distribution to investors (as dividends) or for reinvestment (as retained earnings).

LIQUIDITY RATIOS 流动性比率

We have already noted the importance of liquidity: a sufficiency of cash, and access to cash, is essential to continuing prosperity. Accordingly, finance managers must pay keen attention to various liquidity ratios, most of them based on the working capital accounts. But we've also said that preserving liquidity involves a tradeoff: assets that are kept in liquid form do not earn the same return as those that are committed to medium-or long-term (i. e. less liquid) endeavors. Similarly, while short-term liabilities may be less expensive than long-term liabilities in most market scenarios, they must be managed more actively and can be withdrawn by providers (creditors) very easily. All liquidity measures, including the ones below, focus on the short-term (sub-12 month) horizon.

流动比率

- The current ratio is a version of the working capital measure that compares current assets to current liabilities. It is computed via:

$$\text{current ratio} = \frac{\text{current assets}}{\text{current liabilities}} \qquad [2.8]$$

ABC Co.'s current ratio is equal to 1.6. (£400 million/£250 million), meaning that the firm has £1.60 of current assets that can be liquidated to meet each £1 of short-term liabilities coming due. Though the trend of the current ratio over time and its relation to peer results are again important in interpreting the result, any ratio over 1 × is favorable as it means that liabilities coming due can be properly met by assets.

- The quick ratio is a more stringent version of the current ratio that focuses only on the most liquid of a firm's current asset accounts. This means that the true liquidity available to meet maturing liabilities is based on cash, securities, and receivables, while inventories, which may not be as readily saleable in an emergency, are excluded. The ratio is calculated as:

速动比率

$$\text{quick ratio} = \frac{\text{current assets} - \text{inventories}}{\text{current liabilities}} \qquad [2.9]$$

ABC Co.'s quick ratio of 0.80 × (£200 million/£250 million) reveals that it has 80 pence of cash, securities, and receivables available to cover accounts payable and short-term loans coming due. It is not unusual for firms to post quick ratios below 1.0 ×, but the closer the result is to 1.0 ×, the greater the liquidity buffer. Again, however, the liquidity/return tradeoff has to be weighed.

SOLVENCY (LEVERAGE/CAPITALIZATION) RATIOS 偿付能力（杠杆/资本化）比率

We've noted in the fundamental accounting equation that solvency is one of the most important factors companies must focus on when managing the financial position. Leverage, or the degree of debt (liabilities) contained within the capital structure, is a key measure of solvency. Its impact on a firm's operations can be measured through various ratios:

- Debt to equity, as the name suggests, compares the amount of debt to the amount of equity in the company's capital structure, and can be computed as:

权益负债率

$$\text{debt to equity} = \frac{\text{total debt}}{\text{total equity}} \qquad [2.10]$$

ABC Co.'s payables, short-term debt, and long-term debt lead to a ratio of 1.83 × (£550 million/£300 million). This means that ABC Co. has £1.83 of debt for every £1 of equity. As we shall discover in Chapter 5, debt is cheaper than equity and can help maximize corporate value, but too much debt can threaten financial stability-so, the costs/benefits of leverage have be considered during the financial planning process.

资产负债率

- Debt to assets is similar to the ratio immediately above, except that it focuses on the amount of debt being used to finance the entire asset base. It can be computed as:

$$\text{debt to assets} = \frac{\text{total debt}}{\text{total assets}} \qquad [2.11]$$

ABC Co.'s debt to assets ratio amounts to 0.647. (£550 million/ £850 million), meaning that nearly 2/3 of its asset base is funded through debt, with the remaining 1/3 coming from equity.

利息保障倍数

- Interest coverage is an income statement measure of a firm's ability to pay its interest expense. Any use of debt creates an obligation to pay periodic interest, meaning that a firm must have enough profit on hand to meet the expense. A common interest coverage ratio is:

$$\text{interest coverage} = \frac{\text{EBIT}}{\text{interest expense}} \qquad [2.12]$$

ABC Co.'s interest coverage amounts to 4.5 × (£90 million/£20 million), suggesting that the firm has more than four times the level of pre-tax profit needed to meet its obligations. The interest cover measure is used in conjunction with the previous two measures to indicate how much debt a firm can comfortably support. For instance, even though debt/equity and debt/assets may appear high, they may be acceptable if the interest coverage is also very large. Conversely, if interest coverage is very low (e. g. sub-1) the debt burden is likely to be too large and the company's inability to meet its obligations may threaten its solvency.

Many other ratios can be computed, each measuring slightly different aspects of the key areas noted above. The central point to consider in this discussion is that financial ratios provide an important metric by which company managers can track performance and make decisions. They also allow outside stakeholders, including potential investors and lenders, to compare current and past performance, and the overall position versus other competitors.

Let's expand our example across time and against industry peer averages to consider the firm's financial position more closely. Table 2. 1 contains the current year ratios (as computed above) along with three years of historical data; it also includes the industry average current year ratios for all of the companies operating in ABC Co. 's sector.

These results tell us that ABC Co. 's overall ROA and ROE performance has started to improve, but that it still lags behind the industry average. While ABC Co. 's operating and net margins have improved steadily-to the point where they are coming close to the industry average-its gross margins are still weak. This may indicate that ABC Co. is not charging enough for the goods it sells, or is paying too much for its product inputs (e. g. cost of goods sold). The firm's ROA and ROE underperformance can also be traced back to its very strong liquidity position, which is well above the industry average: the very high current and quick ratios mean that ABC Co. may be holding too much in liquid assets that do not generate much of a return (e. g. £100 million of cash on the balance sheet). However, the firm may be recognizing the problem, as both measures have begun to decline toward industry norms. From a capitalization perspective the company's overall debt levels are only slightly above industry norms and have been declining for the past two years. Interest coverage is extremely strong, indicating that ABC Co. has managed to secure favorable borrowing levels over time.

We can draw various summary points from this simple analysis:

Table 2.1 ABC Co's historical, current, and industry ratio data

Ratio	Year t-3	Year t-2	Year t-1	Current year	Industry average
Return on assets	4.40%	4.50%	5.25%	5.76%	6.25%
Return on equity	15.50%	15.87%	16.05%	16.20%	18.20%
Gross margin	20.05%	17.62%	18.75%	19.00%	23.50%
Operating margin	11.12%	9.62%	10.08%	10.76%	11.00%
Net margin	7.79%	7.35%	7.40%	7.54%	8.20%
Current ratio	1.62 ×	1.68 ×	1.63 ×	1.60 ×	1.20 ×
Quick ratio	0.79 ×	0.90 ×	0.87 ×	0.80 ×	0.75 ×
Debt to equity	1.75 ×	1.90 ×	1.87 ×	1.83 ×	1.75 ×
Debt to assets	0.69 ×	0.68 ×	0.70 ×	0.65 ×	0.58 ×
Interest coverage	3.75 ×	3.90 ×	4.21 ×	4.50 ×	3.75 ×

- Profitability is improving but remains below industry averages; difficulties establishing proper pricing of goods being sold and managing cost inputs appear to be the primary problems, along withholding an excess of non-earning liquid (e.g. cash) assets.
- Liquidity is well above industry norms and can safely be reduced in order to help boost earnings.
- Leverage is close to industry norms and has been in a moderate downtrend; the current level of debt is acceptable given the firm's ability to cover its interest costs so thoroughly.

This example is obviously simplified. Financial managers, investors, credit rating analysts and other interested parties go into considerably more detail to understand the workings and performance of a company on its own, and versus the industry.

FINANCIAL STATEMENTS AND DECISION-MAKING 财务报表与决策

Financial statements and the ratios that can be derived from them are obviously an integral part of the decision-making process because they give interested parties information by which to evaluate a firm's position. They must, of course, be used and analyzed in the context of detailed information contained in the "management discussion and analysis" section, which often provides vital clues about a company's performance, strategies, and future goals. Footnotes to the financial statements, which form part of the company accounts, must also be reviewed as they provide a much greater level of detail than the high-level accounts. In fact, footnotes provide valuable insight into trends and possible problems (e. g. lawsuits or product recalls, growing bad debt problems within the receivables accounts, the nature and extent of financial risks being taken, environmental liabilities, and so forth).

The financial statements we have described above are all related in some fashion: decisions taken by financial managers over the short or long term will have an impact on the balance sheet, income statement, and cash flow statement. Financial statements are clearly an essential component of effective financial management because they inject uniformity into the reporting and decision-making process. For instance, knowing that the balance sheet has a great deal of current liabilities but very little in current 44 The financial statements assets should cause management to make financial decisions that create a stronger position (e. g. lengthening the maturity of liabilities, building up a greater cash reserve). Or, seeing that gross revenue growth in the income statement has started to slow might cause management to examine opportunities to reduce its operating costs and/or expand into new markets via acquisition. Similarly, if the net cash position of the firm as reflected in the statement of cash flows is looking very strong, management may elect to repay some of its debt, issue a special dividend, or invest in a new venture. While each one of these decisions must be supported by proper decision metrics, including the risk/return and net present value frameworks we discuss in the next chapter, financial reporting is the essential starting point in the process.

Let's consider a simple example to illustrate the linkages between statements and the decisions that a financial manager might face. Assume that ABC Co. expects its sales to increase (an income statement item). In order to support this increase it must make sure that its cash and inventory are properly synchronized and that it knows how much it may need to borrow to fund the increased amount of sales (balance sheet items). How might it do so?

Assume that ABC Co. forecasts that sales will increase by £1 million. To support this increase it will need to increase its assets by 60 percent of this amount, or £600,000; this represents the additional inventory needed to produce the greater amount of goods to be sold. Let's further assume that ABC Co.'s policy is to finance 40 percent of any sales increase through accounts payable; this amounts to a £400,000 increase in liabilities. ABC Co.'s net working capital to support £1 million of increased sales is therefore £200,000 (£600,000 less £400,000). If management has a net profit margin requirement equal to 5 percent of sales (i.e. each £1 of sales must generate a minimum profit after expenses and taxes of 5 pence), the firm must therefore be prepared to borrow £150,000 (e.g. £200,000 of available net assets less £50,000 of net profit requirement). This simple example helps demonstrate how a company can use its financial statements to analyze requirements for boosting sales.

Let's consider another simple example based on liquidity.

Liquidity management, as we've noted in Chapter 1, is an essential corporate goal. From a corporate perspective, the process can be monitored and managed through cash budgeting, which involves comparing future cash receipts against cash payments (income statement/cash flow statement items) over specific weekly or monthly time intervals. The cash budget allows a firm's financial managers to detect any surpluses or deficits in a given maturity bucket. Any surpluses can be invested in short-term securities (balance sheet item), while deficits must be funded from the firm's cash account or by drawing down on a credit facility (balance sheet items). Note that the cash budgeting process involves both known receipts/payments and potential/ "what-if" receipts/payments; the latter act as a form of stress-testing to ensure that the company has enough flexibility to meet unexpected payments. Table 2.2 illustrates a simplified example of ABC Co.'s cash budgeting for the coming year, which links together all 3 financial statements in a single framework.

There are, of course, other tools that companies can use to help estimate how much cash they should keep on hand to cover an average level of deficits. One, the cash turnover method, divides annual operating expenses by cash turnover; cash turnover is, itself, a simple computation of 360 days divided by the number of days between the purchase of raw materials and the

短期证券投资

Table 2.2 Cash budgeting framework

Ratio	Jan	Feb	Mar	Apr	May	Jun	Jul	{…}
Receipts	150	125	140	150	160	170	180	
Payments	140	140	140	145	165	175	170	
Net	10	−15	0	5	−5	−5	10	

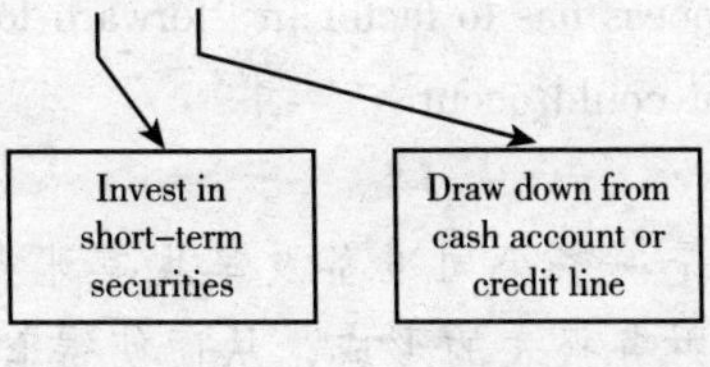

collection of cash from sales (i. e. the entire life cycle of a product). For instance, if ABC Co.'s annual operating expenses amount to £200,000 and its cash cycle is estimated at six times (e. g. 360 days/60 days between production and sales receipt), then the minimum amount of cash the company should keep on hand to cover deficits is £33, 333 (i. e. £200,000/6). In order for ABC Co. to manage its working capital properly it must be sensitive to the minimum level of cash it needs to keep and the maximum seasonal cash it may require; accordingly, it can supplement computation of the average annual operating figures with maximum and minimum figures, which will provide a range of sensitivities. The difference between the two can be factored into seasonal short-term financial planning.

Financial statements must always be viewed in the context of the overall environment. As we've already noted, external forces affect a company every day. This means that analysis and decisions must take account of what's happening with external factors like economic growth, interest rates, inflation, consumer confidence, deregulation, competition, and so forth. Some estimate of how these external forces might impact a firm's financial position is useful, and can often be made through scenario, or "what if," analysis that explores the impact of external variables on a company's position. This brings us to a cautionary note: financial managers, investors, and lenders who rely on financial statements to make decisions on where to lead the company or whether to provide capital must remember that the statements, while vitally important, are "backward-looking." Past trends are obviously important, but the past is history and the future is unknown. Accordingly, to be truly effective the decision-making process has to factor in "forward-looking" assumptions about what could occur.

摘要

财务报告是一家公司准备及呈现其账务状况的过程。它最终会导致财务报表的形成，从而使得管理者、投资者和其他利益相关者能够评估一家公司财务情况的好坏。财务报告基于影响公司运营的所有日常交易的累积，而公司的运营都记录在分类账户中。分类账户用于产生尝试性的报表，这些尝试性的报表逐渐转化为要公布于众的经外部审计的财务报表。财务报告是根据增加了一定程度的统一性和标准性的公认会计准则编制的；然而，会计准则确实需要一定数量的解释。核心的财务报表包括资产负债表（在某时间点的资产、负债和权益表现）、利润表（公司利润和损失的累计记录）和现金流量表（公司的现金流入和流出的累计记录）。这些可以被管理层讨论和分析以及详细的财务脚注所补充。从财务报表中能够得出不同的重要比率衡量法，从而能进一步分析和解释一家公司财务状况、变动趋势以及其与对手相比所处的位置。比率能够计算用于判断一家公司的盈利性、流动性和偿付能力。财务报表和随之产生的比率最终被内部各方用于帮助做出财务决策，被外部各方用于决定承诺资本的可接受性。

FURTHER READING 延伸阅读

Fridson, M., 1995, *Financial Statement Analysis*, *2nd edition*, New York: John Wiley & Sons.

White, G., Sondhi, A. and Fried, D., 1994, *The Analysis and Use of Financial Statements*, New York: John Wiley & Sons.

3

FINANCIAL CONCEPTS AND TOOLS

财务概念及方法

CHAPTER OVERVIEW 本章概述

In this chapter we consider essential financial concepts and tools that financial managers use to make decisions. We begin with a discussion of risk considerations, including the risk/return tradeoff, risk diversification, and the impact of risk on enterprise value maximization. We then describe the general structure of interest rates and stock prices and the determination of the cost of capital. We conclude the chapter with a detailed look at time value of money, including present value and future value, and consider how the time value framework can be used to develop investment decisions rules.

RISK CONSIDERATIONS 风险因素

As we've noted in Chapter 1, a company operating in a free market environment seeks to deliver goods and services to its customers in a timely, cost-effective, and prudent manner so that it can increase its net income. However, a company will only be able to do so if it can balance its risks properly. If it takes too much risk it stands a chance of reducing revenues and/or posting losses. If it takes too little risk it won't be able to generate sufficient revenues or offer investors a suitable return.

RISK VERSUS RETURN 风险与收益

Risk, a reflection of uncertainty, comes in many forms (such as financial risk, operating risk, and legal risk). Return is the amount that a risk-taker requires in order to accept a particular type and quantity of risk. Both elements are intimately related: the greater the risk, the greater the return the risk-taker will demand, and the lower the risk, the lower the return they can expect to receive. This is a fundamental tenet of finance that we will revisit throughout the book.

风险是不确定性的一种反映，表现出多种形式（如财务风险、经营风险和法律风险）。

Risk can be measured in various ways. One common method is standard deviation, or the degree to which an outcome deviates from the norm (or average). Standard deviation (often denoted by the Greek letter σ) can be computed by adding up the probability-weighted outcomes of the squared differences between expected and actual outcomes and then taking the square root; this is shown in (3.1):

收益是一个风险承担者为了接受某一特定类型和数量的风险所要求的数额。

$$\text{std dev} = \sqrt{\left[\text{sum across all observations (actual observation} - \text{expected observation})^2 \times \text{probability}\right]} \quad [3.1]$$

A higher standard deviation means a greater chance that some future outcome will deviate from the average and a lower chance that the expected result will occur. A lower standard deviation means a smaller chance of deviating from the norm and a greater chance that the expected result will occur.

Let us consider a simple example of high and low standard deviation. Table 3.1 illustrates the calculations involved in computing the standard deviations of Project 1 (low risk) and Project 2 (high risk).

Project 2 (standard deviation of 7.71), features more risk than Project 1 (standard deviation of only 2.12); this provides very useful information for financial managers considering capital projects or investments with risky characteristics.

Return is often measured as percentage of the capital invested in, or allocated to, a project or asset; this puts results on an equal footing for comparative purposes. For instance, a 10 percent return means that a company will receive a gain of 10 percent on the amount invested in the risky project, while a 20 percent return means that it will receive a gain of 20 percent.

Table 3.1 Standard deviations of projects 1 and 2

Actual	Expected	(Actual − Expected)	(Actual − Expected)^2	Probability	(Actual − Expected)^2 × Probability
Project 1					
35	40	−5	25	10%	2.5
38	40	−2	4	70%	2.8
41	40	1	1	20%	2.2
				Sum = 4.5	
				std dev =	$\sqrt{4.5}$ = 2.12
Project 2					
Actual	Expected	(Actual − Expected)	(Actual − Expected)^2	Probability	(Actual − Expected)^2 × Probability
30	40	−10	100	20%	20
48	40	8	64	50%	32
45	40	5	25	30%	7.5
				Sum = 59.5	
				std dev =	$\sqrt{59.5}$ = 7.71

Figure 3.1 brings these concepts together: return, as a percentage of capital invested, is depicted on the y-axis, while risk, as the standard deviation of returns, is shown on the x-axis. The upward sloping line suggests that lower risk projects/investments earn a lower return, and higher risk projects/investments earn a higher return. This is consistent with the risk/return tradeoff mentioned earlier.

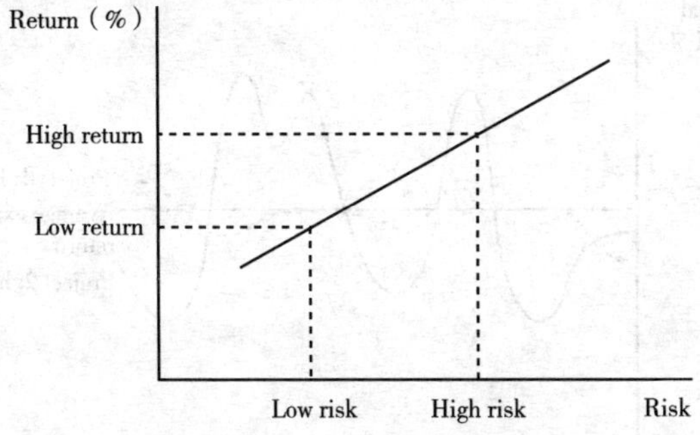

Figure 3.1 Risk and return

It can also be useful examining expected returns versus risk over time to illustrate how two different projects that provide the same expected return might actually expose a firm to very different risks. These profiles are illustrated in Figure 3.2. While Projects 1 and 2 generate the same average expected return, the standard deviation of the return varies significantly: Project 2 exposes the firm to much greater risk, as the realized return might be much higher, or much lower, than expected. In other words, there is a smaller likelihood that Project 2 will achieve the expected return, and a much greater likelihood that it will achieve a return that is either much higher or lower. A company's ability to estimate the actual outcome on Project 2 is lower than on Project 1, which features an expected return pattern that is much closer to the average. A financial manager facing an investment decision will select Project 1: both yield the same returns, but Project 1 does so with less uncertainty. Only when the expected return on Project 2 is higher will the financial manager consider an investment.

风险与回报

We can also examine the likelihood that the return on a project will approximate the expected return. Examining the normal distribution (i.e. the familiar bell-shaped curve), which represents the distribution of all possible outcomes in a population, is central to the process. Given the shape of the

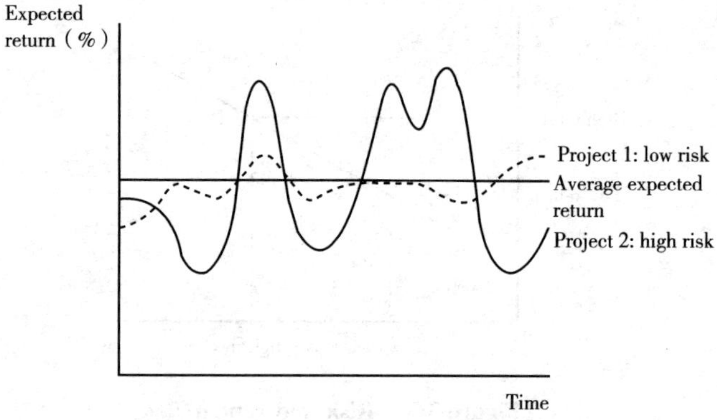

Figure 3. 2 High-and low-risk projects

curve we would expect most observations to occur around the average, and a smaller amount to be above and below; this means that the average has the greatest probability of occurrence. Figure 3. 3 illustrates Projects 1 and 2 in terms of statistical distributions. As before, Project 2 features a wider dispersion from the average, and is therefore riskier than Project 1.

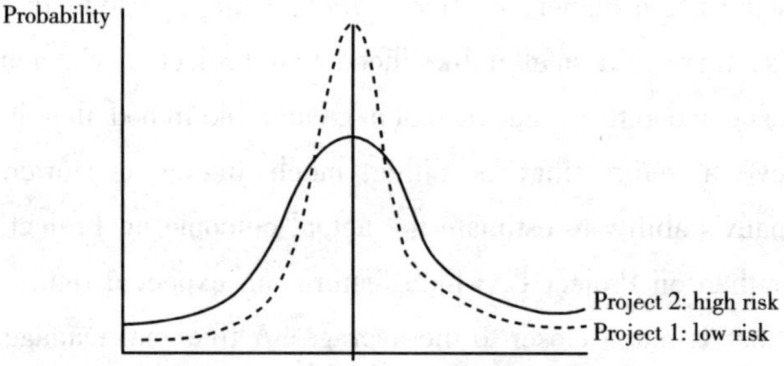

Figure 3. 3 Probability distributions

We've already noted that risk/return is a balancing act-a risky project must always provide a greater return than a less risky one if capital is to be allocated optimally. The actual tradeoff between risk and return can be measured by the coefficient of variation, which is the standard deviation divided by the expected return. So, if Project 1 and Project 2 each feature an expected return of 10 percent, but Project 2 has a standard deviation of 10 percent and Project 1 has a standard deviation of 5 percent, the coefficient of variation on Project 2 is twice as large as that of Project 1. This, again, makes Project 2 appear less attractive from a risk/return perspective.

We can also use the probability distribution and the concept of expected value to measure the relative appeal of different projects. The expected future return that a company can expect to receive on a project or investment is a product of the estimated return and the likelihood that the return will be achieved. Multiplying these two yields the expected value of a project/investment. Consider the hypothetical investments listed in Table 3. 2.

Table 3. 2 Risk/return tradeoffs 1

Investment	Estimated return (%)	Probability (%)	Expected value (%)
1 - low risk	5%	100%	5%
2 - middle risk	7%	80%	5. 6%
3 - high risk	9%	70%	6. 3%

Based on these combinations of returns and risks, a company can select investment 1 and, after adjusting for risk, expect to earn 5 percent. Since the probability of the expected return is 100 percent, the investment is effectively risk-free. If the company wants to take more risk it can choose investment 3, which offers a greater estimated return (9 percent) but injects more uncertainty (e. g. a 30 percent chance that the return won't be realized); this is clearly a risky investment. The expected value, however, is greater than the expected value of investment 1, meaning the risk/return tradeoff is consistent with the relationship illustrated in Figure 3. 1. Investment 2, which is also risky, provides an "intermediate" opportunity: more risk and return than investment 1, but less risk and return than investment 3.

We are most concerned about a scenario where the risk and return appear misbalanced: let's assume that the risk on investment 3 is higher, meaning the probability of obtaining the estimated result is now lower (50 percent). The results, summarized in Table 3. 3, show that the risk/return is no longer balanced-a company can invest in risk-free investment 1 and generate expected value of 5 percent or invest in risky investment 3 and generate expected value of 4. 5 percent.

Table 3. 3 Risk/return tradeoffs 2

Investment	Estimated return (%)	Probability (%)	Expected value (%)
1 - low risk	5%	100%	5%
2 - middle risk	7%	80%	5. 6%
3 - high risk	9%	50%	4. 5%

These simple examples lead us to important conclusions about corporate behavior. First, a "rational" company will want to be paid more when the uncertainty associated with a future event is high. If a firm has an opportunity to invest in a project that will provide a future cash flow, but the likelihood of successfully earning that cash flow is relatively uncertain (i. e. a high standard deviation), it must make sure that the return on that investment is large enough to cover the uncertainty. This is the essence of informed risk-taking. Second, when a company is deciding between two (or more) competing investments that provide the same return, it will choose the one with the lower risk; alternatively, if two projects have the same risk, it will choose the one with the higher return. Proper management of corporate resources therefore requires a strong focus on both risk and return.

RISK DIVERSIFICATION 风险分散

Once a firm has estimated the expected return and risk of a

single project or investment it can apply the same process to all others it might be contemplating. The diversification process helps a firm understand how individual projects/investments interact with one another when they are combined. Sometimes risks can increase when two or more projects/investments are combined, and sometimes risks can actually decrease. Evaluating this relationship is therefore critical.

Let's begin by noting that risks can be classed as diversifiable (idiosyncratic) or non-diversifiable (systematic). A diversifiable risk is a risk that is specific to a project/investment, and which can therefore be changed by adding other projects/investments. Importantly, by creating the right mix of projects/investments, the overall risk of the firm's portfolio can be reduced-without necessarily reducing the overall expected return. This is a key element of financial theory and investment management.

Projects/investments that are uncorrelated or negatively correlated with existing projects/investments can help boost returns and/or reduce risk. Correlation is a statistical measure that is computed from the covariances and standard deviations of two variables (i. e. projects/investments), which we denote as a and b:

$$\text{correlation} = \frac{\text{cov (a, b)}}{\text{std deve (a)} \times \text{std deve (b)}} \qquad [3.2]$$

Correlation measures the variance of variable a relative to variable b, reflecting the degree to which the two variables move together: correlation of +1.0 means that the two projects/investments move in lock-step, suggesting that the risk of the two individual projects is additive; correlation of 1.0 means that the two projects move in opposite directions, indicating that the risks offset one another; and, a correlation of 0 means that the two are independent-whatever happens to one project has no bearing on what happens to the second project.

For instance, if ABC Co. invests in a project that becomes riskier as interest rates rise and another that becomes less risky under the same scenario (i. e. negative correlation), the combination of the two produces a mini-portfolio that is indifferent to the movement of interest rates. By eliminating the risk, the stability of the returns is ensured. In fact, this is the foundation of hedging, as we'll discover in Chapter 7. Conversely, if both react in the same way (i. e. positive correlation), then ABC Co. will either generate a very large return or a very small one; this implies a greater degree of earnings volatility.

分散风险

A non-diversifiable risk is a risk factor that affects all projects/ investments equally and cannot, therefore, be reduced or eliminated by adding additional projects/investments. For instance, if all projects/investments are negatively affected if the economy falls into recession, no amount of new projects can be added to reduce the overall risk of a firm's project portfolio.

非分散风险

We can summarize the risk diversification framework by noting that as more uncorrelated/negatively correlated projects/ investments are added to a firm's portfolio, **diversifiable risk** declines; non-diversifiable risk, in contrast, holds steady, as noted in Figure 3. 4.

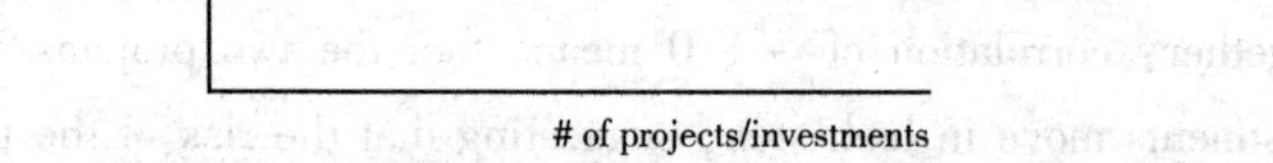

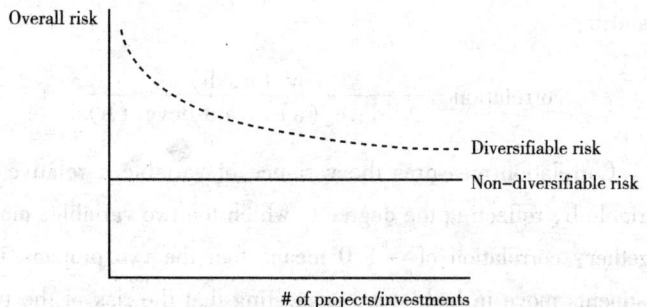

Figure 3. 4 Diversifiable and non-diversifiable risks

We can apply the same logic to entire firms. Firms can be characterized by their degree of diversifiable and non-diversifiable risks. For instance, an auto company has risks that are unique to its operations (e.g. its own balance sheet, management and strategy issues, cost structure, and so on). It is also impacted by factors that affect all auto manufacturers (e.g. fuel prices, consumer demand for large automobiles, emissions standards). An investment manager who is trying to build a diversified portfolio can diversify away the risks to a specific auto company by purchasing the stocks of other auto companies, which have different strategies, financial positions, management and so forth. But this does nothing to eliminate the risk to factors that are common to all auto companies-all are impacted by the same systematic variables. The only way the investment manager can reduce the industry risk is by investing in sectors that aren't impacted by the same factors. It may be able to do so by purchasing the stocks of companies in the technology, banking, and pharmaceutical sector, for instance. Once this portfolio is assembled, the investment manager has a diversified portfolio. However, even these industries may be affected by some of the systematic variables-such as a slowdown in economic growth or rise in inflation. This means that the portfolio will still retain some element of non-diversifiable risk.

A key financial concept known as the Capital Asset Pricing Model (CAPM) is a logical and important extension of the diversification concept. CAPM is a framework that attempts to relate non-diversifiable risk to the expected return of a security, project, or investment. While CAPM is used primarily with stocks, it can also be applied to projects (though care must be taken in defining an appropriate market benchmark).

The first step in the CAPM framework is to divide risk into diversifiable and non-diversifiable components and assume that there is some relationship between the return of individual assets and the return of the market as a whole (in practice there is some debate as to what assets comprise the "market," but in general very broad market indexes are used). The next step is to calculate the degree of risk by determining how sensitive asset returns are to market (or index) returns. A stock that moves more than the whole market is riskier than one that moves less than the market.

This risk sensitivity can be determined by dividing the volatility (standard deviation) of a stock's return by the volatility of the market return, which is then multiplied by the correlation between the stock and the market; this yields a result known as the beta of a stock (i. e. the slope of the line between the stock return and market return). A beta greater than 1. 0 means the stock is riskier than the market; a beta smaller than 1. 0 means the stock is less risky than the market. So if stock A has a beta of 1. 2, we might expect it to rise or fall by 20 percent more than the market; if it has a beta of 0. 8 we expect that it would rise or fall by only 80 percent of the market's move. Beta can therefore be viewed as a relative measure of the non-diversifiable risk associated with the returns of a stock, relative to the return of the market index. Figure 3. 5 illustrates high and low beta stocks.

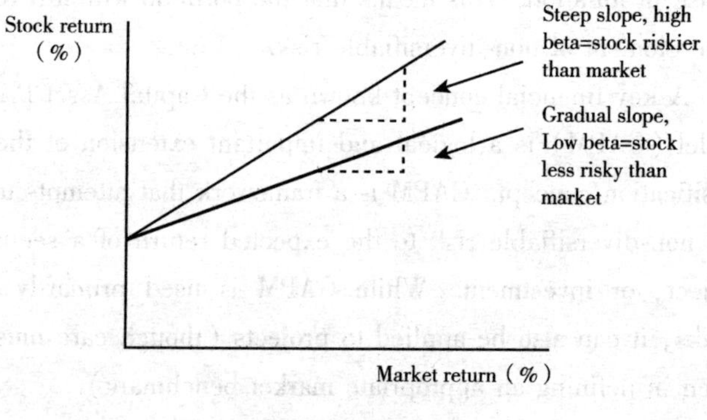

Figure 3. 5 A stock's beta

CAPM states that the actual risk of a stock is equal to a constant (the base risk-free interest rate) plus a market return that is adjusted by beta (plus a minor residual error term):

stock return = constant + (tebeta × market return) + error term [3. 3]

This is a useful relationship that allows a firm to compare the risk of individual stocks or investment projects against the market as a whole. By doing so, a company can create an optimal portfolio-one that provides a maximum amount of return for a given level of risk, or a minimum amount of risk for a given level of return.

ENTERPRISE VALUE MAXIMIZATION 企业价值最大化

Enterprise value maximization is closely related to risk and return. We've outlined the concept of value maximization in Chapter 1 and indicated that, in a free market economy, a company seeks to maximize wealth while complying with various social, legal, and regulatory constraints. This seems like a logical aim. But how does a firm actually accomplish this goal?

The primary way is by using corporate resources as efficiently and effectively as possible. The financial value of a firm is based on its ability to generate net income (or earnings) -the more income the firm produces on a particular base of assets, the greater its worth. Assume Company X and Company Y have the same base of productive assets: Company X, which can only generate $1 million of earnings every year is worth less than Company Y, which can generate $10 million of earnings every year. So, actions taken to maximize the amount of earnings produced will help maximize the value of the firm-the enterprise value.

实现企业价值最大化的主要方式是尽可能有效率地使用公司的资源。

The volatility, or standard deviation, of earnings also plays a role in value determination: the greater the volatility of earnings, the lower the worth of the company, as a strong year might be followed by a weak one. A company with a good record of stable to steadily growing earnings can be regarded as stronger, and more valuable, than one with an erratic pattern of earnings.

Let's refer back to the income statement described in the last chapter to see how a firm might be able to boost its net income. A company can:

- Increase its revenues while keeping cost of goods under control
- Reduce its SG&A expenses
- Reduce its interest expense
- Boost its other operating income/lower its other operating expenses
- Lower its tax bill.

Each one of these will lead to higher net income, and higher levels of (stable) net income mean greater enterprise value.

Let's also remember that active management of the balance sheet can help achieve similar goals. A company can:

- Lower the amount of debt on its balance sheet
- Reduce the amount of non-earning assets on the balance sheet (e. g. cash/equivalents)
- Minimize the amount of inventory on hand
- Invest in projects/investments that reduce risk (i. e. are negatively correlated and thus reduce earnings volatility).

Earnings can also be protected through a proper risk management program that ensures inputs/financial risks, as well as productive assets, are not subject to loss or cash flow interruption. Risks can unexpectedly detract from income, which detracts from value. We'll discuss this concept in Chapter 7.

In fact, proper management of every financial account can lead to efficiencies, and these efficiencies can create greater earnings and, ultimately, enterprise value. Each asset on the balance sheet must create a minimum return for the firm in order to create earnings and enterprise value. So, the disciplined firm focused on financial management will evaluate its assets and returns to determine whether they are adequate. This takes us back to a point we've just discussed: if a firm can allocate its resources in projects that maximize return for a given level of risk, it is helping maximize value.

ESSENTIAL TOOLS OF FINANCE
金融的基本方法

Financial managers use many different tools to make decisions. In this section we consider several fundamental tools, including the general cost of capital, time value of money, and the investment decision framework.

THE GENERAL COST OF CAPITAL
总资产成本

We begin our discussion with a brief overview of interest rates and stock prices and how they impact a firm's weighted cost of capital-or the average cost of the resources companies need to finance productive assets. We'll expand on the topic when we consider capital-raising instruments in Chapters 4 and 5.

An interest rate-or debt cost of capital-is simply the cost of borrowing money, or the amount that can be earned by lending money or depositing funds. The financial markets feature many types of interest rates: government interest rates, private sector (corporate) interest rates, short-term interest rates, long-term interest rates, fixed interest rates, and floating interest rates.

Government interest rates represent a national cost of borrowing via a government treasury or central bank. Highly developed and financially strong nations, such as the US, UK, Germany, Switzerland, Japan, Canada, and Australia, borrow money at the lowest possible interest rates since they are considered good credit risks with essentially no likelihood of defaulting (i. e. not paying) on their obligations. We refer to these as risk-free interest rates (rf). The Government rates of less creditworthy nations (e. g. many emerging market nations) are not considered risk-free, as the likelihood of default is higher. To compensate the lender for this additional specter of default a risk premium (rp) is added to the risk-free rate. The same is true of corporate rates: since all companies have at least some chance of default, they must also pay a risk premium. This is, of course, consistent with the risk/return tradeoff.

Some interest rates are fixed for a particular maturity (such as 3 years, 5 years, or 30 years), while others are variable, changing every 1, 3, 6 or 12 months. For instance, the London Interbank Offered Rate (LIBOR), which represents the borrowing cost for banks in the international deposit market, is a key floating interest rate. The yield curve is a representation of interest rates with respect to maturity-that is, the cost of borrowing across different maturities, from overnight to thirty years. Figure 3. 6 illustrates a hypothetical yield curve built from rates extending from 1 to 30 years. In a normal market environment the yield curve is upward sloping (positive), meaning short-term rates are lower than long-term rates; this means it costs less to borrow in the short term than over the long term. Yield curves that are flat (i. e. short-term rates equal long-term rates) or inverted (i. e. short-term rates exceed long-term rates) are rather less common. These states are depicted in Figure 3. 7. Note that separate yield curves can be created for different types of rates/borrowers (e. g. a US government yield curve, a £ AA corporate curve, and so forth).

What drives the shape of the yield curve? Academic and empirical research points to several forces, including expectations, liquidity, and market segmentation. Expectations embedded in the middle and long maturities of a yield curve are simply an expression of the market's belief of what will happen to rates in the future. An upward sloping curve suggests that the market expects rates in the future will be higher than they are today.

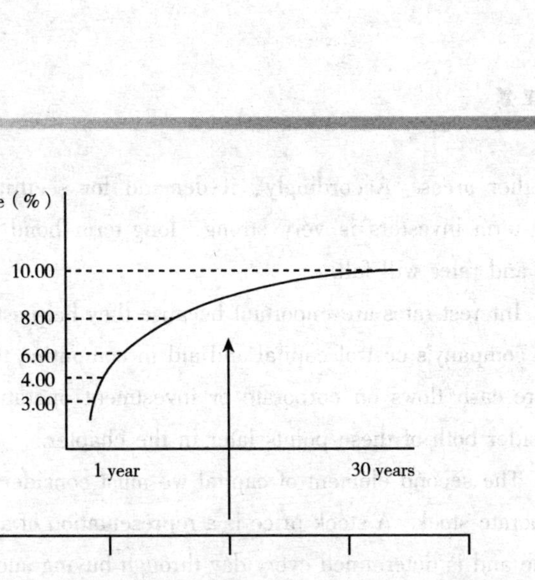

1 year	3 years	5 years	10 years	30 years
3.00%	4.00%	6.00%	8.00%	10.00%

Figure 3.6 Hypothetical yield curve

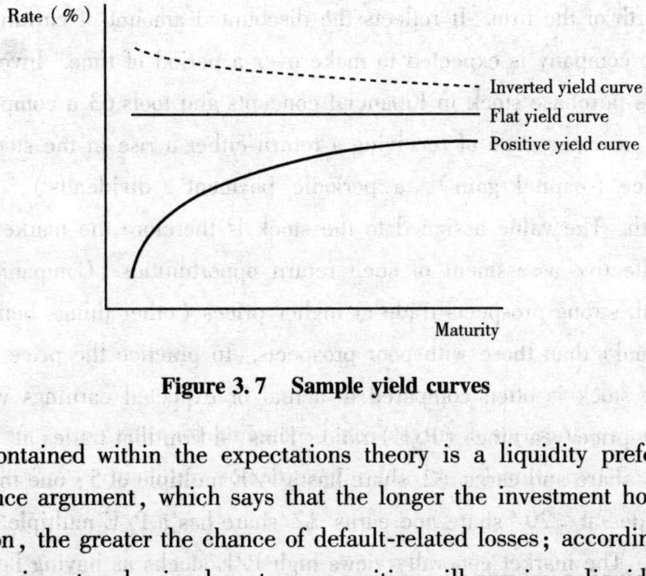

Figure 3.7 Sample yield curves

Contained within the expectations theory is a liquidity preference argument, which says that the longer the investment horizon, the greater the chance of default-related losses; accordingly, investors buying long-term securities will require a liquidity premium in order to accept this risk. The market segmentation theory looks primarily at market structure and the supply/demand forces that exist within different investor groups. This theory suggests that different types of investors concentrate their activities in specific segments of the curve and tend not to invest in other areas. Accordingly, if demand for securities by the long-term investors is very strong, long-term bond prices will rise and rates will fall.

Interest rates are important because they help establish part of a company's cost of capital and aid in computing the effect of future cash flows on corporate or investment operations. We'll consider both of these points later in the chapter.

The second element of capital we must consider centers on corporate stock. A stock price is a representation of a company's value and is determined every day through buying and selling by investors, dealers, and speculators. Though we'll talk more about corporations and the issuance of stock in the next chapter, it is important for our current discussion to note that the fair price of a stock is based on expectations related to the future worth of the firm. It reflects the discounted amount of earnings the company is expected to make over a period of time. Investors purchase stock in Financial concepts and tools 63 a company in expectation of receiving a return-either a rise in the stock price (capital gain), a periodic payment (dividends), or both. The value assigned to the stock is therefore the market's collective assessment of such return opportunities. Companies with strong prospects trade at higher prices (other things being equal) than those with poor prospects. In practice the price of the stock is often compared to actual or expected earnings via the price/ earnings (P/E) ratio. Thus, a firm that trades at $10/share and earns $2/share has a P/E multiple of 5; one that trades at $20/ share and earns $2/share has a P/E multiple of 10. The market generally views high P/E stocks as having better prospects.

If a company wants to issue more stock, it faces a cost that is a direct function of its stock price. A higher stock price means less shares have to be issued to raise a given amount of stock (e. g. if $500 million is required and the stock is trading at $50/share, 10 million shares have to be issued; if the stock is trading at \$25/share, 20 million shares have to be issued). This is important because it lowers the amount of ownership and increases earnings dilution, which we'll consider in the next chapter. In fact, the optimal time to issue stock is when the price is high. Issuing stock is a cost to the company because investors will only supply capital if they receive a fair return. The cost of stock is thus the second major component of corporate financing, and can be used to compute a firm's total cost of capital.

Every company needs some amount of capital in order to operate (e. g. to purchase or lease a factory, hire staff, buy raw materials, and so forth). This capital is not, of course, free. The cost a firm ultimately faces relates to the amount it must pay to generate funds internally or externally. The actual cost assigned to this capital depends on the nature of the funds being raised. Since different forms of capital have different benefits and risks, each has a specific cost. This means that a firm must weigh the relative costs and benefits before deciding on the best possible mix. 资本

Capital can be raised internally and externally. As detailed in the last chapter that a firm's net income, if not paid out as dividends, can be reinvested in productive operations. This is internal capital, reflected in the retained earnings account. External capital comes from outside sources: either lenders or credit investors (in 64 the case of debt [loans and bonds], which is our topic in Chapter 5), or equity investors (for common and preferred stock, which we cover in Chapter 4). We've already noted above that interest rates represent the cost of borrowing, and stock prices represent the amount it costs to raise an incremental amount of stock. For the purposes of our discussion in the rest of this chapter we shall consider the cost of capital to be a generic weighted "average" of a firm's internal and external costs based on its retained earnings, equity and debt (computed on an after-tax basis for reasons we will consider in

Chapter 5). This weighted average cost of capital (WACC), which includes total capital as the sum of debt, equity, and retained earnings, can be computed as:

$$\begin{aligned}\text{WACC} = {} & \text{after} - \text{tax cost of debt} \times \left(\frac{\text{Debt}}{\text{Total capital}}\right) \\ & + \text{cost of equity} \times \left(\frac{\text{Equity}}{\text{Total capital}}\right) \\ & + \text{cost of retained earnings} \times \left(\frac{\text{Retained earnings}}{\text{Total capital}}\right)\end{aligned} \qquad [3.4]$$

We shall note in Chapter 4 that the cost of equity and the cost of retained earnings are actually the same; for now, however, we consider them to be separate. Based on this equation a firm's WACC is a function of both the amount of a particular type of capital in the total capital structure, and the specific cost assigned to that class of capital. It can be used to consider the advisability of investing in one or more investments and of raising an incremental amount of funding for future expansion (i. e. the next dollar or pound of financing).

Consider a situation where ABC Co. has £100 million in total capital, including £50 million of equity, £25 million of retained earnings, and £25 million of debt. Its cost of equity is 10 percent, its cost of retained earnings is also 10 percent, and its after-tax cost of debt is 5 percent. Based on this information, ABC Co.'s WACC is 8.75 percent. It can use this figure to evaluate a series of financing and investing decisions, as noted below.

TIME VALUE OF MONEY 货币的时间价值

Time value of money, one of the most important tools of finance, is routinely used in financial analysis and decision-making. In this section we consider present value and future value, the cornerstones of time value of money.

The value of money is driven by competing forces: its value decreases over time as a result of inflation risk and liquidity preferences, but it can increase as a result of interest rates. Inflation erodes the purchasing value of money over time: as prices rise, each dollar or pound buys less. Similarly, liquidity preferences suggest that institutions prefer to hold cash to meet unexpected payments. That is, institutions prefer to have cash on hand so that it can be invested immediately in productive endeavors or used for emergency purposes. In order to induce these institutions to shift into more uncertain (i. e. longer-term) assets, a premium has to be paid. When interest rates are positive, a sum of money invested today will be worth more in the future. By extension, the value of a future sum of money will be lower today than in the future.

Determining a present value (PV, which is today's value) or a future value (FV, which is the value at some future point) requires three inputs:

- The cash flow (CF) that is to be paid or received today or in the future
- The relevant time horizon
- The proper interest rate, discount rate, or cost of capital (the terms are interchangeable). We will use the generic cost of debt from our discussion above as the discount rate in the formulas that follow. For a risky company or nation this is, of course, equal to the risk-free rate and risk premium described earlier.

While the equations below look somewhat involved, they are intuitively simple and based on the most fundamental algebra.

Let's begin with PV. If we are to receive some cash flow in the future, we know that it will be worth less today than tomorrow. This means we must divide (or discount) the future CF by the discount rate over the time horizon in question. This simple relationship can be captured by the following:

$$PV = \left[\frac{\text{cash flow}}{(1 + \text{discount rate})^{\text{time horizon}}} \right] \quad [3.5]$$

This formula is straightforward and powerful: it reduces the value of a cash flow that we expect to receive in the future by the discount rate, meaning we can make decisions today using today's discounted cash flows. For instance, the PV of a $1 million cash flow to be received in 1 year when the discount rate is 5 percent is simply:

$$PV = \frac{\$1m}{(1 + 0.05)^1}$$

or $952, 380.

We can expand this basic equation in two ways: by adding additional cash flows, and by changing the discounting frequency. Each of these will help us when we begin to value investments or projects with multiple cash flows over time.

To add more cash flows, we simply sum across the individual cash flows and their relevant time periods via:

$$PV = \text{sum across each time period} \left[\frac{\text{cash flow}}{(1 + \text{discount rate})^{\text{time horizon}}} \right] \quad [3.6]$$

So, if we expect to receive $1 million in periods 1 and 2, then the PV (using the same 5 percent discount rate is):

$$PV = \left[\frac{\$1m}{(1 + 0.05)^1} \right] + \left[\frac{\$1m}{(1 + 0.05)^2} \right]$$

or, $1, 859, 409 ($952, 380 + $907, 029). In other words, $2 million that we expect to receive in equal $1 million installments over the next two periods is worth approximately $ 1.86 million today at a 5 percent discount rate. Note that a contract that pays equal cash installments over an extended period of time is also known as an annuity. Individuals that want a fixed income over time can purchase an annuity by making an upfront payment that is based on the discount rate and the size of desired future cash flows.

What happens if the discount rate is greater than 5 percent? We would intuitively expect the result to be smaller, because dividing by a larger figure yields a smaller result. For instance, if the discount rate is 10 percent instead of 5 percent, the two-period cash flows are now:

$$PV = \left[\frac{\$1m}{(1+0.10)^1}\right] + \left[\frac{\$1m}{(1+0.10)^2}\right]$$

or \$1, 735, 536 (\$909, 090 + \$826, 446); this is \$124, 000 less than the cash flows discounted at 5 percent. Accordingly, the larger the discount rate the greater the discounted cash flows, and the lower the resulting PVs. This is an important fact that we will revisit when we discuss risky debt in Chapter 5; we will see that risky cash flows have a higher discount rate, leading to smaller PVs.

What if the cash flows occur twice in a single period (e. g. every six months instead of every year)? We can make the formula above more generic by including a factor that takes account of the frequency of payments, as in:

$$PV = \begin{matrix}\text{sum across each}\\ \text{time period}\end{matrix}\left[\frac{\left(\dfrac{\text{cash flow}}{\text{fractional period}}\right)}{\left(1+\dfrac{\text{discount rate}}{\text{fractional period}}\right)^{\frac{\text{time horizon}}{\text{fractional period}}}}\right] \qquad [3.7]$$

If we assume from the example above that the \$1 million of cash flows for each of two periods is actually paid as \$500, 000 over four periods (e. g. semi-annual instead of annual), and the annual discount rate is 5 percent, the PV is:

$$PV = \left[\frac{\$500,000}{(1+0.025)^{\frac{1}{2}}}\right] + \left[\frac{\$500,000}{(1+0.025)^{\frac{2}{2}}}\right] + \left[\frac{\$500,000}{(1+0.025)^{\frac{3}{2}}}\right] + \left[\frac{\$500,000}{(1+0.025)^{\frac{4}{2}}}\right]$$

or \$1, 939, 394 (\$493, 864 + \$487, 804 + \$481, 819 + \$475, 907). Note that this PV result is greater than the one in the single period payment immediately above (\$1, 859, 409) because it assumes that as the \$500, 000 payments are received each period, they are reinvested at the same discount rate.

As the fractional period gets smaller and smaller (e. g. quarterly, monthly, weekly, daily) we can condense the process by deriving the continuously compounded cash flow as an exponential function (exp); this is equal to instantaneous discounting, and can be computed via:

$$\text{PV} = \text{sum across each time period}\left[\text{cash flow} \times \exp\left(\text{discount rate} \times \text{time horizon}\right)\right] \quad [3.8]$$

For instance, a single \$1 million payment to be received in two years is worth \$904, 837 today when discounted continuously at 5 percent. We can, of course, add multiple cash flows together, as in the examples above.

We can also consider the special case of the perpetuity, which is simply a fixed cash flow that is paid forever (e. g. as in an endowment fund or perpetual bond). Its value can be estimated through a simplification of the PV formula above:

$$\text{PV} = \left[\frac{\text{cash flow}}{\text{discount rate}}\right] \quad [3.9]$$

For instance, a perpetuity might pay \$100, 000 per annum. If the discount rate is 5 percent, the PV of the perpetual stream is:

$$\text{PV} = \frac{\$100,000}{0.05}$$

or \$2 million. If the discount rate is 10 percent, the PV is \$1 million. It is important to remember that, although a perpetuity exists forever, the most distant cash flows PV to a very small amount.

The reverse of the PV calculation is, of course, the FV calculation, or how much a series of cash flows will be worth in the future. If we invest a cash flow today, we know that it will be worth more in the future. This means that we must now multiply, or compound, the current cash flow by some appropriate rate over the relevant time horizon, and can do so via:

$$FV = \text{cash flow } (1 + \text{discount rate})^{\text{time horizon}} \qquad [3.10]$$

For example, a \$1 million sum invested today, for one year, at an annual discount rate of 5 percent, is equal to:

$$FV = \$1m\ (1 + 0.05)^1$$

or \$1, 050, 000. Similarly, if the discount rate is increased to 10 percent, the FV rises to \$1, 100, 000. This makes intuitive, as well as mathematical, sense, since the greater the return on a cash flow invested today, the greater the future value of that cash flow.

The FV of multiple cash flows received over time again requires summation:

$$FV = \begin{matrix}\text{sum across each}\\ \text{time period}\end{matrix}\left[\text{cash flow} \times \begin{pmatrix}1 + \text{discount}\\ \text{rate}\end{pmatrix}^{\text{time horizon}}\right] \qquad [3.11]$$

Thus, \$1 million of cash flows to be received in periods 1 and 2 when the discount rate is 5 percent yields an FV of:

$$FV = \$1m(1 + 0.05)^1 + \$1m(1 + 0.05)^2$$

or \$2, 152, 500 (\$1, 050, 000 + \$1, 102, 500).

When cash flows are invested in fractional periods we can again introduce a fractional multiplier process, as in [3.11]:

$$FV = \text{sum across each time period} \left[\frac{\text{cash flow}}{\text{fractional period}} \times \left(1 + \frac{\text{discount rate}}{\text{fractional period}}\right)^{\frac{\text{time horizon}}{\text{fractional period}}}\right]$$

So, \$1 million received over two semi-annual periods (i. e. CF of \$500, 000 per period) rather than a single annual period, with an annual discount rate of 5 percent, yields an FV of:

$$FV = \$500,000\left(1+\frac{0.05}{2}\right)^{\frac{1}{2}} + \$500,000\left(1+\frac{0.05}{2}\right)^{\frac{2}{2}}$$

or \$1,018,711 (\$506,211 + \$512,500).

Using the logic above, we can summarize the future value of a continuously compounded cash flow as:

$$FV = \text{sum across each time period [cash flow} \times \exp\text{ (discount rate} \times \text{time horizon)]} \quad [3.12]$$

Again, \$1 million compounded continuously at 5 percent for two years yields an FV of \$1,105,170.

In practice the discounting and compounding exercises described above can be performed through financial calculators or spreadsheets with pre-programmed functionality; they can also be estimated through standard discounting/compounding tables. However, understanding the logic and intuition of time value of money is very important, as the framework is fundamental to many financial decisions.

INVESTMENT DECISIONS 投资决策

Financial managers seeking to allocate scarce resources must be able to make rational financial decisions during the financial planning phase. Net present value (NPV) gives managers a measure by which to evaluate multiple projects or investments being considered. The NPV equation, which builds on the time value concepts we have just mentioned, takes an extra step by including initial costs or capital investment.

We know from the section above that a productive project (investment) will yield cash flows over its life, and these can be discounted to provide a PV estimate. In order to receive the benefit of such future cash flows a company must first put up some amount of capital. This initial investment is a cost to the firm and leads to the creation of a simple NPV equation which embeds both costs and benefits. We may express this through:

$$NPV = -\text{investment} + \text{sum across each time period}\left[\frac{\text{cash flow}}{(1+\text{discount rate})^{\text{time horizon}}}\right] \quad [3.13]$$

The initial investment is not discounted by the cost of capital because it is made in the current period. If the project requires interim investment or maintenance costs, these can be subtracted from the positive cash flows directly (i. e. the periodic cash flow is net of additional costs paid). Consider, for instance, a firm that has an opportunity to invest in a simple three-period project that costs \$5 million and yields equal annual cash flows of \$3. 5 million. If the firm's cost of capital is 10 percent, the NPV of the project is:

$$NPV = -\$5m + \left(\frac{\$3.5m}{(1.10)^1} + \frac{\$3.5m}{(1.10)^2} + \frac{\$3.5m}{(1.10)^3}\right)$$

or \$3, 704, 000 (e. g. \$8, 704, 000 - \$5, 000, 000). Let's now assume that the firm can also decide to invest in another project, which costs \$7. 5 million but generates \$3. 75 million per year for four years. Which project is better? The NPV approach allows an examination of the two on an equal basis:

$$NPV = -\$7.5m + \left(\frac{\$3.75m}{(1.10)^1} + \frac{\$3.75m}{(1.10)^2} + \frac{\$3.75m}{(1.10)^3} + \frac{\$3.75m}{(1.10)^4}\right)$$

This yields an NPV of \$4, 386, 000, suggesting the second project is the preferred investment. Alternatively, a company can use the NPV framework to identify projects that meet some minimum rate of return, or hurdle rate. This can be done by computing an internal rate of return (IRR), which is simply the cost of capital that forces the NPV to zero. Converting the example immediately above into the IRR framework looks like this:

$$0 = -\$7.5\text{m} + \left(\frac{\$7.5\text{m}}{(1+x)^1} + \frac{\$7.5\text{m}}{(1+x)^2} + \frac{\$7.5\text{m}}{(1+x)^3} + \frac{\$7.5\text{m}}{(1+x)^4} \right)$$

In this case the firm solves for x, or IRR, to find whether the minimum return meets an internal hurdle rate set by management. In this example the IRR is 10 percent. This framework is particularly useful for comparing amongst several competing projects, all of which demand an investment of the firm's capital. Even though all feature positive NPVs, the IRR rule lets a company make an objective decision. For instance, if a company is presented with the projects noted in Table 3.4, Project 4 appears to be the superior alternative.

When project IRR is greater than the cost of capital, the company achieves a higher return than it is paying for its capital, meaning that investment in the project is sensible. When IRR is less than the cost of capital the company does better not to use its capital to invest in the project. By defining a master IRR curve, such as the one illustrated in Figure 3.8, we create an entire relationship of NPVs and acceptance/rejection decisions.

A firm may assign a different cost of capital to each one of its investment projects, or it may opt for a blended cost of capital (i. e. the WACC). Individual cost of capital may be selected when projects have unique characteristics, such as long maturities, special risks, and so forth; this approach can lead to more accurate decisions as project profitability won't be overstated or understated. A blended WACC approach may be suitable when a firm's investments are largely uniform and no individual project features unusual risks or characteristics.

Table 3.4 Sample projects, NPVs and IRRs

Project	Horizon (years)	NPV, $millions	IRR
1	3	5	8.50%
2	3	6.5	8.75%
3	5	5.5	4.50%
4	**4**	**6**	**9.75%**
5	5	7.25	9.00%
6	5	7	8.75%
7	3	6.5	8.80%

We refine this process slightly to make it even more realistic. Every time a company raises funds to invest or expand, its marginal cost of capital rises; capital is scarce and the limited supply means higher cost for each increment raised. This should make sense: as a firm raises more debt, its financial position becomes slightly more strained, as debt carries with it the obligation to make interest payments. This additional pressure, perceptible by lenders and investors, increases the cost of debt capital slightly. The same is true of equity: each new share that a company issues increases dilution, which causes the value of the shares to drop slightly-again increasing costs. Therefore, if we are considering each incremental dollar or pound of investment, we can't look only at the WACC. We must examine decisions in light of the weighted marginal cost of capital (WMCC), which is an upward sloping function (i. e. marginal cost increases with each incremental amount of capital raised). Figure 3.9 replicates Figure 3.8 with a WMCC curve (rather than a constant cost of capital or WACC curve); we notice in this illustration that the acceptance region for projects becomes smaller, meaning that a firm will have to find projects with a higher IRR in order to satisfy an increasing cost of capital.

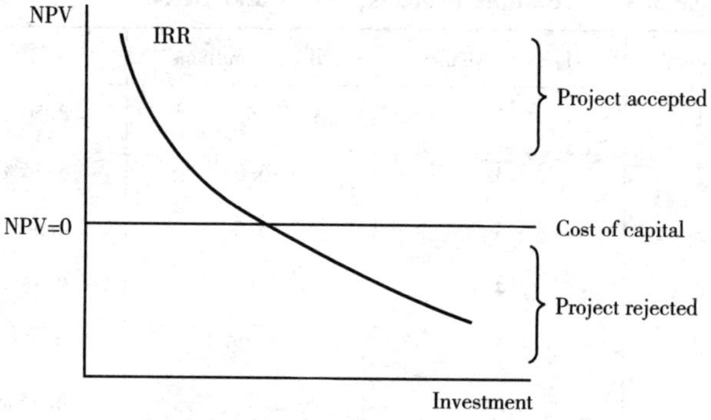

Figure 3.8　IRR, NPV and decision rules

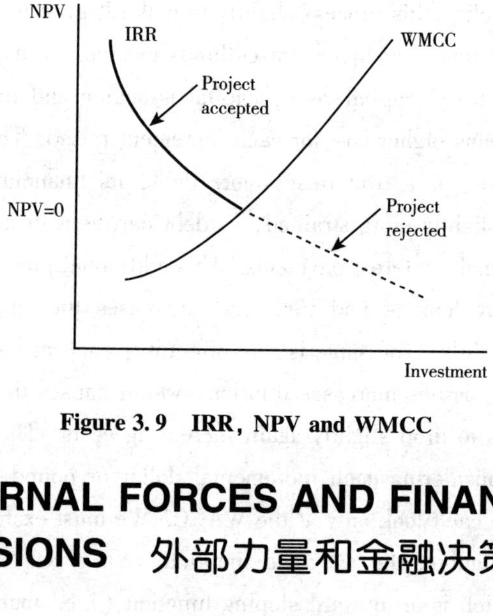

Figure 3.9　IRR, NPV and WMCC

EXTERNAL FORCES AND FINANCIAL DECISIONS　外部力量和金融决策

While our discussion above focuses on internal issues we must not forget our comments from Chapter 1: a firm doesn't operate in isolation, but is impacted by external market forces that must be considered when applying financial concepts and tools to decision-making. It's easy to imagine that the current and anticipated state of the economy, the level of interest rates and inflation, the size and direction of essential capital flows, and the nature of competition and regulation can all play a part in shaping a company's fortunes. The decision-making process must therefore take account of these external variables.

Consider one very simple example: ABC Co. wants to invest in a new project that will expand capacity. Its initial decision on whether to invest will be based on various internal concepts (motivations, optimal financial structure) and its quantitative evaluation of the opportunity (WACC, NPV decision rules). However, if ABC Co. is acting prudently, it must also consider how the expansion will affect, and be affected by, the outside environment. If the economy is in recession and expected to stay that way for several more quarters, it may be prudent to delay the project. If inflation is accelerating and ABC Co.'s costs of production will rise in tandem, the profit margins on the new production may be squeezed to the point where the investment is no longer compelling. Or, if the economy is strong and interest rates are at a low point in the cycle it may be sensible to proceed to lock in a low cost of capital. If competitors are similarly planning to add capacity, ABC Co. may even wish to accelerate the process in order to gain market share more rapidly. Each one of these forces may have a bearing on ABC Co.'s ultimate success/failure with the project.

摘要

为做出合理的决策，金融决策者需要一套概念和方法。风险是金融决策讨论的核心。风险必须总是与潜在的收益相称以便确保一个合适的平衡。一个有较大程度的风险的投资或项目，其风险可以用标准差（或实际结果相对于期望价值的偏离度）衡量，必须赋予比具有较小风险的相似项目更大的收益。为了适当地管理总体风险，必须考虑将多种投资或项目增加到投资组合中的影响；这一进程被称为风险分散。正相关的投资/项目能导致风险增加，而负相关的那些项目能减少风险。企业价值可以通过理解公司运营的风险、输入量和输出量得到管理。具有高收益或低收益波动性的公司可能比那些具有高收益或稳定收益流的公司价值低。资本成本是金融决策工程中的关键因素。它指出了公司为持续经营募集资本的成本。资本成本可以分成负债成本和权益成本（普通股和留存收益）。在资本结构中将每一种组份按适当比例结合起来就得出加权资本平均成本。货币的时间价值是金融的另一个核心建筑基石。现值反映的是将来产生的现金流量在今天的价值；这些现金流量用公司的负债成本折现到现在。未来价值反映的是一串现金流量在将来的某个时点的价值；现金流量用负债成本决定的比率来复合计算。净现值法是估计关于一个项目或投资的现金投入（流出）和收入（流入）相关的决策规则。内部收益率是使净现值等于零的资本成本。

FURTHER READING　延伸阅读

Haugen, R., 2000, *Modern Investment Theory*, *5th edition*, Englewood Cliffs NJ: Prentice Hall.

Maness, T. and Zietlow, J., 2004, *Short-Term Financial Management*, Mason OH: Southwestern College Publishers.

Seitz, N. and Ellison, M., 2004, *Capital Budgeting and Long-Term Financial Decisions*, *4th edition*, Mason OH: Southwestern College Publishers.

第二部分

工具和交易

4

COMMON AND PREFERRED STOCK

普通股和优先股

CHAPTER OVERVIEW 本章概述

In this chapter we consider common and preferred stock, which together comprise equity capital, the first of two major classes of external corporate financing; note that the terms equity capital, stock, and shares are synonymous. We commence with a review of why and how stock is used, the relative costs and benefits of borrowing through the equity markets, and the tradeoffs that exist between using too much and too little equity financing. We then analyze dividend policy and the forces that determine equity costs and share values. We conclude the chapter by describing the characteristics of major classes of stock and how the instruments are issued and traded. The material in this chapter should be compared and contrasted with the debt financing discussed in the next chapter.

USES OF COMMON AND PREFERRED STOCK 普通股和优先股的用途

As we've seen in Part I, a company exists to provide its customers with goods and services while simultaneously creating a profitable business that rises in value; this eventually builds wealth for the proprietors (owners). The actual ownership structure of a firm can take various forms. For instance, a firm can be founded as a sole proprietorship (single owner), a partnership (several partners serving as owners), or a corporation (many investors serving as owners). The corporate structure provides the greatest amount of flexibility, because it allows a firm to raise a much larger amount of capital, it provides for continuity over time, and it shields the owners from unlimited liability. Let's explore each of these characteristics before considering the particulars of common and preferred stock.

First, a firm constituted as a corporation can raise a greater amount of capital as it will have access to the public capital markets, where the pool of investment capital is substantial. Proprietorships and partnerships tend to rely on informal sources of funding (e. g. some amount of bank loans, government grants, personal resources), meaning capital access is quite restricted. This capital restriction invariably constrains growth. Second, a corporation is not identified with a single individual or group since it features large and diffuse ownership. In fact, it is intended to exist as a perpetual entity over many years. Proprietorships and partnerships do not necessarily provide the same continuity: they often rely on a few individuals to guide the business, and their outlook may be threatened if such individuals depart or cannot continue their dealings. This can ultimately lead to an unwinding of the structure. Third, corporations convey the right of limited liability, meaning that owners of a corporation's shares are not liable for more than the amount invested. Partnerships and proprietorships, in contrast, follow the tenet of unlimited liability: owners and partners are responsible and liable for debts they incur on behalf of their organizations, and must repay claims from personal assets if insufficient funds exist within the business. The shortcomings of using the proprietorship and partnership structures for any formal, enduring business are quite apparent. Accordingly, firms seeking to create a robust and scalable structure generally opt for the corporate form.

In most national systems a corporation is created through a corporate charter (a document detailing the scope and nature of business), which is approved by relevant legal and regulatory authorities. A typical corporation features a board of directors, or professionals that are set apart from daily operations of the company in order to fairly represent the interests of investors, and an executive management team, which is granted authority by the board to manage the daily affairs of the company.

The issuance of shares proceeds once all approvals have been obtained and the board and executive management team are in place. Share issuance, which we discuss later in the chapter, is the essential capital-raising effort that allows a corporation to sell to investors transferable interests representing pro-rata ownership of its operations. The proceeds raised through such issuance are used to buy productive assets (e. g. plant and equipment), hire employees, rent or purchase office space, and so forth. This equity capital becomes a permanent form of financing on the company's balance sheet, providing a continuous source of funds that can be supplemented by future share issuance as needed.

股息

Each share issued to investors represents an ownership interest in the company, conveying a series of legal and rent rights. The legal rights entitle the investor to vote on issues of importance to the continuing success of the company and to receive periodic audited financial statements. The rent rights (or economic rights) entitle the investor to a share in the profits of the company. These profits can be conveyed via dividends (i. e. a periodic fixed or discretionary payment) or capital appreciation (i. e. a rise in the share price), or both. Shares can be issued as common stock or preferred stock; we'll consider the differences below, but for now we focus our discussion on common stock, which is the most widely used form of external equity financing.

Let's assume that ABC Co. , currently a partnership, wants to expand beyond the partnership stage, increase the scope of its operations, and repay all of the informal sources of funding it has relied on over the years. It decides to incorporate and sell shares to investors through a public stock offering. Since this deal is its inaugural funding in the stock market, the transaction takes the form of an initial public offering (IPO). The funds raised through the IPO will allow ABC Co. to purchase a bigger factory to expand its product line, and a fleet of trucks to transport the goods to distributors and retailers; it will also permit the firm to buy an office building and hire some additional employees, and repay its outstanding informal funding. The capital that it raises is thus essential to the continued expansion and success of the firm.

ABC Co.'s treasurer, working with a bank, decides to issue £200 million of common stock. In doing so, the firm specifies a par value for its shares, which becomes part of the accounting treatment of the stock after flotation. So, if ABC Co. selects £1 of par value for each share, it can issue up to 200 million shares. After the IPO is completed, ABC Co. , as an enduring corporation with limited liability, will have a capital base of £200 million, which it can use to meet all of the objectives cited above.

As ABC Co. conducts its operations over the coming years, it will (hopefully) begin to generate profits. These profits can be used in various ways once expenses and taxes have been paid. First, after-tax income can be used to pay equity investors-the new owners of the company-a dividend. Corporations regularly pay dividends, which represent a disbursable profit, to common (and preferred) stock investors. But common stock dividend payments are discretionary, rather than mandatory, meaning that a company's board of directors can choose not to pay them if it believes the funds can be put to better use. Second, after-tax income can be reinvested in the company, so that additional productive resources can be acquired to produce more goods and services. This happens by leaving a portion of the profits undistributed-preserving them in an account that is aptly named "retained earnings." As we've noted in Chapter 2, retained earnings form part of the equity account on the corporate balance sheet. Importantly, retained earnings represent an internally generated source of financing (unlike the issuance of equity, which is an external source of financing).

The decision on what to do with after-tax profits is centered on achieving the highest possible return for the owners of ABC Co. shares. If ABC Co. can invest in additional productive endeavors that generate an internal rate of return equal to, or better than, some benchmark, then it may choose to retain most of its earnings and pay only a modest amount (if any) in the form of dividends. Reverting to our discussion from the last chapter, this means approving investments/projects where the NPV is greater than the cost of capital. However, if the company can't identify profitable opportunities that will increase enterprise value (i. e. cost of capital > project NPV), it may decide to pay a larger amount of dividends. In some cases it may even declare a special cash dividend, returning to existing investors a larger portion of their capital. This tends to happen periodically with large companies when it becomes clear that they have capital on hand that they can't invest efficiently. In practice companies tend to pay dividends and reinvest profits so that they can boost the value of their shares and build enterprise value simultaneously. Figure 4. 1 highlights a simple income statement and balance sheet that reflect the flow of net income on the external and internal equity financing accounts.

DIVIDEND POLICY 股利政策

Investors buying stock often expect to receive dividends as a form of risk compensation. Some investors prefer investing in

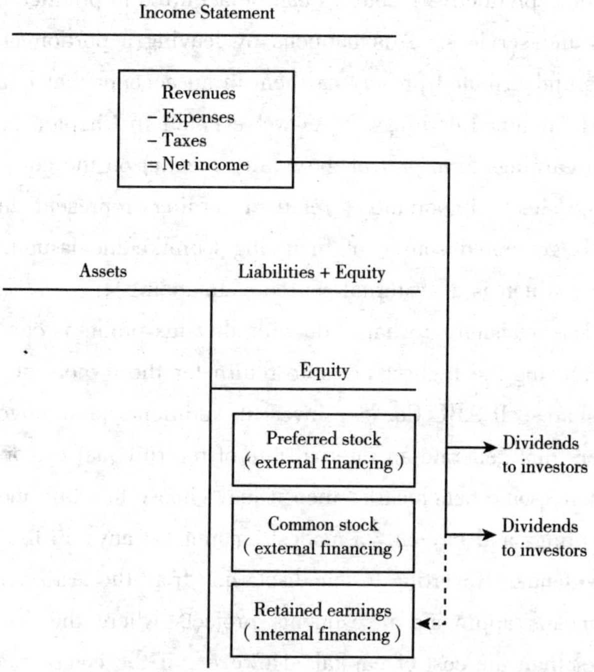

Figure 4. 1 Income statement, balance sheet and net income

the stocks of companies that pay very high dividends, while others are content to buy those that pay lower dividends, under the assumption that net income not paid in the form of dividends will be profitably reinvested in the firm. Since dividends are a representation of a company's ability to generate earnings, both currently and in the future, they affect the value of a company's shares. Dividends also affect, at least indirectly, a company's investing and financing plans. For instance, a company that insists on paying very high dividends will have less internal funds available to pay for new projects or corporate expansion, and may require external financing-which can alter its capital structure and cost of capital, as we'll see in the next chapter.

Financial managers must craft a sensible dividend policy during the planning stage. Finance features competing theories on optimal dividend policies. One theory (put forth by economists Modigliani and Miller) suggests that the value of a firm isn't actually affected by dividend policy. The reasoning is as follows: since dividends are a residual payment they don't form part of the investment decision of a firm and generate no earnings. The cost of capital and the level of earnings therefore don't change when dividend policy changes. A rational firm will reinvest all of its retained earnings as long as the return on investments is greater than the return that can be obtained in the market. In other words, reinvestment will occur as long as returns on reinvested retained earnings are greater than the cost of capital; paying dividends when this condition is true prevents a company from maximizing share value. However, this theory is put forth under a series of assumptions that appear rather restrictive (e. g. a "no tax" regime or one where capital gains taxes are less than ordinary income taxes, no friction costs, perfect capital markets).

Another theory indicates that the value of the firm is, indeed, affected by its selection of a dividend policy. This approach features no assumptions apart from the fact that investors value current cash dividends more than future cash flows obtained from reinvested retained earnings. In effect, payment of cash dividends leads to lower investor uncertainty, which lowers risk and the cost of capital. Some investors also prefer the current income provided by dividends (rather than pure long-term capital gains), and may therefore value such shares more highly. Importantly, dividend payments serve as a signaling device: if investors believe a company intends to pay dividends at a constant or gradually increasing rate over time, they will have greater comfort that future earnings will be strong; the reverse is also true, of course. Either will have an impact on share price.

There is empirical evidence to support the notion that dividend policy has an effect on cost of capital and share valuation. This means that the financial manager faces another balancing act, having to select between maintaining (or gradually increasing) dividends to keep the share price strong and investors satisfied, and reinvesting profits to keep future growth on track. Ideally, dividends should only be paid after all profitable investment opportunities have been reviewed via the NPV/IRR framework.

EQUITY CAPITAL COSTS AND SHARE VALUATION 权益资本成本和股票价格

We know from Chapter 2 that risk/return is the fundamental tradeoff of the financial world. Investors that seek a greater return must be willing to accept a greater amount of risk; those preferring a smaller amount of risk can expect a smaller return. A company arranging financing faces the same tradeoff: if it is funding through an instrument that generates more risk for investors it will have to pay them a greater return than if it uses a less risky instrument. This relationship is central in determining a firm's capital costs and optimal financing mix.

Below we'll see how these tradeoffs relate to a company's funding. First, however, let's consider the position that investors in ABC Co. 's new shares have in the company's capital structure. As owners of the company, equity investors are the first to bear losses should the worst come to pass. When a company experiences financial difficulties that generate large losses, it depletes its retained earnings account, which is held for the benefit of equity investors. As this occurs, the company's stock price is certain to fall, again causing investors some degree of loss (e. g. if they bought shares at £10 and the price falls to £1, at which time they sell, they realize a loss of £9 per share). During this period of financial distress the equity investors effectively bear the first losses. Their capital infusion, which we've said is limited to the amount invested, is used as a buffer to protect all other forms of financing that rank above it, including the preferred stock issues that we discuss below, as well as bond and loan financing that we consider in the next chapter. If bankruptcy occurs investors with a claim that ranks above the equity claim will be repaid first. When all the assets of value are liquidated and outstanding claims are repaid, the residual amount left for the common equity investors may only amount to a few cents on the dollar.

Why would an investor be interested in bearing this first loss risk? Why not sit higher up in the capital structure where there is more protection against losses and a greater chance of a larger recovery if the worst happens? The answer is a higher return. In order to entice investors to supply capital through shares, the company will have to offer a return that compensates for the risk of bearing the first losses. Some investors are willing to accept the increased level of risk associated with stock-but only if they believe they are being appropriately compensated. We can therefore view the common stock buyers as limited liability investors, with voting power, who receive a higher return than other capital suppliers because they bear first losses and are subordinated in bankruptcy. We must also bear in mind that the higher cost of equity capital-the equity risk premium-must also compensate for time: an equity security is a perpetual instrument that will never mature or be redeemed. Accordingly, the probability that an investor may one day bear some degree of first loss is higher than it is on a dated security. Finally, we must note that in most jurisdictions investors are taxed on their dividend income. In order to entie investors to commit capital to the purchase of stock, a company must make the after-tax return sufficiently attractive, meaning a gross-up of the dividend payment, which adds to the cost of equity.

So, how much does equity capital cost? How much will ABC Co. have to offer investors in order to raise the type of permanent financing that it needs to fund its operations? The answer depends on various external and internal factors.

Let's start with the external factors. Market supply of, and demand for, equity capital influences the cost of equity for all firms. When investors believe the market provides a proper equity risk/return, they will be inclined to participate. This means liquidity flows into the market and the overall cost of equity declines (but bear in mind that costs for individual firms may still be higher or lower than the overall market, depending on the internal factors noted below). In other words, a market that features a greater amount of liquidity in search of fair return is going to lead systematically to lower equity financing costs. This tends to happen when an economy is stable, corporate earnings are strong, and financial volatility is low. The opposite scenario also holds true. If investors don't believe that equity prices correctly reflect risk they will withhold their capital, causing a supply shortage that leads ultimately to a rise in overall equity financing costs. Companies that want to issue stock will have to entice investors to supply funds, and will only be able to do so by offering them greater returns (i. e. selling stock at a cheaper price, which means a higher cost of financing). In practice, this scenario appears when economic growth is sluggish, investors are nervous, corporate earnings are poor, and/or the financial markets are very volatile. In fact, all new equity issuance may be temporarily curtailed if the market environment is especially unstable.

Internal company-specific factors play an equally important role in establishing equity costs. Once market forces establish the minimum expected equity return, the ability of a company to generate earnings that create value for shares (via dividends and capital appreciation) helps define the actual cost of accessing equity capital. As we know, the greater the risk, the greater the return capital suppliers will require, so a risky company that has uncertain earnings-generation power will have to pay more for its capital than one that has a stable, gradually expanding, earnings stream. If a company regularly misses its earnings targets because it cannot properly control its revenues or costs, then investors will view this as an extra risk that demands compensation; this additional compensation is obviously a cost to the company, which will be reflected in the premium over the market return paid to attract investor capital. Naturally, other financial variables can impact the stability of the company and affect the perceived riskiness of the firm-these can include insufficient liquidity, failed expansion or merger attempts, significant legal/regulatory issues, weak management, and so forth.

The opposite is also true: a firm that is able to manage its business and financial position properly, expand its revenues, control its costs and flow more dollars or pounds to the bottom line will regularly meet or exceed its earnings targets, providing investors with a proper degree of comfort. This ultimately translates into a lower equity risk premium.

Though exogenous and endogenous forces clearly affect costs, actually estimating the cost of equity capital can be a complicated endeavor. One method is to use a form of CAPM we described in the last chapter as a risk value proxy. Remember, we are attempting to estimate the cost of equity capital for a single company, and this will be influenced by the external and internal variables described above. We know that beta is a measure of a company's riskiness versus the market at large. Accordingly, the cost of equity can be set as a function of beta, the risk-free rate and the market return:

$$\text{cost of equity} = \text{risk-free rate} + \text{beta}(\text{market return} - \text{risk-free rate}) \qquad [4.1]$$

For instance, if ABC Co.'s market beta is 1.25, the market return is 10 percent and the risk-free rate is 4 percent, ABC Co.'s estimated cost of equity capital-the return investors will demand for holding ABC Co.'s equity-is 11.50 percent. While this approach is widely used and perfectly valid, it obviously requires comfort with the assumptions underlying CAPM.

While our discussion has intentionally focused on externally generated equity, we must not forget that retained earnings also involve a cost. Though there are no fees associated with retained earnings since they are generated by post-tax/post-dividend income, they attract a cost of capital that is generally set equal to the cost of common stock. This approach is appropriate because if a company doesn't have any retained earnings, it will have to issue common stock to fund its balance sheet (i. e. it cannot be purely debt financed, for reasons that we explore in Chapter 5).

A firm does not face a single cost of equity capital. We can generalize overall costs by noting that a company faces a situation where:

$$\begin{aligned}\text{cost of common stock} &= \text{cost of retained earnings}\\ &> \text{cost of preferred stock} \quad [4.2]\\ &> \text{cost of debt}\end{aligned}$$

This relationship holds true because of claims seniority in the capital structure and the order in which losses are allocated.

Once a company's cost of equity has been estimated, it is possible to value preferred or common shares that have been, or are about to be, issued. This process is based primarily on discounting of future dividends, which we know represent a company's earnings power. Estimating dividends is not a precise science since it involves unknown future cash flows. We cannot be precisely certain, for instance, how much ABC Co. will earn in the future or how much it might choose to pay in dividends. Nevertheless, some estimates have to be made to produce a fair value. The general valuation framework depends on three key variables: the cost of equity, dividends, and dividend growth rate.

Before looking at various dividend-based valuation models, let's consider a few general issues regarding dividends. Dividends are often paid on a quarterly basis to investors holding shares as of a particular record date; an ex-dividend date occurs up to four days before record date and indicates which investors are entitled to the dividends. When a stock goes "ex-dividend," its price declines by the dividend per share value, since this is value existing within the company that is being paid away. While most dividends are paid in cash, some non-cash exceptions exist: the stock dividend, which involves the issuance of a fractional quantity of new shares in lieu of cash (e. g. each investor receives 0. 05 new shares for every ten shares owned) and the stock split, which is similar but often much larger in scope (e. g. each investor exchanges one old share for two shares, though the value of the stock is reduced by the same proportion).

Naturally, not every company pays dividends. For instance, when a firm is in a start-up phase and prefers to reinvest its capital in growth opportunities, or if it is in a poor financial state and can't generate a profit, shareholders may not receive any dividend payments. Furthermore, it is illegal in some jurisdictions for a firm to borrow funds to pay dividends, as this simply places the compensation of equity investors on the shoulders of creditors. Similarly, bank lenders may bar a firm from issuing dividends if it breaches any financial ratios in its lending facilities.

As we've noted, dividends are paid from after-tax earnings, meaning they generate no tax advantage; this represents an additional cost to investors, which we'll discuss in more detail in the next chapter. The dividend yield of a security, computed by dividing the current dividend by the current stock price, is an important measure of the current return of an equity security, allowing investors to compare returns across companies and industry sectors. The dividend payout ratio indicates how much of a company's net earnings is going to investors rather than the retained earnings account; this is computed by dividing dividends per share by earnings per share. A company that has predictable earnings growth is more likely to pay a high portion of its earnings out in the form of dividends. But a high dividend payout ratio doesn't imply earnings stability. A company may pay large portions of its earnings in dividends in order to attract investors, but may also suffer from volatile earnings that can jeopardize its ability to deliver dividends. In fact, investors view companies that cut their dividends in an unfavorable light, and often sell their holdings. A rational dividend policy requires directors and executives of a firm to determine future earnings growth and analyze sensitivity to changing market circumstances and economic cycles. For instance, one approach calls for dividend payouts to remain low until a company's earnings base is stable and well established.

The dividend growth rate is another important tool used in valuations, and can be estimated via:

$$\text{growth} = \frac{\text{net income}}{\text{equity}}\left[1 - \left(\frac{\text{dividends per share}}{\text{earnings per share}}\right)\right] \qquad [4.3]$$

We note in Equation 4.3 that the growth rate is a function of both return on equity (net income/equity) and the dividend payout ratio (dividends/earnings). We shall return to the dividend growth rate below.

With these basic thoughts, let's begin our share valuation analysis with preferred stock, the simplest of the equity claims. We know that preferred stock is an equity-like security that grants the investor access to a fixed dividend payment stream in perpetuity; this means valuation of the security is quite simple: the future dividend cash flows are contractually fixed and there is no need to take account of the future value of the principal, as the security is never redeemed. So, if we assume a share of preferred stock pays a periodic dividend (quarterly, semi-annually, or annually), the value of a share of stock is simply the PV of the dividend stream in perpetuity, discounted by the firm's cost of preferred equity. This is shown in [4.4] as:

$$\text{price of preferred} = \frac{\text{dividends}}{(1+\text{cost of preferred})^{\text{time 1}}} + \frac{\text{dividends}}{(1+\text{cost of preferred})^{\text{time 2}}} + \cdots \quad [4.4]$$

$$\Rightarrow \frac{\text{dividends}}{\text{cost of preferred}}$$

For instance, if we assume ABC Co. 's cost of preferred is 15 percent and a share of its preferred stock pays an annual dividend of £2. 50/share, the fair price of the preferred is £16. 67/share. This formula also suggests that as the price of the dividend rises, the value of the preferred increases, and vice-versa-a perfectly logical relationship. Thus, if the annual dividend increases to £3. 50/share, the price of the preferred rises to £23. 33/share; if it declines to £1. 50/share, the price of the preferred falls to £10/share. In practice preferreds with fixed dividends tend to pay the same fixed dividend over a long period of time, so that upward and downward moves tend to be relatively small.

The same general approach can be used to value a share of common stock. Common stock, like preferred stock, will never be redeemed so there is no need to account for the PV of the redemption amount. Unlike preferreds, however, common stock does not always pay dividends-we recall that the dividend payment is at the discretion of a company's directors. And, if a company does pay dividends, those payments are likely to change over time.

Accordingly, common stock can be valued using one of several approaches, including the constant dividend model (which is the same as the process above), the growing dividend model, or the discrete dividend model. Regardless of the method used, we recall that cost of common equity used to discount common dividend cash flows is higher than the cost of preferred equity used to discount preferred dividend cash flows, since common stock is riskier than preferred stock.

When the dividend on a common stock is expected to grow at a constant rate we adjust estimated dividends to reflect that growth, and can do so via dividend payments × (1 + growth rate); this is simply a scaling of the dividend payment for each period. However, we also have to adjust the cost of capital by the same growth rate to take account of the fact that additional returns will be earned. This yields the following formula:

$$\text{price of common} = \frac{\text{dividends } (1 + \text{growth rate})}{\text{cost of common} - \text{growth rate}} \quad [4.5]$$

Let's assume that ABC Co.'s cost of common stock is 18 percent, its current dividend is £1/share, and the expected dividend growth rate is 3 percent. The fair value of ABC Co.'s common stock under the constant dividend growth model is £6.87. Under this scheme it is relatively easy to deduce that if earnings increase and dividends expand in tandem, the cost of equity capital will decline. This finding is consistent with our earlier statement: companies with a stronger base of earnings and growth are perceived as less risky than those with weak and/or volatile earnings, meaning the returns payable to investors are lower.

Valuing a share of stock based on discrete dividends, or individual dividend payments that vary from period to period, follows the same approach but requires a more precise estimate of how much a company will pay in each period. This can be a complicated process, as it demands a reasonably realistic method of forecasting potential earnings and dividend payouts. Once the estimate is obtained cash flows are simply discounted back using the cost of common equity, which yields an estimate of the value.

Determining the value of an IPO share is slightly more involved, because the firm issuing stock is a private company or partnership with no historical price record of its own. To get around this problem market participants typically rely on one of several different techniques. The first is to use comparable public firms as a proxy. Thus, if ABC Co. has several publicly traded competitors in its market sector, it can examine how those companies have traded over a period of time and what specific differences exist between those firms and ABC Co. The price of the stock can then be set in relation to what the comparables suggest might be a fair value.

A more precise approach involves using comparables data in the constant dividend model, and then making an adjustment for the target company's specific forecast earnings. Rearranging the terms from equation [4.5] to solve for the cost of common equity, we note:

$$\text{cost of common} = \frac{\text{dividends}}{\text{price of common}} + \text{growth rate} \quad [4.6]$$

Thus, if comparable company XYZ Co. is trading at a price of £30/ share, pays £3/share in dividends every year, and features earnings growth of 5 percent, its cost of capital is 15 percent. If we assume for simplicity that ABC Co. expects to earn £500,000 in year 1 which it will pay out as dividends, and plans to issue 500,000 shares of stock, then the price of the stock, based on the comparables' constant growth dividend model, is £6.67/share (£500,000/0.15 = £3.33 million/ 500,000 shares). If the bankers and ABC Co.'s management don't believe the same growth rate parameters apply, they can adjust the growth rate and, by extension, the cost of capital (i.e. a lower growth rate will translate into a lower stock price, and vice-versa). Note that if the company wants to raise a specific amount of equity, such as £20 million, it can use the same share price and simply adjust the number of shares it plans to issue, e.g. £20 million/£6.67 = 3.03 million shares, rather than 500,000 shares.

We see that dividends play a significant role in all of the valuation methods noted above. As a result, a proper dividend policy, based on a company's fundamental earnings strength, capacity, and volatility, along with attention to what competitors/industry peers are doing, is an effective way of avoiding any surprises that can hurt the share price. It's worth noting that analysts, investors, and financial managers commonly use the methods of share valuation we have described above. There are, of course, other ways of estimating value, including frameworks that make use of balance sheet information and earnings per share information. While these are valid, they are beyond the scope of our discussion.

While most of the cost of equity financing is covered by the external and internal variables noted above, a company still needs to pay its bankers for arranging a transaction. Bankers arranging new or secondary issues are responsible for coordinating the entire process and charge fees for doing so. In fact, the fees payable by a company for an equity issue can be significant, ranging in most markets from 4 percent to 7 percent. This, as we'll see in the next chapter, is relatively expensive, and adds considerably to an issuer's total funding expense. In practice, the size of an equity issue can be scaled up to take account of the fees, or reduced by subtracting the fees. Thus, if ABC Co. requires a minimum of £500 million of common stock on a net basis and must pay a 4 percent fee, it will need to raise a total sum of approximately £52 million. Alternatively, if it simply wants to raise £500 million on a gross basis, its net proceeds will be £480 million.

INSTRUMENT CHARACTERISTICS
工具特征

Equity comes in various forms, each with unique characteristics. In this section we describe the features of the main types of external equity instruments, which are summarized in

Figure 4. 2.

KEY CHARACTERISTICS 关键特征

Common and preferred stock issues are defined by a number of characteristics, all of which are negotiated in advance of flotation. These include size, dividend, maturity, placement mechanism, market, and seniority.

- Size: The amount of stock being placed with investors. This can range from less than $1 million to well over $1 billion, depending on the issuing company, its needs, investor appetite, and market circumstances. For instance, ABC Co. may decide to issue £200 million in common stock and £100 million in preferred stock as part of its overall financing plan. 规模
- Dividend: The specific dividend being paid for a given series of shares. This applies primarily to preferred stock issues, which may feature a fixed or variable dividend payable on a cumulative or non-cumulative basis. Remember, common 股利

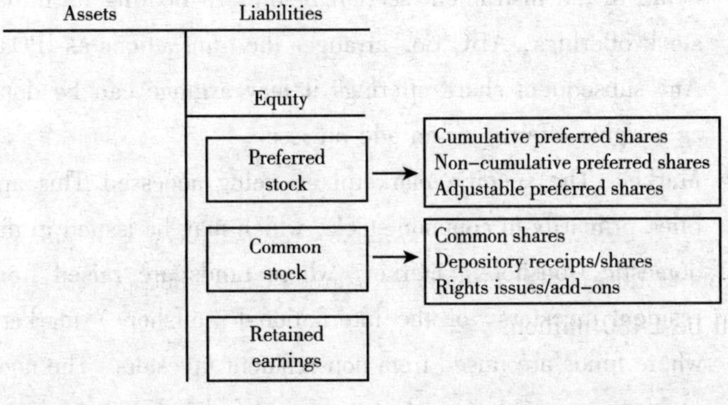

Figure 4. 2 Equity accounts on the corporate balance sheet

stock often pays a dividend (generally every quarter), but such payments are entirely discretionary and cannot therefore be included as a defining characteristic of an issue. ABC Co., for instance, may pay an annualized dividend of 7 percent every quarter on its preferred stock issue, which becomes a contractual characteristic of the security. (It may also pay 3 percent dividends on its common stock, but since these are discretionary and changeable, they do not form part of the ex-ante definition of the security.)

到期日

- Maturity: The specific term of the issue. This is quite an exceptional characteristic, and relates only to a small minority of preferred stock issues with redemption features. In all other cases, e. g. common stock issues and conventional preferred stock issues, the securities are perpetual, and can only be retired or redeemed through a specific repurchase mechanism.

募集机制

- Placement mechanism: The manner in which securities are placed with investors. Inaugural issues of stock form part of the IPO mechanism, meaning the securities can be offered to a broad range of investors. Any subsequent issues (e. g. secondary placements) may be offered as rights issues (to existing investors) or add-on issues (to all investors). We consider rights issues, which are relatively common, in more detail in the instrument section below. In floating its initial stock offerings, ABC Co. arranges the transactions as IPOs. Any subsequent share offerings it may arrange can be done as a rights offering or an add-on issue.

市场

- Market: The specific marketplace being accessed. This applies primarily to common stock, which may be issued in the domestic (onshore) market, where funds are raised from resident investors, or the international (offshore) market, where funds are raised from non-resident investors. The non-resident issues are raised in the form of global depository receipts (GDRs), global depository shares (GDSs), American depository receipts (ADRs) or American depository shares (ADSs); we discuss these in the next section. The selection of a market depends on various factors, including cost (i. e. where a company can issue stock on the best terms), availability (i. e. which pools of investors are willing to supply capital), and overall market conditions (i. e. where market stability (volatility) may attract (repel) capital). Preferred stock tends to be issued mainly in domestic markets, though some offshore exceptions occur. Since ABC Co. is UK-based and is well known to UK investors, it may choose to float sterling-denominated common and preferred shares in the domestic market.

- Seniority: The priority of the stock regarding claims on the issuing company's assets. The seniority of shares dictates the priority of payments to equity holders should a company declare bankruptcy. While all forms of debt rank senior to equity (as we shall discuss in more detail in Chapter 5), preferred stock ranks above common stock. This means that in a bankruptcy situation, preferred stock investors will be repaid from the company's assets before common stock investors-but only after debt holders (creditors) have been repaid. Since all forms of stock rank below debt, recovery levels in bankruptcy are generally very low-perhaps only a few cents for every dollar invested.

求偿等级

KEY INSTRUMENTS 主要工具

The key instruments of the equity sector include:

- Common stock. Common stock can be issued in the local market, or it can be floated in the offshore markets in order to attract a base of international investors As noted, the initial launch of common stock is known as an IPO, and any subsequent secondary issues take the form of rights issues or addons-though both ultimately lead to the creation of additional common shares. Common stock is typically issued as a scripless (dematerialized) ownership interest with a stated par value; it is a perpetual security that can pay dividends, though is not contractually obliged to do so. As we've indicated above, non-resident issues can be issued in various

普通股

forms. Depository receipts (GDRs, ADRs) are securities that are issued by a depository on behalf of the issuing company; the company lodges shares with the depository, which then issues tradable receipts to investors (with each receipt often representing a single share). Depository shares (GDSs, ADSs) function in a similar manner, except that the depository issues shares rather than receipts to investors. Note that both forms can be traded as any normal stock offering.

配股

- Rights issues. Rights issues are secondary placements of stock that are offered initially to existing shareholders, giving them the right of first refusal to invest in the new shares; the rights effectively allow existing investors to control dilution: by exercising the rights to take up new shares (generally at a small discount to the prevailing market price), existing investors retain the same proportion of ownership and control, meaning dilution is avoided. Rights can be issued in transferable or nontransferable form: transferable rights can be sold by existing investors to other investors, while non-transferable rights cannot be conveyed to third parties and simply expire if they are not used. Once issued and taken up, the shares form part of the company's common stock base.

优先股

- Preferred stock. Preferred stock is a security that pays investors a periodic dividend, and does not generally permit any participation in capital gains (i. e. its price is quoted in a relatively fixed range) Preferred stock dividends are generally constant. Some forms of preferred, known as adjustable rate, or money market, preferred stock, link their dividend payments to a spread over a floating rate index. The dividends established for a preferred stock can be structured in several forms. The most common type of preferred stock is cumulative, which means that dividends that are due to preferred investors accumulate in cases where the company is unable to make a current dividend payment. No other dividends can be paid to other equity investors until any dividend arrears have been settled. Another form of preferred stock is the non-cumulative structure, which does not allow for dividend accrual; if a dividend is skipped, non-cumulative investors have no continuing claim on that dividend.

ISSUING AND TRADING 发行和交易

ISSUING 发行

Before any stock issue can be launched in the market, the appropriate securities commissioner or regulator must approve it. Once this occurs, the stock issue becomes known as "authorized." When a company decides to issue a certain amount of stock, the actual shares that are floated are known as "authorized and issued," and these become part of a company's permanent capital base. In practice, a company generally only issues a portion of its shares initially so that it can preserve additional capacity for future issues (and employee stock plans). Any additional capacity is shown as a note on the financial statements as stock that is "authorized but not issued" (e. g. the regulator approves up to £1 billion of shares but ABC Co. elects to float only £200 million, leaving an unused balance of £800 million). The equity account is not affected as shares that have not been floated obviously raise no funds; still, investors are alerted to the fact that future issuance may occur. Conversely, if ABC Co. decides to repurchase some of its outstanding stock issue (e. g. £50 million), it can do so by buying them in the open market for cash; when this happens the treasury stock contra-account is debited by the amount of the repurchase (i. e. the common stock account is reduced by the amount of the repurchase to reflect the fact that the capital base has actually declined). These shares are known as "issued but not outstanding." We summarize these states of the common stock account in Figure 4.3.

Paid-in capital account	
Authorized and not issued (1 billion shares at £1 par value)	…
Authorized and issued (200 million shares at £1 par value)	£200 million
Issued and not outstanding (50 million shares)	—£50 million
Total paid-in capital account	£150 million

Figure 4.3 Impact of shares on paid-in capital

Raising equity capital begins when a bank, working closely with the issuing company, establishes necessary equity financing requirements, prepares detailed preliminary disclosure (known as a "red herring") and registers the proposed issue with the national securities commission. Once regulators approve the disclosure (which becomes known as the prospectus) the bank begins a pre-marketing phase to determine investor appetite and potential pricing levels (i.e. a price that will be attractive to investors); this process involves a detailed analysis of where the stock prices of comparable companies are trading. Not surprisingly, the best time to issue stock is when a company's stock price is already strong; this means less shares have to be issued for a given amount of equity, which decreases the effect of dilution. In large deals the bank is likely to assemble a syndicate of other banks to help distribute the shares. The final price of the shares is established on launch date and securities are placed with investors based on an allocation method determined by the lead bank.

In most instances a bank arranging a stock issue is not required to deliver a specific amount of funds to the issuing company. Thus, if ABC Co. seeks £500 million of common stock but investors are only interested in purchasing £350 million at the quoted price, the company only receives £350 million.

However, in some instances (mainly those involving add-ons), a bank may agree to purchase the entire block of £500 million at a fixed price, and then distribute the shares to investors. These "block trades" ensure that companies like ABC Co. receive the full amount of equity they are seeking-but are relatively risky for the arranging bank, because the price may fall before the bank can place all of the shares. In order to protect itself from any possible losses, the bank generally purchases the block at a discount to the prevailing market price. For example, if ABC Co. wishes to raise an additional £500 million through the issuance of 500, 000 shares at a current market price of £10/share, the bank may agree to buy the entire block of 500, 000 at a price of £9. 95, meaning the net proceeds to ABC Co. amount to £497. 5 million-a £2. 5 million shortfall to the firm, which must be factored into the overall cost of capital.

SECONDARY TRADING 二级市场交易

Major banks and securities dealers actively quote prices on a range of small and large capitalization stocks on a continuous basis. Dealers provide a buy (bid) and sell (offer) price on individual issues, allowing investors to enter or exit the market once an issue has been launched. The prices that dealers are willing to quote are based on the macro and micro variables we've discussed. If these factors are favorable/benign, dealers will be willing to quote tighter bid-offer spreads than if they are unfavorable/volatile. For instance, if the market environment is positive and the outlook for ABC Co.'s earnings is strong, a dealer may quote shares at £10. 00 – 10. 02, meaning it stands ready to buy a share at £10 and sell the same share at £10. 02, making a profit of £0. 02 in the process. Conversely, if the markets are volatile, investors are nervous, or ABC Co.'s earnings prospects are weakening, the dealer may widen the spread to £10. 00 – 10. 07; this wider spread is intended to compensate the dealer for the additional risk taken in owning the shares.

Most secondary equity trading occurs through conventional exchanges, such as the London Stock Exchange, New York Stock Exchange, Tokyo Stock Exchange, and NASDAQ (among many others), which feature "physical" open-outcry trading floors or electronic matching systems. However, a growing amount of volume now flows through electronic communications networks (ECNs), which are electronic conduits that allow participants to trade directly on screen. In fact, the advent of computing power and advanced networking has led to the creation of many such platforms, which have increased the competitive threat to traditional exchanges. Not only do these platforms increase efficiencies and price transparency, they extend trading hours. The migration to 24-hour trading-certainly in many of the largest stocks around the world-is very nearly a reality as a result of this type of electronic trading.

摘要

每一个以公司制建立的企业必须在其资产负债表有一些数量的股票，这表明通过普通股和优先股的权益融资是公司融资的主要组成。权益资本的成本高于负债资本是基于三个原因：第一，权益投资者比债权人接受更多的风险，如果公司破产就承担第一损失。第二，权益不能像负债那样获得同样的税收挡避，因为股利是由税后利润支付的，而不是税前利润。以及第三，投资者经常要为其收到的股利纳税，这意味着他们需要通过较高的股利收益被诱使去乐意投资股票。确定资产负债表上权益的合适数额是重要的：太少的权益意味着太多的负债，这可能会导致财务压力。

FURTHER READING 延伸阅读

Damodaran, A., 1994, *Damodaran on Valuation*, New York: John Wiley & Sons.

Koller, T., Goedhart, M. and Wessels, D., 2005, *Valuation*, *4th edition*, New York: John Wiley & Sons.

Schwartz, R. and Francioni, R., 2004, *Equity Markets in Action*, New York: John Wiley & Sons.

5

LOANS AND BONDS
贷款和债券

CHAPTER OVERVIEW 本章概述

In this chapter we examine loans and bonds, which together comprise debt capital, the second major class of external corporate financing. We commence with a review of why and how loans and bonds are used, the relative costs and benefits of borrowing through the debt markets, and the tradeoffs that exist between using too much and too little debt financing. We then consider the macro and micro forces that drive borrowing costs, and conclude by describing the characteristics of loans and bonds, and how they are created and traded. The concepts of debt financing covered in this chapter should be compared and contrasted with the equity financing material discussed in Chapter 4.

USES OF LOANS AND BONDS
贷款和债券的用途

In our last chapter we noted how equity can be used to finance corporate operations. While equity is obviously essential to any financial plan, it is not the sole source of funding. In fact, the availability of debt capital is critically important to companies attempting to maximize enterprise value, as we shall discover.

We've already seen that ABC Co. can use the equity markets to meet its financing requirements. But we know that equity can be expensive. Since investors in ABC Co.'s common shares bear the risk of first losses, they demand a higher return on their invested capital. The higher return to investors is, of course, reflected in a higher overall cost of capital for ABC Co. We have also indicated that in some markets equity dividends aren't tax deductible, meaning that they are paid from after-tax, rather than pre-tax, income. This also adds to the company's cost of capital, because in order to persuade an investor to buy the dividend-paying shares, the pre-tax cost of funding has to be increased to reflect the additional tax burden.

So, are there cheaper ways for ABC Co. to fund its operations? Are there other financing instruments that can help the company lower its costs, so that it can allocate more of its income to retained earnings or pay it out to shareholders as dividends?

Fortunately ABC Co. can turn to the loan and bond markets to finance a significant portion of its operations, generally at a much lower cost. In fact, debt can be up to several hundred basis points (100 basis points = 1%) cheaper than equity, and the cost savings can lead to an increase in enterprise value.

We recall that ABC Co. can issue equity in the market for the equivalent of 11.5 percent, so each £100 million that it has to raise for its operations costs £11.5 million. If ABC Co.'s total assets amount to £1 billion, total financing costs through equity add up to £115 million. But what if ABC Co.'s treasurer found that the company could raise debt at a cost of only 5 percent? That's a saving of £6.5 million for every £100 million raised. If ABC Co. decided to do the majority of its funding (i.e. 99.9 percent) in the form of debt rather than equity, its total financing cost would amount to just under £50 million-a compelling savings versus the £115 million required for equity financing. ABC Co. could reinvest the extra funds in productive operations that help generate more earnings (and value). In fact, this savings is one of the key reasons companies use loans and bonds so actively.

Such big savings might bring to mind two questions: why is debt so much cheaper than equity? And, if it is so cheap, doesn't this means the financing decision is relatively easy-all debt and no equity?

Let's start with the first question. Debt financing is cheaper than equity financing for two reasons, both of them running parallel to what we've already mentioned about equity. First, debt is an IOU, or corporate promise to repay a lender or investor any amount borrowed, plus interest, in the future. Equity, in contrast, represents a perpetual ownership claim. Debt holders are therefore creditors, while equity investors are owners. In fact, unsecured debt holders have no ownership claim on a firm's assets because they are not owners of the firm. In order to protect against this lack of ownership claim and ensure equitable treatment in the event of default and bankruptcy, debt holders are given payment priority over equity investors. This priority means that if a company goes into bankruptcy, assets with value are used to repay debt holders first (the actual order of claims priorities within the debt capital structure varies, as we'll discuss later). Because of this bankruptcy claim priority, debt holders bear less risk than equity investors, and we already know that lower risk investments command lower returns. This translates into a lower cost of financing for the company.

Second is the fact that the interest expense used to pay debt holders for the use of their capital is tax deductible. That is, interest expense is paid from operating revenues, before taxable income is computed. This deductibility generates what is commonly known as a tax shield. Equity dividends are generally not tax deductible and don't create the same shield. Let's consider the simplified income statements in Table 5. 1 to demonstrate the tax effect of debt and equity financing. The debt-financed income statement carries £10, 000 of interest expense while the equity financed income statement features £10, 000 of dividend expense. We immediately note that the equity-financed income statement features a higher tax bill since no interest expense is incurred and no tax shield is generated; the debt-financed income statement, in contrast, creates an extra £2, 000 of retained earnings through the shield.

Table 5. 1 Debt and equity-financed income statements

Debt financed income statement, 000s		Equity financed income statement, 000s	
Revenues	£200	Revenues	£200
Cost of goods sold	– £100	Cost of goods sold	– £100
Gross profit	= £100	Gross profit	= £100
Interest expense	– £10	Interest expense	– £0
Pre-tax profit	= £90	Pre-tax profit	= £100
Tax at 20%	– £18	Tax at 20%	– £20
After-tax profit	= £72	After-tax profit	= £80
Dividends	– £0	Dividends	– £10
Net profit to retained earnings	= £72	Net profit to retained earnings	= £70

We see, then, that the cost of debt must be adjusted to reflect the tax benefit, helping generate an after-tax cost that is lower than the cost of equity. This can be calculated as:

$$\text{after tax cost of debt} = (1 - \text{tax rate}) \times \text{cost of debt} \quad [5.1]$$

Thus, if ABC Co. 's borrowing rate on a loan is 7 percent and its tax rate is 27. 5 percent, its effective after-tax cost of debt is just over 5 percent. Again, this is a significant savings compared to the 11.5 percent it is paying for its equity capital.

This brings us back to our second question. If debt is inexpensive compared to equity, it seems that ABC Co.'s treasurer has a simple decision: issue as much debt as possible so that financing costs are as small as possible. Unfortunately, the answer is not this easy. Just as too much equity can be extremely expensive, too much debt can create significant financial burdens. A company that borrows creates a fixed charge, because the borrowing commits it legally to paying interest and principal on a pre-set schedule. The company must make the agreed principal and interest payments on schedule if it wants to avoid default. This means a portion of every pound or dollar earned has to be earmarked for this fixed charge (commonly known as debt service), which reduces the company's financial and operating flexibility (i. e. no longer can it do precisely what it wishes to do with its revenues and income). The same obligation doesn't exist with equity. Even though a company might pay its shareholders dividends-the equivalent of an interest payment-we recall that dividends are entirely voluntary (apart from certain mandatory dividends for preferred shares). A company doesn't have to pay dividends, so it creates no fixed charge against its operations.

Too much debt can therefore lead to an excessive burden on operating revenues and reduce corporate flexibility; it can also lead to more volatile earnings, as noted below. In fact, the burden can become so large that a company might even enter into a state of financial distress, where the likelihood of bankruptcy rises dramatically. Once the specter of financial distress appears, the company's cost of debt will soar-remember, the greater the risk, the greater the return demanded by investors/lenders, so the greater the company's cost of capital.

Knowing this, we can conclude that there is some point where too much debt and too little equity is not an optimal financing strategy. In practice the best mix of debt and equity on a company's balance sheet depends on its business, expansion plans, investment opportunities, relative debt and equity financing costs, and tax rates. It also tends to vary by industry. Some industries, like those involved in heavy industrial manufacturing with considerable long-term plant and equipment requirements (steel, shipbuilding, auto manufacturing), might favor a greater amount of permanent financing via equity and long-term debt. Others, like financial institutions making short-term loans or buying securities, might prefer a greater amount of short/medium-term debt to equity. Credit rating agencies and bank lenders monitor the debt levels of companies and industries, and tend to penalize those that stray too far from industry norms or those that cannot handle the financial burden.

FINANCIAL LEVERAGE 财务杠杆

During the financial planning process managers can consider the proper amount of debt by determining the impact of financial leverage, or the degree to which debt can be safely used to fund investment and operations. We know that interest cost generates a tax shield as well as an interest burden, so a financial manager trying to determine the optimal level of capital must focus on both earnings before interest and taxes (EBIT) and earnings per share (EPS). To consider the impact of debt on these two measures, let's examine a very simplified example based on ABC Co.'s capital structure in two forms-unleveraged and leveraged. Table 5.2 contains sample data.

The degree of financial leverage can be computed via a simple formula:

Table 5.2 **ABC Co.: leveraged and unleveraged results**

	ABC Co. unleveraged	ABC Co. leveraged
Total capitalization	£200m of equity (10m shares outstanding), £0 debt	£100m of equity (5m shares outstanding), £100m of debt
EBIT	£100m	£100m
Interest expense (at 8%)	£0	£8m
Operating profit	£100m	£92m
Tax expense (at 20%)	£20m	£18.4m
Net income	£80m	£73.6m
EPS	£8/share	£14.7/share

$$\text{financial leverage} = \text{EBIT} / (\text{EBIT} - \text{interest expense}) \qquad [5.2]$$

The unleveraged ABC Co. has financial leverage equal to 1.0, while a leveraged ABC Co. has financial leverage of 1.087. This means that for every unit increase in EBIT, unleveraged ABC Co.'s net income increases by 1 unit, while leveraged ABC Co.'s net income increases by 1.087 units. Unfortunately, the reverse holds true for every unit of decline: the leveraged ABC Co.'s net income falls by 1.087 instead of just 1.0.

We notice through these results that a leveraged ABC Co. features higher EPS as a result of the tax shield and the smaller number of shares included in the total capital base. This means that as the business environment strengthens and ABC Co. sells more goods and generates more profits, it delivers greater EPS to its shareholders than if it were unleveraged. We recall from Chapter 3 that higher earnings lead to higher stock valuations, which generate greater returns for investors. But the downside is also clear: if the economy weakens, ABC Co.'s revenues and profits may decline but its interest burden will remain the same, squeezing profits and reducing EPS. This increases financial pressures, raises the cost of capital and lowers the firm's stock price. It's worth noting that one theory of finance, based on arguments put forth by Modigliani and Miller, says that changes in a company's capital structure won't affect its cost of capital; this theory is based on rather restrictive assumptions, however, and is challenged by competing theories and empirical evidence. We assume in our discussion that changes in capital structure do, indeed, have an effect on cost of capital.

Earnings (or EPS) volatility is directly related to the degree of financial leverage a firm chooses. We recall from earlier that companies seek to minimize earnings volatility in order to strengthen their share prices: managing financial leverage properly is thus essential in creating enterprise value.

盈余波动性

We can therefore summarize by saying that if too little debt is used the benefits derived from financial leverage are greater than the cost of capital, meaning more debt can be added. Conversely, if too much debt is used, the interest burden rises, earnings and EPS decline, investors will demand a higher return, the cost of capital rises and the stock price declines. How is the optimal degree of leverage determined? Primarily through a trial and error process, where each company experiments with different levels of borrowing; some guidance can also be sought by examining peer and industry groups. Ultimately, a proper mix of debt and equity serves a company best-it optimizes the balance sheet, dampens earnings volatility, lowers the prospect of financial distress, allows proper use of tax shields, provides good access to different sources of funds (which lowers risk in case one source disappears) and generates the lowest prudent weighted cost of financing.

BORROWING COSTS 借款成本

Borrowing costs are a function of several variables. Like equity financing, some of these are external, or market-related, while others are internal, or company-specific. The two ultimately dictate how much a company will pay for its debt financing and how it can optimize its capital structure.

Let's begin with the external factors. The level of market interest rates is the base variable that impacts every company's debt funding. We know from Chapter 2 that interest rates represent the general cost of borrowing, or the level at which debt capital can be attracted from investors/lenders. Since interest rates represent some minimum cost of accessing debt capital, it is clear that they have a bearing on what ABC Co. can expect to pay for funds. If the market interest rate environment is low, overall corporate borrowing costs will be low, and if they are high, costs will be high. Of course, this is just a benchmark level because when we refer to interest rate levels generically we refer to the risk-free market rate accorded to high-quality government borrowers, such as the US, UK, Japan, Switzerland, Canada, Australia, and Euro zone countries. But we know that individual companies are riskier than government borrowers-certainly in the case of industrialized markets-meaning they will have to supplement the base interest cost with some premium related to their own level of riskiness; we'll defer this point until later since it is an internal factor.

We also recall that the maturity of borrowing has an impact on costs. In a "normal" upward sloping yield curve environment rates are lower in the short term than in the medium or long term, meaning that those wanting to borrow short-term will pay less, and those wanting to borrow long-term will pay more. The opposite is true when the yield curve is downward sloping. Figure 5. 1 highlights sample high-, mid-, and low interest rate environments and associated upward sloping yield curves; these are key macro drivers in determining borrowing costs.

This fact raises another question: if short-term rates are lower in an upward sloping yield curve environment-the most common market scenario-shouldn't a company always borrow short-term funds? Not necessarily. Short-term funding (out to 6 or 12 months) requires a company to continuously roll over its obligations in order to maintain the same level of funding. If rollovers are not possible as a result of market disruptions (i. e. investors or lenders don't want to provide short-term capital) a company risks getting caught in a liquidity funding squeeze, which can have dangerous financial consequences-including bankruptcy in the most severe instances. In addition, short-term rates can always rise. A company that borrows medium-or long-term funds locks in its interest costs for an extended period of time and therefore isn't susceptible either to funding withdrawal or a rising rate scenario. There is thus a tradeoff: in a normal positive yield curve environment a company can pay lower costs by borrowing short-term, but also increase the risk that it will be unable to roll over funding when needed, or it can pay higher costs by borrowing long-term and remove the risk that its funding will disappear. In practice companies often "match fund" their assets and liabilities: that is, they finance their long-term assets, such as plant and equipment, with long-term debt, and their short-term, or seasonal, assets, with short-term debt.

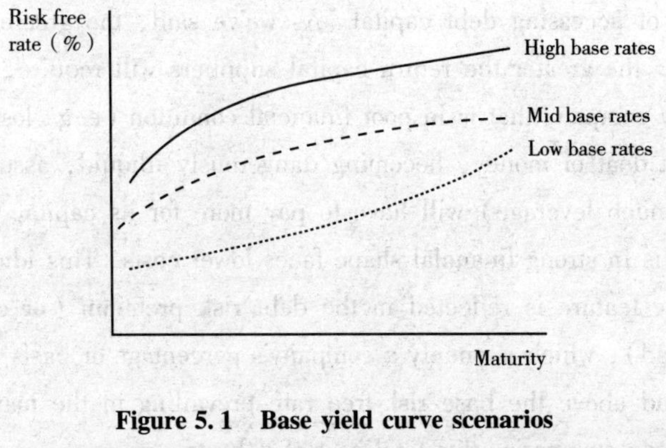

Figure 5. 1 Base yield curve scenarios

The overall market supply and demand of capital is another external factor that can influence borrowing levels. When lenders and bond investors feel the market properly compensates them for providing risk capital, they will be inclined to participate. This means liquidity flows into the market and overall credit borrowing levels can decline-again, with due reference to the fact that individual borrowing costs may be higher or lower, depending on company-specific factors. A system that features a larger amount of liquidity in search of fair return is going to lead systematically to lower debt financing costs. This tends to happen when an economy is stable, rate levels are reasonable, and financial volatility is low. The opposite scenario also holds true. If investors and lenders feel that rate levels do not provide fair compensation they will withhold capital, causing a supply shortage and a rise in overall borrowing costs. Companies seeking funding will have to entice investors/lenders to supply funds, and will only be able to do so by offering them greater returns-a higher cost of financing. This scenario appears when economic growth is sluggish, investors/ lenders are nervous, or the financial markets are very volatile.

Internal factors play an important role in setting borrowing costs. Once market forces establish the minimum base borrowing rate, a company's financial condition crystallizes the actual cost of accessing debt capital. As we've said, the greater the risk, the greater the return capital suppliers will require, so a risky company that is in poor financial condition (e. g. losing a great deal of money, becoming dangerously illiquid, assuming too much leverage) will have to pay more for its capital. One that is in strong financial shape faces lower costs. This idiosyncratic feature is reflected in the debt risk premium (or credit spread), which is simply a company's percentage or basis point spread above the base risk-free rate prevailing in the market. We can summarize this total cost of debt as:

$$\text{cost of debt} = \underbrace{\text{risk-free rate}}_{\text{External influence}} + \underbrace{\text{risk premium}}_{\text{Internal influence}} \qquad [5.3]$$

Credit spreads, as a debt risk premium, reflect creditworthiness. As we've noted, rating agencies evaluate and rate companies prior to the issuance of debt and bank lenders perform a similar exercise before extending loans. These analyses and ratings, which reflect financial standing, have a decided impact on borrowing levels; the lower the rating, the greater the risk of default, and the larger the risk premium investors/lenders will demand.

Still, we have to bear in mind that credit spreads are dynamic, just like other financial indicators, and can be partially influenced by market forces. Short-term supply and demand levels can move spreads, meaning borrowing levels can change. Although ABC Co. might be able to borrow at 50 bps above the risk-free government rate today, it may only be able to do so at 60 bps in one month's time if supply/demand conditions become unbalanced-even though ABC Co. 's credit might be unchanged. Naturally, there are limits to how much these spreads can move due to market circumstances alone. At some point idiosyncratic factors have to return to the equation; astute market participants help make sure this happens, because they will supply capital to those that have been unfairly penalized by excessive market forces, bringing spreads back in line.

Factors driving credit spreads are based on financial actions that are within a company's control-and which can affect its financial standing. For instance, if ABC Co. decides to increase its debt load by a significant amount, the action will reshape its financial standing. Similarly, the company's financial standing will change if it enters a new line of business that makes its cash flows more volatile than before, or buys a competitor for a large premium and finances the acquisition by borrowing, or develops a new product that triples sales. Changes may therefore be positive or negative, and they may have a small or large impact on a company's financial condition.

Recalling our discussion in Chapter 2, financial strength

and stability are analyzed by looking at a company's liquidity, leverage, capital base, revenue generation, income generation, and cash flow volatility-at a point in time, as a trend over time, and versus the competition. These factors are supplemented by examining less tangible variables, such as management quality, company strategy, and industry competition. A very financially stable company is regarded as being of the highest quality (AAA-rated) and may only pay a few basis points above the base risk-free rate. One that is of middle quality (BBB-rated) may pay 50 – 150 basis points above the base rate, while one that is of weak quality (BB and lower), may pay several hundred basis points above the base rate. The market thus distinguishes between high-grade companies (AAA—BBB—) and high-yield companies (BB + and lower), and any actions taken to strengthen or weaken financial standing will change market perception and, by extension, borrowing costs.

We now know that total borrowing costs on a bond or loan are a function of the level of the base yield curve rate, certain capital supply/demand forces, and company-specific financial standing or creditworthiness. Let's assume that ABC Co., rated AA, is interested in borrowing five year funds when the middle interest rate scenario is in force. This means that its borrowing costs will be a function of five-year risk-free rates dictated by the sterling gilt curve, as well as the credit spread accorded to AA-rated companies-which we assume, for purposes of this example, is 10 bps over the gilt curve. If 5-year gilts are quoted at 4 percent, ABC Co.'s 5-year borrowing rate is 4.10 percent. But we needn't stop at the 5-year point. Let's also assume that ABC Co. might be interested in borrowing for 3 years or 7 years, and the market quotes AA-rated 3-year credit spreads at 5 bps and 7-year spreads at 15 bps. If the 3-year gilt is 3.75 percent and the 7-year gilt is 4.25 percent, ABC Co.'s total financing costs would amount to 3.80 percent for 3 years and 4.40 percent for 7 years.

In fact, the market features separate yield curves for each credit rating class, each serving as a borrowing cost benchmark. Naturally, these curves are a composite of all AA or BBB borrowers, so they do not imply that any single AA or BBB company will always be able to borrow at the level indicated by the AA or BBB curve; remember, every company is still subject to market perceptions regarding its financial stability, so two AA companies may borrow at slightly different levels (though the differential is unlikely to be more than a few basis points, at most).

Let's now assume that ABC Co. is a BBB-rated company, meaning it faces larger credit spreads. If 3-, 5-, and 7-year BBB credit spreads are 30, 40, and 50 bps above the gilt curve, then ABC Co.'s borrowing costs will amount to 4.05 percent, 4.40 percent, and 4.75 percent, respectively. We summarize these results in Table 5.3 and Figure 5.2.

Table 5.3 ABC Co.'s borrowing costs

	Gilt base rate	AA spreads	AA borrowing costs	BBB spreads	BBB borrowing costs
3 years	3.75%	0.05%	3.80%	0.30%	4.05%
5 years	4.00%	0.10%	4.10%	0.40%	4.40%
7 years	4.25%	0.15%	4.40%	0.50%	4.75%

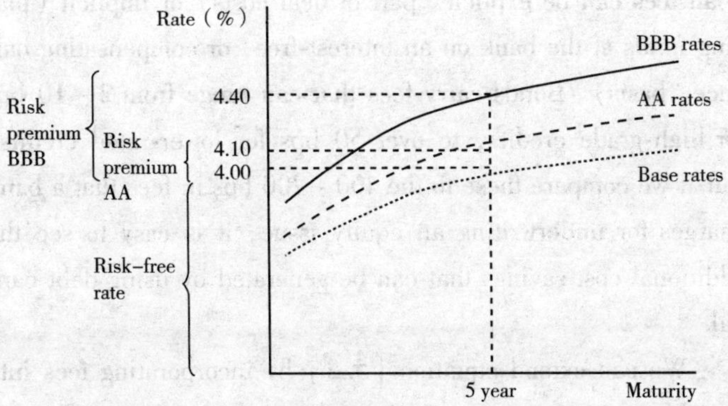

Figure 5.2 ABC Co.'s borrowing costs

Before we continue, it is worth noting that the credit spreads we have used in our example rise as maturity extends. Thus, the 3-year AA spread is 5 bps and the 7-year AA spread is 15 bps, while the 3-year BBB spread is 20 bps and the 7-year BBB spread is 50 bps. This characteristic is evident for virtually all credit classes, because the chance of default increases with the passage of time-particularly for companies that are financially weak. Since the probability of default rises over time, the compensation to investors willing to supply longer-term capital must increase-which means the credit spread curve has to be upward sloping. The only exception to this occurs with companies that are on the brink of default (e. g. CCC-rated). The market expectation in these instances is that if a CCC company can survive over the short term (by securing its liquidity, or cash, position) it will then be able to shore up its overall financial position and improve its creditworthiness; the CCC curve is therefore downward sloping.

While most of the cost of funding is incorporated in the base rate and the credit spread, we know that banks arranging loans and bonds don't work for free. As such, certain fees need to be added to the equation. Loans to high-quality borrowers command quite small fees, perhaps as little as 5 – 10 bps upfront; those to lower-quality borrowers can rise to 25 – 50 bps. Loan fees can be explicit (part of deal costs) or implicit (placing funds at the bank on an interest-free, or compensating balance, basis). Bonds carry fees that can range from 2 – 10 bps for high-grade credits, to over 50 bps for lower-rated credits. But if we compare these to the 400 – 700 bps in fees that a bank charges for underwriting an equity issue, it is easy to see the additional cost savings that can be generated by using debt capital.

We can extend equation [5. 3] by incorporating fees into total borrowing costs; to remain consistent with per annum interest rate costs, upfront fees can be amortized annually over the life of the financing.

cost of debt = risk-free rate + risk premium + fees [5. 4]

To summarize our example, if ABC Co., rated AA, is borrowing £100 million via 5-year bonds in the middle interest scenario (and paying a 5 bps upfront fee for doing so), its total annual pre-tax borrowing costs are £4. 1 million, plus an additional £50, 000 in upfront fees (or £10, 000 per year, if amortized over the 5-year horizon). The after-tax equivalent can be computed using equation [5. 1].

INSTRUMENT CHARACTERISTICS
工具特征

Debt comes in many varieties, each with unique characteristics. In this section we describe the features of the main types of loans and bonds, with a caveat that many other variations exist.

We can classify debt instruments by focusing on the liability portion of a typical corporate balance sheet. In many accounting regimes liabilities are segregated by maturity, ranging from short-term (sub-1 year), to medium-term (1 – 5 years) and long-term (over 5 years); this is consistent with the current-and noncurrent liability classification discussed in Chapter 2. Each maturity sector features its own types of instruments, as highlighted in Figure 5. 3.

Short-term liabilities include debt obligations that provide a company with short-term credit or cash to meet liquidity needs, seasonal cash flow aberrations, or emergency payments, or to serve as a temporary "bridge" until longer-term financing can be arranged. Short-term financing needs are a function of a company's liquidity position, seasonal supply and demand forces, expected short-term cash inflows and outflows, and the perceived need to maintain a buffer for emergency purposes.

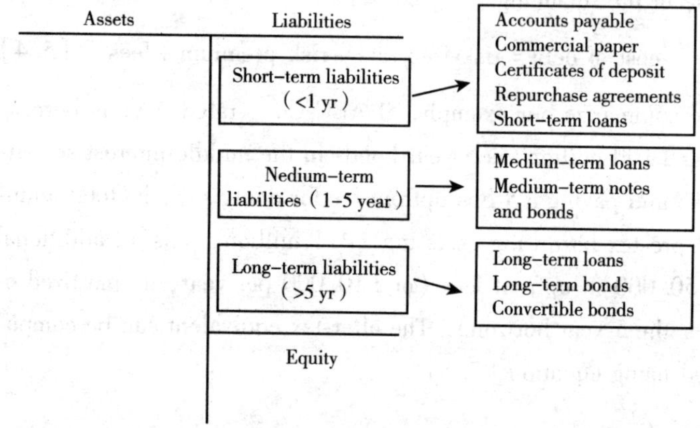

Figure 5. 3 Loans and bonds on the corporate balance sheet

Medium and long-term liabilities include obligations that provide funding for semi-permanent expansion and investment requirements, such as purchase/ upgrade of factories or financing of long-term research and development. Since this medium/long-term funding covers a multi-year period, it isn't intended to be drawn and repaid repeatedly. Accordingly, it is best suited for capital projects/ investments, rather than seasonal or emergency financing. Medium and long-term financing requirements are typically a function of a company's expected growth plans, economic/ industry sector outlook, competitive pressures, customer demand, inflation, and interest rates. Each may have a bearing on how much debt is required and desirable. Semi-permanent debt financing is often supplemented by the external and internal equity financing we've discussed in Chapter 4.

KEY CHARACTERISTICS 主要特征

Securities and loans are characterized by a number of key features, all of which are negotiated in advance of borrowing. These include deal size, coupon/ rate, maturity, repayment schedule, placement/ borrowing mechanism, optionality, market, and seniority.

- Size: The amount being placed with investors or borrowed from banks or other creditors. This can range from less than $1 million to well over $1 billion, depending on the borrower, its needs, investor appetite, and market circumstances. For instance, ABC Co. may decide to borrow up to £100 million to fund its operations. 规模
- Coupon/rate: The specific interest rate being paid for the funds, which is a reflection of the borrowing costs discussed above. The coupon may be set in fixed or floating rate terms: fixed rates remain unchanged for the life of the financing; floating rates reset periodically, generally every 3, 6, or 12 months, meaning a borrower's funding cost will change. A company may also issue a zero coupon bond, selling the security at a deep discount but paying no interest; the bond redeems at par value (100 percent) at maturity, meaning the investor earns an "implied" interest rate. In our example ABC Co. may borrow its £100 million for a fixed rate of 5 percent or, if it prefers floating rate funds, £LIBOR + 50 bps. 利息率/利率
- Maturity: The specific term of the liability. As noted above, the maturity may be short-, medium-, or long-term. The decision on optimal maturity depends on a company's goals (i. e. whether it is attempting to manage liquidity or a capital investment program) and overall market conditions (i. e. whether the yield curve is relatively flat, suggesting an opportunity to lock-in cheaper long-term funding, or very steep, indicating a short-term rollover strategy may be preferable). In our example, ABC Co. opts to borrow intermediate 5-year funds through its bond issue. 到期日
- Repayment schedule: The manner in which the principal amount of the bond or loan is to be repaid. Common mechanisms include amortizing repayment (where the borrower repays a portion of the principal on every interest payment 偿还时间表

date, so that there is no large principal payment due at maturity), bullet repayment (where the borrower makes no principal payment until the final maturity), and balloon repayment (where the borrower makes small principal payments for the first few years of the borrowing, followed by a large payment at maturity). When bullets or balloons are used, lenders/investors may still want the borrower to set aside some amount of funds every year to make sure the principal amount can be safely repaid at maturity; this is done through a sinking fund, which is a special account created to accept and hold periodic principal payments. In borrowing £100 million via its bond issue, ABC Co. may select a bullet structure, repaying the entire principal in five years. In fact, bullets are very common in bond financings.

募集/借款机制

- Placement/borrowing mechanism: The manner in which funds are placed with investors or drawn from banks. Bonds can be placed on a public or private placement basis. Public bonds are securities registered with regulators that are accompanied by detailed information on the issuer (i. e. financial statements and projections) and the deal (i. e. terms and conditions). They are often listed on a national exchange, though secondary trading tends to occur in the over-the-counter (OTC) market. Private placements, in contrast, are exempt from regulatory registration and may not feature much disclosure. These deals are designed for sophisticated institutional investors that can bear more risk than the average individual investor. Private placements need not be listed on an exchange and have limited resaleability, meaning investors originally buying the securities often hold them until maturity. In issuing its bonds, ABC Co. may choose a standard public deal in order to increase the universe of investors and add to market liquidity.

期权性

- Optionality: The inclusion of issuer or investor options in bonds that enhance yield or lower funding costs. During some market cycles it can be attractive to float a callable bond, or a bond that grants the issuer the right to call (buy back) the bond from investors; this option gives investors an enhanced yield. Alternatively, it may be wise for a firm to issue a puttable bond, or a bond that gives investors the right to put (sell) the bond back to the issuer; this gives the issuer a lower funding cost. In arranging its bond, ABC Co. could consider including put options to lower its funding cost by several basis points.

- Market: The specific marketplace being accessed. This feature is especially relevant for bonds, which may be issued in the domestic (onshore) market, where funds are raised from resident investors, or the international (offshore, or Euro) market, where funds are raised from non-resident investors. The selection of a market depends on various factors, including cost (i. e. where a company can borrow on the best terms), availability (i. e. where investors are willing to supply capital), overall market conditions (i. e. where market stability (volatility) may attract (repel) capital), and regulatory restrictions (i. e. where barriers may impede domestic or offshore access). Loans can also be raised in a domestic or offshore setting. Since ABC Co. is UK-based and is well known to UK investors, it may choose to float a £-denominated bond in the domestic market. 市场
- Seniority: The priority of the liability regarding claims on the borrower's assets. Recalling our discussion from Chapter 3, we know that the seniority of claims dictates the priority of payments to creditors and equity investors should a debtor company declare bankruptcy. Equity investors, bearing the first loss, are the most junior in the capital structure, ranking below all forms of debt capital. Loans or bonds that are secured by a company's assets (such as receivables, cash/securities, or hard assets, like plant and equipment) receive first repayment priority; in fact, the source of repayment for 求偿等级

such secured creditors is the very asset being held as collateral. Within the general class of unsecured creditors, loans or bonds that are accorded senior status are repaid before those with a junior ranking. Because junior creditors are exposed to greater losses (i. e. insufficient funds in liquidation to repay junior liabilities at the same level as senior liabilities), the return they expect is higher. This treatment is consistent with the general risk/return trade-off we've discussed. The general sequence of seniority, from senior (lowest risk) to junior (highest risk) is:

- Senior, secured (with specific assets used to collateralize the liability)
- Senior, unsecured
- Junior, unsecured
- Subordinated
- Junior, subordinated

When considering the seniority of a transaction and the creation of payment priority in default, we can look to historical statistics on recovery rates to see that senior, secured creditors receive, on average, 60 – 80 percent of their capital upon default, senior, unsecured creditors may receive 40 – 60 percent, and the broad class of junior creditors as little as 10 – 30 percent. Priority in the capital structure does, indeed, matter. In our continuing example, ABC Co.'s 5-year bond may be issued as a standard senior, unsecured instrument. If the company were rated sub-investment grade, it might choose to secure its bond with specific assets rather than face the high interest costs of an unsecured issue; this would make bond investors senior, secured creditors.

KEY INSTRUMENTS 主要的短期债务工具

The key short-term debt instruments (< 1 year) include:

- Accounts payable: These accounts comprise the general class

应付账款

of trade credit described in Chapter 2. Trade credit serves as a *de facto* short-term loan, because if a company borrows from its suppliers and chooses not to take advantage of a discount by paying within an allotted time frame, it begins accruing a finance charge-just as it might under a revolving loan facility. Accounts payable can extend out to 360 days, though maturities in the 30 – 180 day sector are more common.

商业票据和欧洲商业票据

- Commercial paper (CP) and Euro commercial paper (ECP). These instruments are senior, unsecured, discount instruments issued almost exclusively by the very best companies. CP/ECP facilities must typically be rated by one or more of the rating agencies, and may be supported by bank lines that allow the issuer to replace its funding if notes cannot be rolled over at maturity. In the US market CP has a maximum maturity of 270 days (to avoid registration requirements), while in the non-US domestic markets and the Euromarkets maturities can extend to 360 days. In practice most issuance occurs in the 14 – 30 day sector, with outstanding notes rolled over on each maturity date. Though the instruments can be traded on a secondary basis, many investors purchase and hold the securities until maturity, rolling them into new issues on a continuous basis. CP and ECP are institutional instruments, with minimum denominations of $100,000.

存款凭证

- Certificates of deposit (CDs): CDs are unsecured, discount or coupon instruments issued exclusively by banks; coupon-bearing CDs may have fixed or floating coupons. CDs are marketable bank deposits that are routinely traded on a secondary basis. CDs can be issued in various currencies in the domestic or offshore markets. The instruments have maturities ranging from 1 week to 1 year (though certain 1 – 5 year instruments are also available, and would thus form part of the medium-term funding noted below) and are available in both small and large denominations (e.g. $

1, 000 to $100, 000 +). In some national systems CDs benefit from deposit insurance, which protects depositors against default by the bank issuer (up to certain maximum amounts).

回购协议

- Repurchase agreements: Repurchase agreements (repos) are a popular form of secured financing for securities firms and other financial institutions that deal actively in portfolios of government and corporate bonds. Repos are collateralized borrowings, where the financial institution sells securities to another party for cash (the borrowing), agreeing simultaneously to repurchase them at a future time, which can range from overnight to one year; the securities sold serve as collateral against the cash loan. Though repos are generally designed to be held until maturity, they can be sold in the secondary market, particularly when the underlying collateral is based on high-quality government bonds, such as US Treasuries, gilts, bunds, or Japanese Government Bonds.

短期贷款

- Short-term loans: Short-term loans, with maturities ranging from 3 to 12 months, are interest-bearing liabilities used by companies requiring additional liquidity. The facilities may be secured or unsecured, fixed or floating rate, and are typically of large size (e. g. millions of dollars). They may be arranged as straight term loans, or as revolving credit facilities that can be drawn down and repaid during a particular horizon.

The primary medium-term (1 – 5 year) and long-term (5 years +) debt instruments include:

中期票据和欧洲中期票据

- Medium-term notes (MTNs) and Euro medium-term notes (EMTNs): These securities, which can be likened to long-term versions of the CP and ECP described above, have become a popular form of financing as they can be launched very quickly, from shelf registered programs that require only a minimum amount of documentation. MTNs and EMTNs feature maturities ranging from 1 to 30 years (though most issuance activity is in the sub-10-year sector), and can be structured with fixed or floating rate coupons and callable or puttable features. Issues are generally unsecured and can be floated in a variety of currencies. Issuance is generally targeted towards institutional investors with minimum denominations of $100,000; secondary trading tends to be quite active.

- Bonds and Eurobonds: Standard fixed and floating rate bonds and Eurobonds are similar to MTNs and EMTNs-featuring 1 to 30 years maturities, fixed or floating rate coupons, and callable/puttable options-except that the issues are floated on a "one time" basis rather than through a shelf program. This means registration and disclosure are generally required for each new issue (though the Eurobond market has less formal standards than many domestic bond markets). Bonds issued by the best quality companies are considered high-grade securities; those issued by sub-investment grade companies form part of the high yield (or junk) bond market. Secondary trading in many issues is extremely active. 债券和欧洲债券
- Convertible bonds: Convertibles are hybrid debt/equity instruments that can be considered debt or equity, depending on the dominant characteristics of the security at any point in time. Convertibles pay a minimum coupon, generally on a fixed rate basis, and allow investors the option of converting the bond into common shares if a conversion level is reached. Once (or if) converted, the bond is extinguished and bondholders become equity investors. The conversion premium, or the level at which investors can exchange their bonds for stock, is often set in the range of 15 – 30 percent above the market price at launch. This means the company's stock has to rise by that amount before the investor will convert. Convertibles carry maturities of 1 to 30 years, and can be issued in the domestic or offshore markets. The securities 可转换债券

are institutional investments with large minimum denominations and are actively traded in the secondary market by both bond and stock investors.

中期和长期贷款

- Medium-and long-term loans: Medium-and long-term loans, with maturities ranging from 1 to 30 years, are interest-bearing liabilities used by companies requiring semi-permanent financing. The facilities may be secured or unsecured, fixed or floating rate, and are typically of large size. Loans can be structured as conventional term loans or revolving credit facilities with multiple drawdown/repayment opportunities. As we've noted, principal repayment may be on an amortizing, bullet, or balloon basis. Though banks often hold loans until they are repaid, there is a growing market for transferable loans, which can be traded by institutions in the secondary market.

租赁

- Leases: Leases are liability financing contracts, which, depending on accounting convention and product type, may appear on or off the balance sheet. However, even when a lease appears off balance sheet it acts as a form of debt, and any reasonable analysis of a company's liabilities must incorporate its effect. A lease is a private transaction between the lessor, who owns an underlying asset (e. g. computer, factory, airplane), and the lessee, who wishes to use/rent the asset in exchange for lease payments. At the end of the lease contract the lessee returns the leased asset (though they may be given the option to purchase the asset at a pre-defined residual value); the asset's ownership is never transferred from lessor to lessee. The lessee thus obtains "financing" from the lessor in exchange for periodic payments that are similar to interest payments on a loan. The lessee benefits from not having to borrow and make an investment to buy the underlying asset being used; the lessor benefits from the tax advantages that accrue from depreciating the asset. A lease can be structured as an operating lease or capital lease. The operating lease has a maturity of less than five years and is generally cancelable by the lessee; maintenance and repairs are the responsibility of the lessor and the contract is generally shown off balance sheet. The capital lease, in turn, is a long-term, non-cancelable, contract, where the lessee is responsible for maintenance and repairs; in many jurisdictions the capital lease must be shown directly on the balance sheet. Other forms of leases are available, including the sale and leaseback (the lessee sells the lessor an asset and then leases it back), and the leveraged lease (the lessor borrows to buy the asset, which it then leases to the lessee); each of these has unique tax and depreciation features.

In addition to the securities noted above, there exists a thriving market for structured bonds that are created by combining pools of assets and issuing securities to finance the pools. The resulting bonds are not specific to a single company or issuer, but serve as a reference to a broader portfolio of borrowers. Common securitized bonds include mortgage-backed securities (backed by pools of home or commercial mortgages), asset-backed securities (backed by auto loans, credit card receivables), and collateralized debt obligations (backed by other bonds and loans).

BORROWING, ISSUING AND SECONDARY TRADING 借款、发行和二级市场交易

BORROWING AND ISSUING 借款和发行

The process of creating the liabilities described above varies according to instrument type.

Borrowing via the loan markets is based on a well established procedure where a bank, working closely with a company, arranges a loan facility that suits the company's funding needs, drafts and executes a loan agreement (with details on terms, conditions, collateral requirements, and any financial ratios to which the borrower must adhere), and then provides funds based on the terms contained in the documentation. The bank may then retain the entire loan in its portfolio until maturity, or sell a portion to other banks or loan investors in the secondary markets. A large loan, generally in excess of several hundred million dollars, may be syndicated, or divided, among a larger group of banks during the primary market phase. The arranging bank creates a syndicate of banks, where each bank commits to funding a portion of the loan; this mechanism allows risk to be more sensibly distributed.

Raising debt capital via the securities markets is based on a slightly different process. In a public deal a bank, again working closely with the borrowing company, establishes funding requirements, prepares detailed preliminary disclosure and registers the issue with the national securities commission. Once regulators approve the disclosure (which becomes known as the prospectus), the bank begins a pre-marketing phase to determine investor appetite and potential pricing levels (e. g. a coupon/yield that will prove attractive to investors). If a deal is particularly large, the bank may again assemble a syndicate to help in the distribution efforts. The final bond price/yield is established on launch date and the syndicate places securities with investors. To speed up the issuance process a company can also choose the shelf registration noted earlier, meaning it can issue securities as needed during a particular period of time (generally two years) without needing to go through an extensive registration and documentation process.

If a bond deal has been arranged as a "best efforts" transaction, the bank places as many bonds as it can, but is not required to deliver the full amount the company needs if it cannot do so. So, if ABC Co. wants £100 million of 5-year funds but investors are only interested in purchasing £75 million at the quoted yield, the company only receives £75 million. However, if the bank agrees to a "firm underwriting" or "bought deal," it must deliver the full amount to the company and then try to place the securities with investors. If it cannot do so, the bank retains the securities until it can place them-generally by lowering the price (i. e. increasing the yield). Since the bank bears more risk under the bought deal structure, it charges the issuing company more in fees.

The issuance process is quite similar for private placements, except that disclosure is not as extensive and the pool of investors to which banks can pre-market is much smaller. The process for other "exempt securities," such as CDs, CP, and ECP, is similar: securities are issued with a minimum of disclosure through a shelf or tap mechanism that allows for quick distribution. Unlike private placements, however, a broader range and number of investors can purchase these exempt instruments.

In some cases companies are able to eliminate the role of the bank by placing securities directly with end investors, saving themselves a few basis points in fees. This process of direct placement (a form of disintermediation, as we shall discuss in Part Ⅲ), is increasingly common in the millennium, but still reserved for large, creditworthy borrowers that have strong name recognition.

SECONDARY TRADING 二级市场交易

Most debt trading occurs in bonds and other securities rather than loans. Though a secondary market has developed for loans, total turnover is still small compared to what is found in the largest domestic bond markets and the Eurobond market. As such, we'll focus our discussion on secondary trading of bonds.

Major banks and securities dealers actively quote prices on

a range of bonds on a continuous basis. This market-making role, providing a buy (bid) and sell (offer) price on individual securities, allows other investors to enter or exit the market once a particular issue has been launched-that is, once the primary market phase of a deal has been concluded. The prices that dealers quote are a function of the variables we've already discussed, including external factors (i. e. overall interest rate levels, market conditions/outlook, supply of investment capital) and internal factors (i. e. specific creditworthiness of a company and/or its sector). These factors dictate perceived risk levels and, by extension, the required price or return.

The secondary marketplace quotes in price terms rather than yields. Thus, ABC Co.'s £100 million 5-year bonds, launched 12 months ago at par (100), may now be quoted at 101.79 – 101.89. This means a market maker will buy bonds from existing investors at 101.79 and will sell them to new investors at 101.89. The 0.10 points is the market maker's compensation for assuming the credit risk that ABC Co. will default before the bonds have been resold, and the liquidity risk that investors will suddenly become disinterested in the bonds (leaving the market maker with a "stuck" position).

Let's run through several simple scenarios to see how ABC Co.'s secondary prices can change as risk-free rates and credit spreads change. We begin by adapting the basic PV equation from Chapter 3. Since a bond is simply a series of future cash flows (interest and principal) and we are interested in determining its value today, we need only discount the cash flows by the relevant cost of debt, as in:

$$PV = \text{sum across all periods}\left[\frac{\text{interest coupon}}{(1+\text{discount rate})^{\text{time horizon}}}\right] + \left[\frac{\text{principal}}{(1+\text{discount rate})^{\text{maturity}}}\right] \quad [5.5]$$

Assume ABC Co. launched its original 5-year £100 million

bond at par 12 months ago with a coupon of 5 percent; for simplicity we assume that the 5-year gilt rate at that time was 4.50 percent and the company's credit spread was 50 bps, or 0.50 percent. Through the equation above, the price at launch was precisely equal to par:

$$P=\frac{5}{(1.05)^1}+\frac{5}{(1.05)^2}+\frac{5}{(1.05)^3}+\frac{5}{(1.05)^4}+\frac{105}{(1.05)^5}$$

or:

$$100=4.7619+4.5351+4.3192+4.1135+82.227$$

Let's now assume that gilt rates fall from 4.50 percent to 4.00 percent and ABC Co.'s spread remains unchanged at 0.50 percent. With four years left to maturity the new price is:

$$P=\frac{5}{(1.045)^1}+\frac{5}{(1.045)^2}+\frac{5}{(1.045)^3}+\frac{105}{(1.045)^4}$$

or:

$$101.79=4.7847+4.5786+4.3815+88.0480$$

Even though only four years remain until maturity, the price has risen from 100 to 101.79 because base rates have fallen by 50 bps. A market maker quoting ABC Co.'s bond in this market may thus be willing to buy at 101.79 and sell at 101.89. This illustrates an important fact concerning bond prices and rates: there is an inverse relationship between the two, meaning that when rates rise bond prices fall and when rates fall bond prices rise. This is true because new bonds issued in a higher rate environment with high coupons will appear more attractive than those with lower coupons; investors will sell the old bonds (causing their yields to rise) and buy the new ones (causing their yields to fall) until an equilibrium point is reached.

What if base rates remain unchanged from the time of issuance (4.50 percent) but ABC Co.'s creditworthiness has deteriorated dramatically? In this case the credit spread may have risen from 50 bps to 100 bps (1.00 percent), meaning the cost of debt is now 5.50 percent. The secondary price of the bond, with four years until maturity, is thus:

$$P = \frac{5}{(1.055)^1} + \frac{5}{(1.055)^2} + \frac{5}{(1.055)^3} + \frac{105}{(1.055)^4}$$

which gives us a price of:

$$97.9014 = 4.3933 + 4.4923 + 4.258 + 84.758$$

This makes intuitive, as well as financial, sense: ABC Co.'s credit standing has deteriorated, meaning that its prospect of default has increased; investors will only be willing to pay a lower price (i.e. they will demand a higher yield) to own the bond.

The process of establishing secondary prices is therefore based on the PV equation, adjusted for changing base rates and credit spreads. As base rates rise, secondary prices fall, and vice-versa; as credit spreads widen secondary prices fall, and vice-versa; these are summarized in Table 5.4. Market makers must therefore remain vigilant to changes in both before quoting prices.

In practice the actual bond price quote must also take into account the fact that buying and selling activity doesn't occur precisely on each coupon date, but at some point in between. Accordingly, interest that accrues between coupon dates is factored into the pricing: the new buyer of the bond pays a price that reflects that interest that has accrued from the last coupon date, and is entitled to the full coupon when it is paid.

Secondary bond trading can occur via an exchange or OTC. Though the market has long favored voice-based OTC trading, the advent of computing power and advanced networking has led to the creation of new electronic bond trading platforms, and more volumes are gradually being directed through such conduits. Some of these electronic communications networks (ECNs) are supported by major financial institutions, which place their bond inventories online with indicative prices so that institutional clients can trade directly on screen. Brokers, who seek to match buyers and sellers in an electronic environment, operate ECNs of their own. Though these efforts are still in a relatively nascent stage, they are gaining acceptance.

Table 5.4　　Impact of interest rates on bond prices

Risk-free rate	Bond price	Credit spread	Bond price
↑	↓	↑	↓
↓	↑	↓	↑

摘要

通过贷款和债券的负债融资是整个公司融资的关键要素。负债资本的成本一般比通过权益市场的融资更有利，因为债权人通过比权益投资者更优先的清偿权在资本结构中占据了更安全的位置，而且负债利息抵扣可以获得税盾。一家公司应该承担的最佳债务数额是由它的流动性和资本投资需要以及行业标准确定的；太少的债务能够导致对于昂贵的权益融资的过度依赖，而太多的债务能够造成巨大的固定费用负担并增加财务恶化的可能性。实际借款成本是通过市场相关和内部因素的组合确定的。有利的市场能够导致较低的基准利率，而强劲的财务状况能够导致较低的信贷息差；相反的情况也是对的。贷款和债券能够以不同的方式发行或推出，而且由包括交易规模、利息/利率、到期时间、偿还时间表、募集/借款机制、期权性、市场和求偿等级的主要特征来描述。一个活跃的二级市场上存在多种形式的债务，特别是公开登记发行的债券；许多这种交易活动正在从交易所和以喊价为基础的机制转移到纯粹的电子环境。

FURTHER READING　延伸阅读

Donaldson, J., 1982, *The Medium-Term Loan Market*, London: Palgrave Macmillan.

Einzig, P., 1969, *The Eurobond Market*, *2nd edition*, London: St Martin's Press.

Fabozzi, F. (ed.) 2003, *Bond Markets*, *5th edition*, New Jersey: Prentice Hall. —— 2005, *Handbook of Fixed Income Instruments*, *7th edition*, New York: McGraw-Hill.

Stigum, M., 1989, *Money Market Instruments*, *3rd edition*, New York: McGraw-Hill.

6

INVESTMENT FUNDS

投资基金

CHAPTER OVERVIEW 本章概述

In this chapter we examine investment funds, which are financial products that combine into portfolios the debt and equity securities discussed in the last two chapters. We begin with a review of why and how investment funds are used and the role diversification plays in the creation of funds. We then consider the main types of investment funds, including open-end funds, closed-end funds, hedge funds, and exchange-traded funds, and the strategies that portfolio managers use to create investor returns. We conclude by describing how different classes of investment fund shares are created, traded, and redeemed.

USES OF INVESTMENT FUNDS 投资基金的用途

In the last two chapters we've described capital securities that firms issue to fund their balance sheets. We know that an investor buying securities supplies capital in exchange for a return. Each individual stock or bond that the investor purchases represents a separate exposure to the stock or bond issuer. The investor holds a concentrated position in the risk of the issuer, and if something goes wrong-perhaps the issuing company sustains large financial losses or even falls into bankruptcy-some amount of invested capital may be lost. While the return the investor earns is supposed to compensate for such risks, there are times when it may prove insufficient.

Naturally, many investors are comfortable bearing this "concentrated" risk, especially when they feel the returns are appropriate. Some, however, are less willing to do so-particularly if they feel that they lack the knowledge needed to properly evaluate potential risks and returns. In these cases they may prefer allocating capital across many stocks or bonds. This spreads the risk: if one of the issuing companies has trouble and the others remain sound, the investor continues to earn an acceptable return. To facilitate this process investors can use investment funds, or conduits that purchase a wide range of securities on behalf of investors. In fact, the market for investment funds has grown at a fast pace over the past few decades, and now represents several trillion dollars' worth of investable assets.

The investment fund framework involves various parties. Investors provide capital to a portfolio manager, who then purchases relevant securities; the returns generated by the underlying securities are paid to investors periodically. In exchange for performing the management function, the portfolio manager charges a fee. A separate trustee oversees the process and ensures safekeeping of securities. Note that once investors give capital to the portfolio manager, they have no say in the actual purchase/sale of securities in the fund's portfolio; the manager has complete discretion to invest as he or she sees fit (within the confines of the investment mandate, as discussed below). The only recourse available to an investor who disagrees with the investment decisions (or is otherwise dissatisfied with a fund's performance) is to exit by selling the position in the fund.

While diversification is perhaps the most important characteristic of many investment funds, the product also features other advantages. Some investors are drawn to funds because they provide for continuous, professional management of capital. Seasoned portfolio managers constantly monitor the performance of their funds, buying and selling securities based on the strategies that they have developed. Investors therefore needn't depend on their own research skills and monitoring efforts. Funds are also efficient transactions. While an investor can create a diversified portfolio by buying a large number of individual stocks or bonds, the process can be tedious, time-consuming, and expensive. Buying shares in a fund that is already based on a desired portfolio is much easier.

Let's note at this stage that certain investment funds are created primarily to provide investors with the possibility of enhanced returns-and not necessarily to reduce risk through diversification techniques. Some funds specialize in particular market sectors (e. g. by industry, country, and so forth) and thus take a greater degree of concentrated risk. Other classes of funds often thrive on risk: they deliberately assume a great deal of exposure in hopes of creating very large returns for investors. These specialized investment funds, known as hedge funds, are intended only for the most sophisticated investors-those that can stand to lose a significant amount of their capital should markets or positions turn against them.

PORTFOLIO DIVERSIFICATION
投资组合分散化

We indicated in Chapter 3 that an investor can reduce or eliminate diversifiable risk of a security by holding other securities that are either uncorrelated, or negatively correlated, with the target security. It comes as no surprise that this concept is the linchpin of the investment fund world: combining the right mix of uncorrelated/negatively correlated securities creates diversified portfolios of securities. (This does not hold true, of

在一定水平的风险下的有效的投资组合

course, for investment funds that are deliberately established to take concentrated or large risks, i. e. certain hedge funds.)

An efficient portfolio generates high returns for a given level of risk, while an inefficient portfolio generates lower returns for the same level of risk, as noted in Figure 6. 1. The rational investor will always prefer the efficient portfolio. For instance, if investors can earn a 10 percent return on a portfolio with a risk level of 20 percent, or earn a 10 percent return with a risk level of 50 percent, they will obviously choose the first portfolio. Similarly if they must invest in a portfolio with a maximum risk level of 20 percent, and can select between a portfolio generating a 7 percent return and a second one generating a 12 percent return, they will opt for the latter-earning an extra 5 percent for taking the same amount of risk.

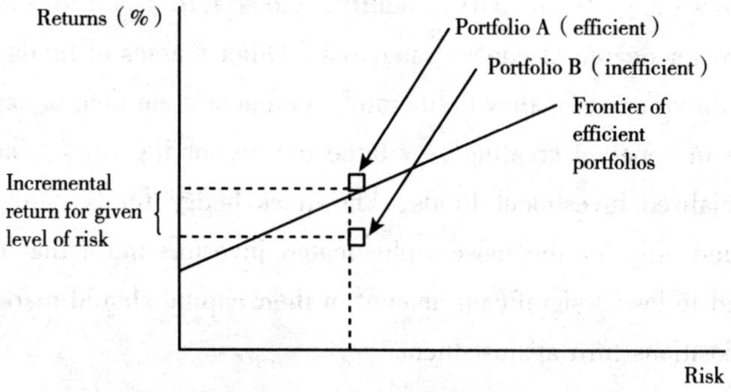

Figure 6. 1 Risk, return and efficient portfolios

Selecting securities with the right correlation characteristics is the key to diversification and the creation of an efficient portfolio. The lower the correlation between securities, the greater the diversification, and the more diffuse the risk. Portfolio managers are responsible for identifying securities that will create a portfolio with the desired characteristics. So, if an investor invests in a diversified fund, the portfolio manager must ensure that an appropriate level of risk diversification actually exists. Conversely, when an investor wants a more focused or concentrated exposure, the portfolio manager is free to select assets with a greater degree of positive correlation.

Empirical studies conducted over the years have focused a great deal of attention on the existence of market efficiency, or the degree to which the market prices of securities absorb and reflect all known (public) and unknown (non-public) information. The existence of this relationship is important in determining whether a portfolio manager can create a diversified portfolio that regularly "beats the market." In the weakest form of the so-called efficient market hypothesis (EMH), information is not regularly or accurately absorbed, suggesting that the prices of assets may not be accurate. This means a portfolio manager can actually outperform a market or index with some frequency. In the strongest form of the EMH the market reflects all public and non-public information; asset prices contain all information and are an accurate representation of value, meaning that it is very difficult, if not impossible, for a portfolio manager to regularly beat the market. Many practitioners believe that an intermediate form of market efficiency exists, suggesting that it may be difficult for a portfolio manager to create a strategy that regularly outperforms the market. Accordingly, some fund managers choose simply to try and match the market-through a process known as indexing. Indexing can be implemented in different forms:

- Pure index tracking: Target returns of a fund are precisely equal to the benchmark index.
- Enhanced index tracking: Target returns may be up to 1 percent away from a benchmark index.
- Constrained active management: Target returns may be 2 – 4 percent away from the benchmark.
- Unconstrained active management: Target returns may be more than 4 percent away from the benchmark.

The farther a portfolio manager moves away from the pure index tracking strategy, the more active the management of the portfolio becomes. At the extreme end of the spectrum we encounter hedge funds, which feature no index relationship at all; that is, they seek to generate absolute returns of any magnitude, rather than returns relative to an index.

INSTRUMENT CHARACTERISTICS 工具特征

In this section we consider several of the most popular types of investment funds, including investment companies (open-end funds, closed-end funds, and unit investment trusts), hedge funds, and exchange-traded funds. Open-end funds comprise the largest segment of the investment fund market and are designed for the broadest group of individual and institutional investors. Closed-end funds, which operate in a similar fashion but with greater restrictions, represent a much smaller portion of the market. Hedge funds, designed for sophisticated investors, often take a great deal of risk. Exchange-traded funds (ETFs) are "hybrids" that combine the structural features of open-end funds with the trading and liquidity features of actively traded corporate securities.

KEY CHARACTERISTICS 主要特征

THE FUND BALANCE SHEET 基金的资产负债表

We can examine an investment fund in light of the balance sheet presented in Chapter 2 to establish a frame of reference. Though a fund can be legally structured in various ways-such as a registered investment company, a special purpose entity (SPE), a trust, or a limited partnership-it always has assets, liabilities, and capital, which we know are the essential ingredients of any balance sheet.

The asset portion of the fund consists of the securities the portfolio manager has purchased, along with a small cash balance reflecting funds awaiting investment and any extra liquidity needed to meet redemptions (i. e. sales of fund shares by investors). The equity account consists of the capital that investors in the fund have given to the portfolio manager for investment. Depending on the nature of the fund and its specific authorizations, the balance sheet may also feature a certain amount of short-or long-term debt. Not all funds are allowed to incur debt, as debt increases leverage and leverage magnifies risks. Those that are so authorized, however, can use the extra liabilities to purchase more securities. Some funds are also allowed to use off balance sheet contracts-primarily derivatives-which we discuss in the next chapter. The general structure of a fund's balance sheet, shown under US GAAP, is illustrated in Figure 6. 2.

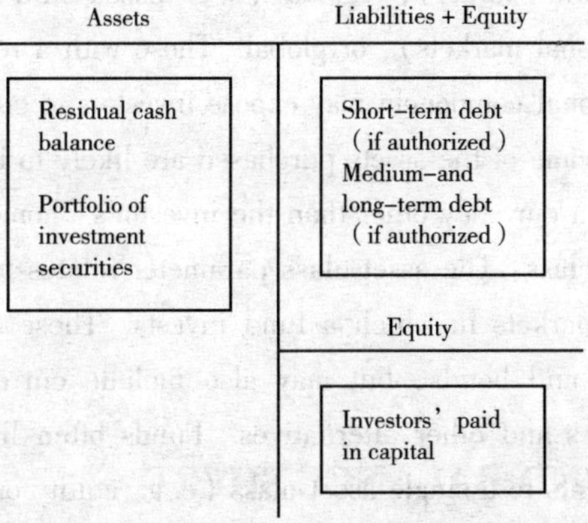

Figure 6. 2 General fund balance sheet

GENERAL FUND CATEGORIES 一般基金类别

Funds can invest in a wide range of asset classes and employ different types of investment management techniques. But they must always operate under rules specified by their investment mandates. This ensures that investors are getting the type of investment they believe they are getting. For instance, if a fund is marketed as a low-risk fund and is restricted by its mandate to investing in short-term government treasury bills, it cannot then purchase high-yield bonds or stocks.

Investors can select funds that match their risk and return goals. For purposes of our discussion we can divide fund categories into earnings type, geographic focus, asset class, and sub-asset class.

收益类型

- Earnings type: The earnings dimension relates to the specific source of a fund's income, which may include dividends, interest, and/or capital gains. Funds that rely on dividends and interest (so-called current income) tend to be less risky than those that rely on capital gains, since current income cash flows are a great deal more certain.

地理重点

- Geographic focus: The geographic dimension relates to a fund's spatial focus, which may be national (e. g. confined to a specific country), regional (e. g. based on a related group of national markets), or global. Those with a regional or international component may expose investors to currency risks, since some of the assets purchased are likely to be denominated in a currency other than the investor's "home" currency.

资产类别

- Asset class: The asset class parameter relates to the general asset markets in which a fund invests. These are generally stocks and bonds, but may also include currencies, commodities and other alternatives. Funds often limit their investments to a single asset class (e. g. equity only), though most also hold a certain amount of cash equivalents to meet redemptions. Equity funds represent the single largest asset class in the investment sector. Large funds often hold positions in hundreds or thousands of individual issues in order to boost returns for a given level of risk. Bond funds are also popular, and may invest in domestic/foreign money market instruments, government bonds, municipal bonds, corporate bonds, mortgage-backed securities (bonds comprised of pools of mortgages), asset-backed securities (bonds comprised of pools of receivables) and/or collateralized debt obligations (bonds comprised of pools of corporate bonds/loans). Balanced funds can incorporate stocks, bonds, preferred stock, convertibles, and other securities.

- Sub-asset class: A sub-asset class distinction is relevant in some instances. For instance, an equity fund might invest only in large capitalization stocks (e.g. companies with $5 billion + in market capitalization), mid-cap stocks ($1 – $5 billion), small cap stocks ($500 million – $1 billion), or micro-cap stocks (up to $500 million); each market sector is considered a distinct sub-asset class. Similarly, sector funds invest in stocks from a single industrial or market sector (e.g. real estate investment trusts, pharmaceutical stocks, technology stocks); since their focus is much narrower, security concentrations are typically much higher (e.g. some funds are permitted to invest up to 25 percent of their assets in a single stock or bond). Similar sub-asset class sector distinctions can be created for bond funds (e.g. a focus on municipal securities, government securities, high-grade corporate bonds, money market securities, and so forth), currency funds [e.g. Group of Ten (G10, the largest industrialized nations) currencies, emerging market currencies, and so on], and commodity/alternative funds (e.g. precious metals, energy, catastrophe/weather, and so forth).

次资产类别

These general fund categories are summarized in Figu-re 6.3.

KEY FUND CLASSES 主要基金类别

OPEN-END FUNDS 开放式基金

Open-end funds also known as mutual funds in the US and unit trusts in the UK-are the single most common form of investment fund; most individuals and institutions have some quantity of open-end funds shares in their investment or retirement accounts. Open-end funds are available across asset classes and many are structured to provide some form of indexed returns.

Earnings Source	Geographic Focus
Current income/capital preservation Capital gains Both	National/single country Regional International

Asset Class	Sub-asset Class
Equity Bond Currency Commodity/Alternative Balanced	Market type Index Sector

Figure 6.3 General fund categories

The mechanics of the open-end fund are straightforward: investors give a fund capital in exchange for shares of the fund. With rare exceptions, open-end funds can create new shares at will-hence the name "open-end." As long as investors continue to contribute capital, a fund continues to create new shares. As capital is received from investors the portfolio manager purchases securities for the portfolio. Every publicly traded open-end fund is valued at the net asset value (NAV), which is computed via:

$$\text{total net assets} = \text{cash and equivalents} + \text{market value of securities held in the portfolio} - \text{current liabilities (including accruals)} \quad [6.1]$$

This result can be converted into a per share figure via:

$$\text{NAV per share} = \frac{\text{total net assets}}{\text{shares issued}} \quad [6.2]$$

An investor wanting to buy or sell shares in the fund will do so at the NAV (plus any applicable fees or commissions, which may be payable upfront, upon exit, or annually); trading generally occurs once a day, at the market closing NAV. Let's assume Fund XYZ has a total of £100 million of cash on hand, £1.5 billion of equity securities, £50 million of liabilities, and 100 million shares outstanding. The NAV, per the equations above, is £15.5/share. If the value of the stocks that XYZ holds rises tomorrow so that the worth of the portfolio increases from £1.5 billion to £1.7 billion (and all other account balances remain unchanged), the NAV increases to £17/share.

Since open-end funds are intended for distribution to the public at large (including individual investors who may need extra protection) they must adhere to legal and regulatory requirements. Investment companies must generally register their funds with the national securities regulator and comply with minimum standards related to disclosure, diversification, reporting, dividend policy, and income distribution. Depending on the specific jurisdiction, regulatory authorities may monitor a fund and its activities formally or informally to ensure compliance; further oversight may be provided by the listing stock exchange.

An open-end fund is often structured in corporate form so that new shares can be created with ease. The investment company acting as sponsor is responsible for organizing the fund, making operating and investment decisions, and marketing the fund to investors. Each fund has its own investment mandate, which outlines permissible investments, strategies, and risks. For instance, some funds can only buy securities with capital on hand, while others can borrow or use derivatives. Similarly, some can invest in very risky securities while others can buy only the safest of instruments. The prospectus given to each investor contains details on the fund's investment mandate, goals, strategy, risk factors, sales charges, operating expenses, financial history, annual return history, purchase/redemption mechanisms, portfolio manager (fund advisor) experience and fees, and shareholder distribution mechanisms.

Various other parties are involved in the operation of an open-end fund. An independent custodian holds a fund's assets and monitors cash inflows/outflows on behalf of investors. A transfer agent tracks share purchases and sales, maintains shareholder records, computes the daily NAV, and arranges for dividend/ interest payments and capital gains disbursements. Many of the largest fund companies also have fund distributors (underwriters), who are affiliates responsible for marketing fund shares to investors. Participants involved in the creation and management of an open-end fund are summarized in Figure 6. 4.

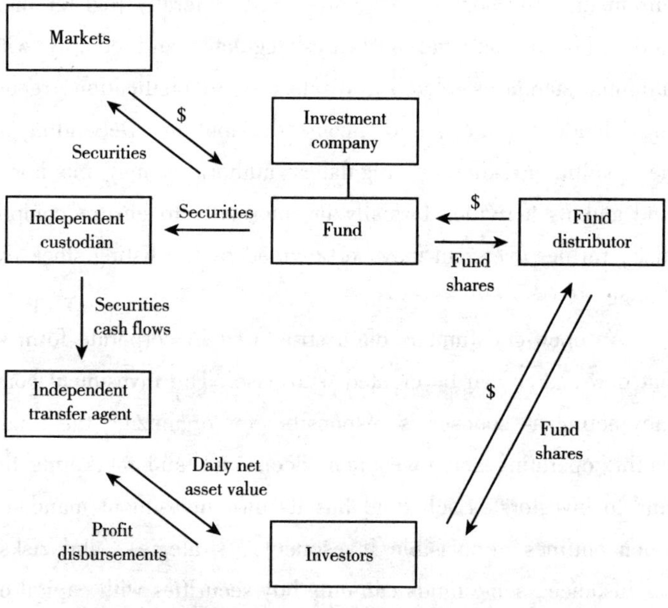

Figure 6. 4 Open-end funds legal vehicles/participants

CLOSED-END FUNDS 封闭式基金

Closed-end funds represent a much smaller portion of the investment fund sector. Closed-end funds, like their open-end counterparts, are professionally managed portfolios that are listed and traded on exchanges. But closed-end funds can issue only a limited number of shares and cannot create new ones at will. In some cases the combination of a fund's investments and its limited ability to create new shares leads to illiquidity, or difficulty on the part of investors in selling shares at the quoted price when needed. Accordingly, closed-end funds are considered to be most suitable for investors with a medium-to long-term investment horizon. The most active element of the closed-end market is centered on bonds issued by municipal/local authorities and stocks of companies in emerging markets.

The unit investment trust (UIT), a subset of the closed-end fund class, features a specific, rather than indefinite, maturity date. A UIT is a "passive" fund that accepts an initial (and limited) amount of investor capital, purchases a target portfolio of securities, and holds the securities until the maturity of the fund. The portfolio of a UIT is not actively managed or rebalanced. In fact, the trustee simply holds the securities that have been purchased and collects and distributes cash flows to investors. In practice most UITs invest in bonds rather than stocks, since bonds have defined maturities/redemption dates. Once the final securities mature the UIT is liquidated and investors receive their principal.

HEDGE FUNDS 对冲基金

Hedge funds are flexible investment conduits intended primarily for sophisticated investors who can absorb greater risk than the average individual. In fact, minimum amounts of income and/or net worth are usually required. As we've noted, hedge funds attempt to create absolute returns through active management, regardless of what is occurring in a specific market. They do not benchmark to, or replicate, indexes or engage in passive investment strategies. Hedge funds may increase their risks (and potential returns) by using borrowed funds to buy securities, taking concentrated positions, short-selling securities, and buying/selling illiquid assets and derivatives. Contrary to popular belief, not all hedge funds trade their portfolios actively (e. g. buying/selling securities repeatedly throughout the trading day); some feature relatively low portfolio turnover as they try to generate value over the medium term.

We've already said that hedge funds enjoy considerable flexibility in allocating investors' capital across markets and strategies. Common hedge fund strategies include:

- Directional asset allocation: Buying/selling securities in one or more asset classes to take advantage of the direction of the market. For instance, a fund may buy a portfolio of auto company stocks if it perceives them to be undervalued, or may sell a portfolio of emerging market bonds if it thinks they are overvalued.
- Relative value: Buying/selling securities in one or more asset classes to take advantage of the differential between the assets, rather than the absolute direction of the market. For instance, a fund might sell the stocks of high-priced retailers and buy the stocks of discount retailers if it believes that consumer spending and economic growth are about to slow dramatically. Alternatively, it might buy a company's convertible bonds and short sell its stocks to capture any value differential between the two.
- Event driven: Buying/selling securities of companies that are subject to possible "events" such as takeovers, bankruptcy, or recapitalization. For example, a fund might buy the stocks of several companies that are likely to be takeover candidates in an industry that is consolidating. Or, it may buy the bonds of a company that has defaulted in hopes of earning a profit once the company emerges from bankruptcy.

A key segment of the market centers on funds of funds (FOFs) and funds of funds of funds (F3s). Following the concepts of portfolio theory we have already discussed, these entities try to diversify hedge fund performance risk by using investors' capital to invest in 5 – 20 + different hedge funds (or funds of funds). While the concept is appealing, FOFs and F3s add an extra layer of costs that subtract from investor returns. So, to be truly appealing to investors, fund of fund and F3 managers must have proven skills in selecting above-average hedge fund performers.

Many hedge funds are exempt from regulations that are applied to open-and closed-end funds. In fact, most hedge fund managers are considered to be unregistered investment advisors, and cannot therefore advertise or market their funds directly to the public. But they must still distribute to prospective investors an offering memorandum with essential details on the fund, its activities, and its risk factors.

Hedge funds are typically structured as private partnerships rather than investment companies, using a general partner (GP) /limited partner (LP) framework. The fund's portfolio management team acts as the GP, making all investment management decisions and retaining unlimited liability in the business. Investors in the fund act as the LPs, holding passive interests in the fund and remaining liable up to the amount of the capital they have invested in the venture. The partnership structure can only accommodate a small number of large investors.

Funds are often set up with multiple entities that cater to domestic and offshore investors. For instance, a US-based hedge fund may establish an offshore partnership in a tax-and regulatory-friendly environment (e. g. in the Caymans, British Virgin Islands, Bermuda) to handle the requirements of offshore investors and non-taxable US investors (e. g. pension funds, endowment funds, foundations), and an identical US partnership (e. g. Delaware) to serve taxable US investors. Even though the fund might use multiple partnerships, it invests capital in the same strategies. Figure 6. 5 summarizes this process.

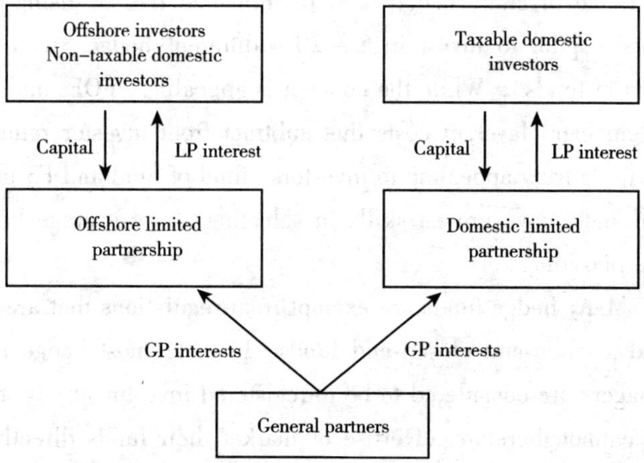

Figure 6. 5 Onshore/offshore hedge fund structure

Hedge funds generally charge asset-based fees (just as any other fund might) and performance fees. For instance, a fund may charge between 1 – 2 percent p. a. on assets under management, and a 20 percent performance fee on any gross earnings generated; this compares to all-in fees of sub – 1 percent – 2 percent for other types of funds. So, the general partners of a hedge fund with £100 million under management that posts £20 million in returns will receive £5 million (i. e. 2 percent of £100 million and 20 percent of £20 million). The returns paid to investors (limited partners) come from the earnings that remain after all asset and performance fees have been paid. Some hedge funds protect investors by including a minimum hurdle rate that must be achieved before managers receive any performance bonuses. A "high water mark" test may also be included. The high water mark means that fund managers will only be paid if they create value year over year. For instance, a fund with £100 million under management and a 20 percent payout that generates £20 million of earnings in year 1 pays £4 million in performance fees to the managers. If markets are difficult in year 2 and the managers lose £10 million, they receive no payout. If performance improves in year 3 and the funds generate £10 million of earnings, the managers still receive no payout as a result of the high water mark: the fund has not yet exceeded the performance position held in year 1.

EXCHANGE TRADED FUNDS 交易所交易基金

Exchange traded funds (ETFs) are popular investment funds that combine features of the open-end fund sector with standard securities trading. ETFs allow new shares to be created and redeemed at will, and permit continuous intra-day trading (just as in standard stocks and bonds), rather than the typical end-of-day trading characterizing open-end and closed-end funds. The cost structure of ETFs also tends to be lower than that of open-end funds. All of these features have helped the instrument build a critical mass of interest in recent years. ETFs are available on baskets, industry sectors, country sectors and broad market indexes (e. g. NASDAQ 100, S&P 500, Dow Jones Industrials, FTSE 100); bond-related ETFs have also become prevalent. In fact, the most popular index ETFs are among the most actively traded financial instruments in the marketplace.

ETFs can be created using an investment company structure, where a fund manager is responsible for all coordination and investment allocation decisions. Under this scheme the investment company tracks (but does not precisely replicate) a reference index, and can use derivatives and physical securities to achieve desired investment results. ETFs based on the UIT concept noted above are similar to investment companies, but somewhat less flexible-primarily because they must replicate a target index very closely. ETFs created as trusts are used primarily for smaller baskets of securities that track specific sectors. All ETFs, regardless of legal structure, are sponsored by major financial institutions/exchanges and must meet certain regulatory requirements (e. g. disclosure by the trust bank of the next day's creation/redemption baskets; purchase/redemption of ETF receipts with the underlying securities; and use of a central clearing/depository). As noted, ETFs generally feature lower costs than equivalent open-end funds; management fees and annual expenses are generally very modest, and processing fees associated with the creation/redemption of ETF shares are small.

ISSUING, REDEEMING, AND TRADING 发行、赎回和交易

ISSUING AND REDEEMING 发行和赎回

The creation and redemption of investment fund shares (or partnership interests) depends on the type of fund being considered. Let's analyze these differences in light of the four major classes described above.

An investor wishing to buy shares in an open-end fund transfers a specific minimum amount of cash to the fund distributor, who forwards the cash to the fund; the fund then buys the securities forming part of the investment strategy. Since the fund is structured as an open-end vehicle it can create new shares at the NAV without limitation. Although open-end funds almost always accept new funds from investors, some eventually accumulate too much and may close to further subscriptions, either temporarily or permanently. This is a defensive mechanism that helps ensure portfolio managers do not suffer from "style drift" -investment outside of a given area of expertise that can result in a misbalancing of risk/return. An investor selling (redeeming) shares submits instructions to the fund, which uses its cash reserve or liquidates a pro-rata amount of securities to meet the redemption. Open-end funds generally preserve a cash buffer of 5 – 10 percent of assets in order to meet redemption orders. Fund managers attempt to minimize the size of the cash buffer, as holding too much cash reduces fund earnings.

As we've noted, closed-end funds do not issue new shares regularly; they nearly always arrange for a single issue of capital, which is preserved over time. While the constant level of capital may be seen as a limiting factor, it can also be regarded as an advantage: fund managers don't have to be concerned about continuous cash inflows and reinvestment, and are unlikely to suffer from style drift. Closed-end funds do not redeem outstanding shares; all shares issued remain outstanding until (or if) a fund is liquidated or restructured. Investors wanting to sell their shares must find other investors willing to buy them, and do so through a standard brokered transaction.

The supply of shares in a hedge fund is strictly limited. Partnership shares are generally arranged as private placements sold directly to accredited investors through the onshore or offshore entities mentioned above. Once the initial capital has been raised, (sometimes in tranches) proceeds are invested in one or more strategies. In some cases a fund may arrange a new issuance of capital to finance another fund strategy. But this has to be seen as an independent transaction, rather than a continuous creation of capital. Similarly, redemption of fund shares is very limited. Investors who want to sell their interests may only be able to do so at defined points during the calendar year (e.g. every month or quarter), and may be required to provide several months' advance notice. Since hedge funds don't have to worry about daily liquidity they can optimize their portfolios by holding less cash.

The ETF share issuance and redemption process is rather more involved because it is based on unlimited share creation and continuous share trading. In a typical ETF an authorized participant (e.g. a financial institution) purchases a portfolio of securities representing the underlying reference index, which it deposits with a trust bank. The trust bank places the securities in a trust account and issues divisible depository receipts. Once the receipts are issued, they can be subdivided and bought and sold through an exchange, just like any other listed corporate security. If an investor wants to sell ETF shares they have purchased, the shares are not redeemed by the fund (as in a standard open-end fund transaction), but are simply sold to another investor. If overall demand for the ETF declines-that is, no further buying interest exists-the authorized participant can gather up the receipts, reassemble them, submit the single receipt to the trust bank, and receive the underlying portfolio of securities in return. It can then liquidate the securities, thus returning investors to their original cash position. This process is summarized in Figure 6. 6.

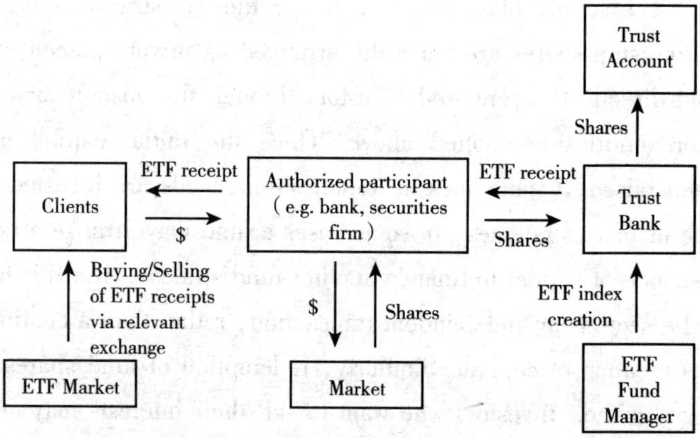

Figure 6. 6 Process of creating/trading an ETF

SECONDARY TRADING 二级市场交易

The degree of secondary trading in investment funds again depends on structure.

ETFs feature the greatest amount of secondary trading. Investors can purchase and sell shares in the fund several times during the trading day, or they can hold them for the intermediate or long term (note, of course, that each purchase and sale attracts a bid-offer spread and a brokerage commission charge). Since ETFs can be traded at current market prices they are eligible for short selling. The existence of continuous pricing and the depth of liquidity in the most popular indexes have led to the creation of derivative contracts on select ETFs. This, in turn, helps promote further activity and liquidity in the ETF, in a self-fulfilling cycle.

The shares of major open-end funds are actively traded as well, but can only be bought or sold at the end-of-day NAV-not at continuous prices. However, since new shares can be created constantly and existing shares can be redeemed without difficulty, turnover can be reasonably good-particularly for large, well known funds with a strong performance record. The same is obviously not true for closed-end funds or hedge funds, which have very low levels of secondary trading volume. Hedge fund shares can be particularly illiquid: as noted, investors may only be able to sell their shares every few weeks or months, and must generally give the fund administrator several weeks (or months) advance notice of their intention of doing so.

Figure 6.7 summarizes the spectrum of secondary trading activity, from the most active (or most liquid) to the least active (or most illiquid).

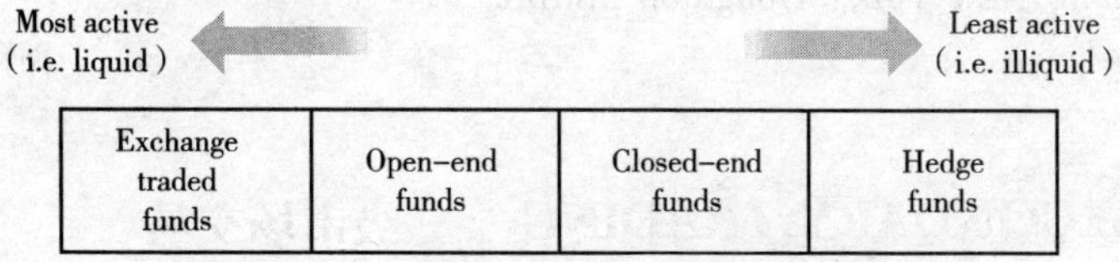

Figure 6.7 Secondary trading activity in funds

摘要

投资基金将债务和权益证券结合成单一的投资组合，已经变成重要和流行的投资渠道。基金具有几个重大的优点：它们提供给投资者受到专业管理的证券投资组合，其风险和收益特征同步地可适应广泛的投资者风格和目标；它们利用投资组合分散化在给定的风险水平下最大化收益；它们通过允许经由单一交易执行多项交易活动创造了效率；而且它们在投资组合中产生了持续性，特别是对于那些具有有限到期时间和标明回购日期的资产。基金可以由几项主要的特征来描述，包括收益类型（经常收入、资本利得或两者兼备）、地理重点、资产类别和次资产类别。投资基金主要的种类包括开放式基金，或允许在连续的基础上创建新份额并且被以每日结束时净资产值（NAV）报价和赎回的投资渠道；封闭式基金是发行固定数量的份额并也能以每日净资产值（NAV）交易的投资渠道；对冲基金是投机的手段，能够投资到广泛的金融工具和战略中去，而且仅仅允许投资者每月或每季度结算；以及交易所交易基金（ETFs）是允许创建无限数额的份额并可以在交易日随意交易的投资渠道。基金具有不同程度的流动性：交易所交易基金（ETFs）是最富流动性的（因为在连续的基础上存在购买和出售的可能），而紧随其后的是开放式基金、封闭式基金和对冲基金。

FURTHER READING 延伸阅读

Lake, R., 2003, *Evaluating and Implementing Hedge Funds Strategies*, *3rd edition*, London: Euromoney.

Pozen, R., 2002, *The Mutual Fund Business*, *2nd edition*, New York: Houghton Mifflin.

7

DERIVATIVES AND INSURANCE

衍生品与保险

CHAPTER OVERVIEW 本章概述

In this chapter we examine derivatives and insurance, financial contracts that companies can use to manage different types of risks. We begin with simple definitions of the instruments, a review of why and how derivatives and insurance are used, the similarities and differences between the two, and the types of risks that each class is designed to create, reduce, or transfer. Following this we consider speculation and arbitrage, two activities that are unique to derivatives. We conclude by analyzing the characteristics of each class; although the two share certain similarities, this section will reveal in greater detail important differences between the two.

USES OF DERIVATIVES AND INSURANCE 衍生品和保险的用途

RISK MANAGEMENT 风险管理

Before beginning a detailed discussion of derivatives and insurance, let's first consider simple definitions of the two (which we shall expand in subsequent sections).

衍生品

- Derivative: A contract that derives, or obtains, its value from some other market or asset. It has no value on its own and must be tied to some other reference asset. For instance, a €/$currency derivative is a contract that derives its value from the €/$currency rate.

保险

- Insurance: A contract that insures, or provides financial restitution when a loss-making event occurs. For instance, a fire insurance policy is a contract that provides a payment if a fire destroys valuable property.

On the surface these two contracts may seem quite different. They do, in fact, have very different characteristics, as we'll discover later in the chapter. But they also share a significant commonality-namely, they can both be used to manage risks.

Recall from our discussion in Chapter 1 that risk, which we have defined as the uncertainty (or variability) surrounding an outcome, affects every company. Though the actual nature and magnitude of risks can vary across companies, every firm is exposed to some type of risk. Some of the key risks a company can encounter include:

经营风险

- Operating risk: The risk of loss arising from a firm's inability to sell its goods or obtain raw material inputs; it can also include risk of loss stemming from plant and equipment damage or destruction, or technology/systems failure.

财务风险

- Financial risk: The risk of loss coming from an adverse movement in financial markets/prices (such as interest or currency rates) or the failure of a client/counterparty to perform on its contractual obligations (such as accounts receivable). The former is often referred to as market risk, while the latter is considered a credit risk.

法律风险

- Legal risk: The risk of loss arising from litigation (individual, regulatory, or "class action") or other legal/documentary errors.

环境风险

- Environmental risk: Risk of loss arising from the firm's willful, unknowing, or accidental damage to the environment (such as an oil spill).

We recall from Chapter 1 that a key corporate financial goal is prudent management of risk. If ABC Co. can keep its risk exposures properly balanced, then it stands a better chance of avoiding surprise financial losses and reducing its earnings volatility, which ultimately helps boost enterprise value. We must consider an important point here: managing risks properly does not mean eliminating or shifting all risk. There are times when it makes economic sense for a company to preserve certain types and amounts of risk. This happens when risk-taking activities have the potential of being profitable, or when the cost of obtaining risk protection is very expensive. In fact, every risk management decision can be evaluated in a cost-benefit framework by focusing on the costs a company incurs in reducing or eliminating the risk against the benefits it obtains from doing so; conversely, it may consider the costs of retaining the risk versus the benefits it derives from doing so.

Though risk can be categorized according to the classes described above, it can also be distinguished more broadly as being "speculative" or "pure." A speculative risk lends itself to three possible states: profit, loss, or no profit/loss. For instance, if €/$ currency rates move in a particular direction, a company with a currency exposure may generate a profit; if rates move in the opposite direction it will post a loss. Many financial risks are speculative. Reducing or eliminating a financial risk is done through a process known as hedging (which we consider later) or through risk diversification (as described in Chapter 3). A pure risk, in contrast, features only two states: loss or no loss. In other words, there is no chance of generating a profit. For example, a company operating a factory is exposed to the possibility of damage or destruction by fire. If the fire occurs and damage is done the company loses money, and if no fire occurs, it loses no money. Reducing or eliminating a pure risk is done through insurance, derivatives, or diversification, depending on the nature of the risk.

The basic decision states related to risk costs and benefits are summarized in Table 7. 1.

Table 7. 1　　Risk decision framework

Decision	*Cost*	*Benefit*
Preserving risk	A possible loss from the source of risk	A possible profit from the source of the risk (if speculative) and no costs associated with a risk management solution
Reducing/eliminating risk	Costs associated with a risk management solution (e. g. fee, insurance premium) and no possibility of profit from the source of risk (if speculative)	No/reduced potential for loss from the source of risk

A firm that is deciding how to manage its risks often does so in a formalized way, as part of long-term financial planning. This adds rigor and discipline to the process, and helps ensure that the right kind of risk is preserved or eliminated. A proper risk management framework can be created by first defining a risk mandate, which reflects two important concepts:

风险理念

- Risk philosophy: An explicit statement developed by the board of directors and executive management that reflects the nature of the risks the firm is willing to bear.

风险承受能力

- Risk tolerance: A definition of the actual amount of risk the firm is willing to bear.

The mandate can then be converted into a sequential, four-step process:

风险鉴定

- Risk identification: An analysis of the kinds of risks the firm faces

风险量化

- Risk quantification: A quantitative description of how large risk exposures are (or may become) and what size profit and/or loss might be generated

风险管理

- Risk management: A determination, based on cost/benefit

analysis, of how the firm can best manage its exposures
- Risk monitoring: A process of tracking risk exposures over time.

风险监测

The cycle then repeats, so that the process can be considered dynamic. With this type of risk process in place a company can create a risk profile that makes optimal use of risk management tools like derivatives and insurance. The ultimate goal of the process is, of course, value maximization.

Figure 7.1 summarizes the risk framework.

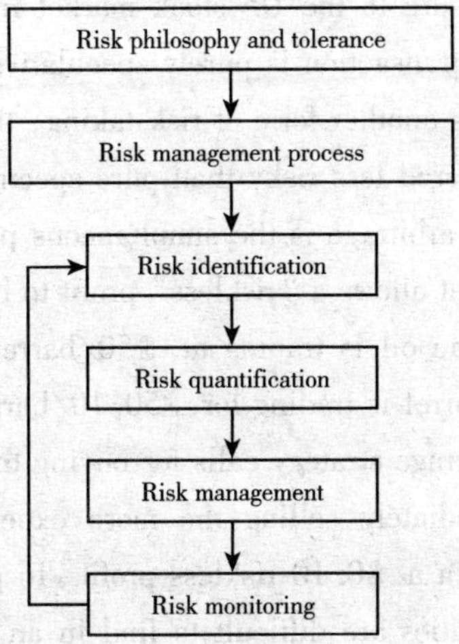

Figure 7.1 The risk management framework

SPECULATION AND ARBITRAGE
投机和套利

Not all risk-related activities are based on reducing or eliminating risk. Some firms are in business to actively take risk. Banks, securities firms, insurers, and investment funds, for example, regularly take risk, as this represents the core of their business and how they actually make money. They are motivated by speculation and arbitrage rather than pure risk management.

Speculation involves creating a risk position that has the potential of generating a profit or loss, depending on which way a particular market or reference asset moves. Unlike hedging or risk protection, speculative positions are subject to unrealized gains or losses; once a position matures or is reversed, the gain or loss is crystallized in the income statement. Thus if ABC Co. believes that the US stock market is poised to rise, it can create a speculative position that will benefit from a market rise (and which will lose if the market falls). Because ABC Co. has no underlying exposure to the US stock market in its normal core operations, the transaction is purely speculative.

Arbitrage is another form of risk-taking, though one that is generally considered less risky than pure speculation. The classic definition of arbitrage is the simultaneous purchase and sale of some asset that allows a "riskless" profit to be locked-in. For instance, if crude oil is trading at $50/barrel in one location and the same barrel is trading for $50. 10/barrel in another location, the arbitrage strategy calls for buying the cheaper oil for $50 and immediately selling the more expensive oil for $50. 10, locking in a $0. 10 riskless profit. In practice such arbitrage opportunities are difficult to find in an era where information is disseminated globally on an instantaneous basis and technology allows for rapid trading execution. In fact, arbitrage is generally defined to include any relatively low-risk strategy that involves the purchase and sale of similar assets. The intent is not to generate a riskless profit, but a low-risk profit-one that is more predictable and less volatile than is possible through pure speculation.

We've noted above that insurance contracts provide compensation in the event that a defined loss occurs; under no circumstances can insurance-which is a contract of indemnity-be used to create a profit. Accordingly, firms speculating or arbitraging must turn to the stocks and bonds we have described earlier in the book, along with other financial instruments such as foreign exchange. They can also use derivative contracts based on the same stock, bond, or currency references.

RISK REFERENCES 风险参照

Derivatives and insurance can be arranged on a broad range of risk references, making them suitable for companies from all industries. In general, derivatives are based on financial risks, while insurance contracts are based on insurable operating risks. That said, there are areas of "overlap" that are starting to emerge as the financial and insurance markets draw closer together.

Derivatives can be bought and sold on any of the following references:

- Equities: Individual stocks, baskets of stocks, and broad indexes
- Debt: Money market instruments/rates, government bonds/rates (e.g. risk-free bonds), and corporate bonds/rates (e.g. risky bonds)
- Currencies: G10 and emerging market currency rates
- Commodities: Precious metals (e.g. gold, silver, platinum), industrial metals (e.g. copper, zinc, aluminum), energy products (e.g. oil/distillates, natural gas, electricity), agricultural products (e.g. corn, soybeans, coffee, sugar), commodity indexes, and other non-commodity references (e.g. inflation, gross domestic product, weather, catastrophe)

Insurance can be purchased on the following:

- Property and casualty (P&C): Damage/destruction to property caused by non-catastrophic or catastrophic events, and losses related to liability
- Business interruption: Temporary loss of business revenues as a result of non-catastrophic or catastrophic events
- Marine insurance: Damage/destruction to hull, cargo, or

freight, along with liability-related losses

- Health and mortality: Long-term disability and death
- Automobile: Damage/destruction, bodily injury, and liability

From a corporate perspective most focus is placed on the P&C, business interruption, and liability sectors; the health, life/mortality, and automobile sectors, while of vital importance, relate more specifically to individual insurance contracting.

INSTRUMENT CHARACTERISTICS: DERIVATIVES 工具特征：衍生品

While the derivatives sector is based on a large variety of unique contracts, we can condense the essential instruments to a more manageable number that includes over-the-counter (OTC) forwards, swaps and options, and exchange-traded (or listed) futures, options, and futures options. We shall not consider the subclasses of "exotic" derivatives (e. g. complex swaps and options, structured notes) as these are beyond our scope. Figure 7. 2 summarizes key types of derivative instruments.

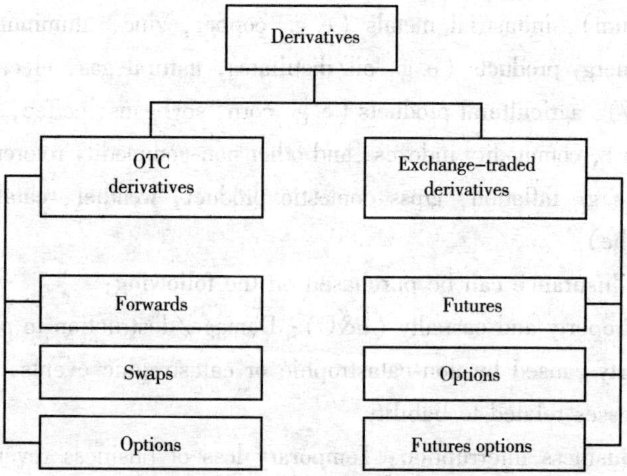

Figure 7. 2 Derivative classes

Derivatives have certain features that can make them very appealing: some contracts are very actively traded and therefore cost-effective; transactions arranged through the listed market eliminate credit risk; transactions structured through the OTC market are highly customizable and flexible; and, contracts serving as hedges don't require demonstration of "proof of loss" (as an insurance contract does). Some risks and disadvantages also exist, of course: credit risks for OTC transactions can be significant; the costs for exotic contracts can be high; and bilateral derivative contracts, like swaps and forwards, expose a firm to downside payments.

KEY CHARACTERISTICS

Derivatives can be defined by various key characteristics, including notional, reference asset, maturity strike (for options) and payment/receipt flows (for swaps/forwards), settlement, and trading mechanism.

- Notional: The value amount of the transaction being arranged. This ranges from several million dollars up to $1 billion or more, depending on the instrument, market, and motivation. Apart from a few exceptions noted below, the notional amount of a derivative serves only as a reference to compute amounts due or payable, and not as an actual sum that is paid or received. For instance, ABC Co. may decide to arrange a swap with a notional value of £100 million to hedge its interest rate risk. It will not exchange the £100 million notional, but use it to compute the amount that it must pay, or expects to receive, each period. 名义值
- Reference asset: The specific financial asset to which the contract relates. We have noted above that a derivative can be arranged on a very broad range of reference assets from the debt, equity, currency, commodity, non-commodity, and credit markets. The reference asset must be defined 标的资产

specifically, rather than generally. Thus, if ABC Co. is arranging a £100 million notional swap on interest rates, the actual reference rates must be properly defined, e. g. the company will pay 5 percent £ fixed rates and receive £ 6-month London Interbank Offered Rate LIBOR.

到期时间

- Maturity: The duration of the derivative contract. This can range from overnight to more than ten years, though in practice most activity takes place in the 1 – 5 year range. ABC Co.'s £100 million swap, for instance, might have a five-year maturity, indicating that it is contractually obliged to fulfill the terms of the deal for the full five years. The maturity of a derivative contract can sometimes be altered by mutual agreement of the contracting parties.

行权/付款/收款

- Strike/payments/receipts: The relevant financial parameters that dictate the economic flows of a transaction. A strike price is used for options contracts, while pay/receive flows are used for forwards and swaps, as we shall discuss in the next section. For example, we have noted that ABC Co.'s swap involves a payment of 5 percent per year on £100 million versus receipt of LIBOR. If LIBOR at the end of year 1 sets at 4 percent, ABC Co. pays its counterparty £1 million (£100 million × (4 percent – 5 percent); if LIBOR sets at 6 percent, ABC Co. receives £1 million (£100 million × (6 percent – 5 percent)).

结算

- Settlement: The means by which the underlying economics of a transaction are settled at maturity. Settlement may be arranged in physical or financial terms. A physical settlement involves the actual delivery/acceptance of any asset or instrument that can be physically conveyed, such as oil, gold, or various types of financial instruments. A financial settlement involves a pure exchange of cash value. Thus, in ABC Co.'s £ interest rate swap, any settlement of the fixed and floating interest rate flows is done in financial terms. Had ABC Co. sought to hedge an exposure to copper rather than interest rates, it could have selected a physical or financial settlement, depending on its need for, or access to, physical copper.

- Trading mechanism: The actual forum through which the derivative is arranged, revalued, and terminated. As we shall see below, this can be done through the OTC market (telephonically or electronically) or through the exchange-traded market; each trading mechanism has advantages and disadvantages. In arranging its swap, ABC Co. uses the OTC market, negotiating terms and conditions verbally with its bank, which then documents details through a confirmation.

交易机制

KEY INSTRUMENTS 主要工具

We begin our review of derivatives with a look at OTC contracts, or financial assets that are arranged on a customized basis between two parties.

OTC DERIVATIVES 场外交易衍生品

OTC derivatives, as the name suggests, are arranged and traded between two parties on an off-exchange basis. Each contract represents a customized negotiation of terms and conditions, with the parties agreeing to specific characteristics related to notional, term, reference market/asset, payoff profile, and so forth. Since each contract is tailor-made, liquidity or resaleability may be lower than in markets where standardization is mandatory (i. e. the exchange-traded market we consider below). Lack of liquidity access adds to total costs, as expressed through the bid (buy) and offer (sell) spread. In fact, some OTC contracts can feature relatively wide spreads, which can impact the economics of a hedge or speculative trade. However, some OTC contracts, such as standard, on-market interest rate, currency, and equity derivatives on major references, feature good liquidity.

Dealing occurs off-exchange (either telephonically or via electronic communications networks) rather than through formalized exchanges; though there is no "central forum" for OTC dealing, most activity is arranged and transacted by major financial institutions and their clients via the major financial centers of the world, including New York, Toronto, Chicago, Tokyo, Singapore, London, Frankfurt, and Zurich. Since OTC derivatives are arranged between two parties with no intermediate clearinghouse, aspects of credit risk can arise. Indeed, in the absence of any specifically negotiated collateral/margin agreement between the two parties to a transaction, credit exposure arises for one or both parties (depending on the nature of the contract).

FORWARD 远期

远期合同是一种单期合同。

A forward contract is a single-period contract that allows one party, known as the seller, to sell a reference asset at a forward price for settlement at a future date, and a second party, the buyer, to purchase the reference asset at the forward price on the named date. A forward is considered a bilateral contract since either party may be obliged to make a payment at maturity. Market terminology indicates that the party that has sold the position is "short" and the one that has bought the position is "long"; this is true of all other derivative (and financial asset) positions, so we'll use the terms throughout this chapter. A notional amount is used as a reference to compute the amount payable/receivable at maturity; in fact, the two parties exchange no initial or intervening cash flows. Settlement of the contract at maturity may be set in physical or financial terms. If the market price at maturity is greater than the contracted forward price set at trade date, the buyer makes a profit and the seller a loss. If the market price is lower than the forward price, then the seller profits and the buyer loses. These relationships hold true for all price-based forwards, including those involving equities, bonds, indexes, currencies, and commodities. The profit positions of generic long and short forwards are summarized below, and the flows are illustrated in Figure 7.3.

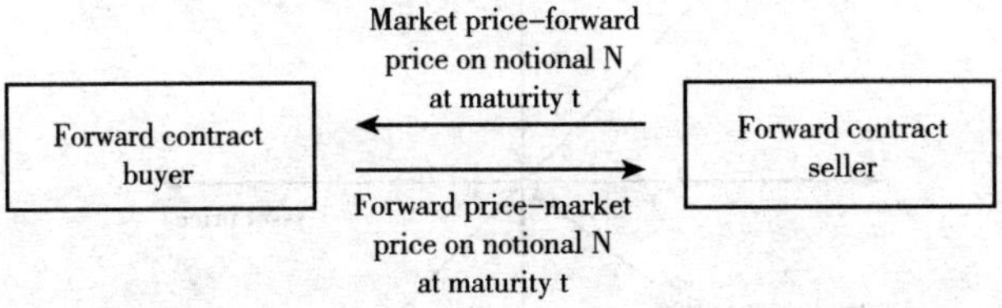

Figure 7.3 Forward contract flows

Table 7.2 describes how the value of long and short forwards change as the reference asset increases or decreases, while Figures 7.4 through 7.5 depict the same information in graph form.

Table 7.2 Long/short forward relationships

Position	*Reference asset* ↑	*Reference asset* ↓
Long forward	Gains value	Loses value
Short forward	Loses value	Gains value

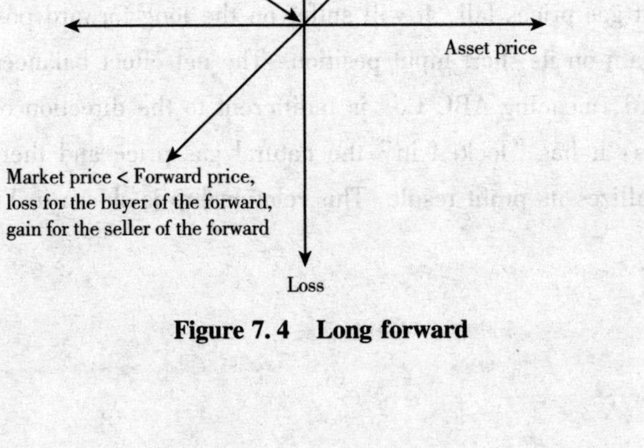

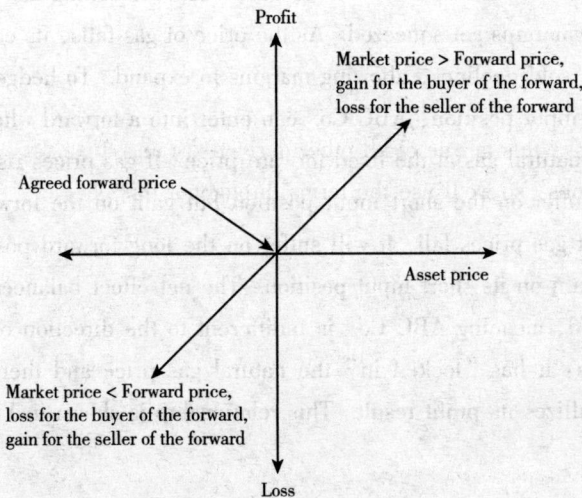

Figure 7.4 Long forward

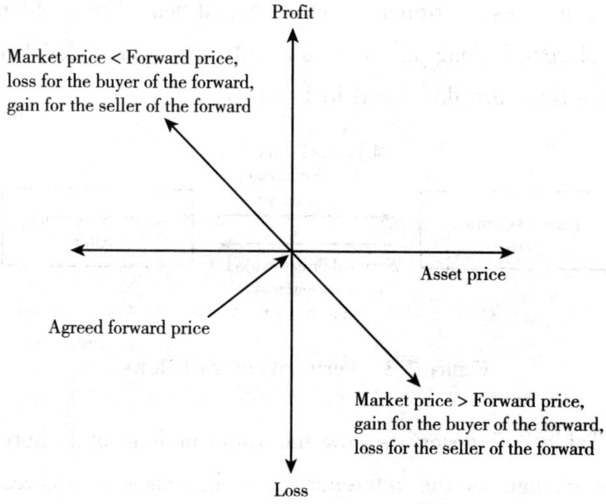

Figure 7.5 Short forward

We've noted that forwards can be used to hedge other positions. To illustrate this in graph form, let's imagine that ABC Co. has a short position in some input that it uses in its production. For instance, the firm may use natural gas to power its assembly lines. As the price of natural gas rises, the firm suffers from an increase in its cost of goods sold, meaning its gross profit margins get squeezed. As the price of gas falls, its cost of goods sold declines, allowing margins to expand. To hedge this short input position, ABC Co. can enter into a forward where it buys natural gas at the fixed forward price. If gas prices rise, it will suffer on the short input position but gain on the forward, and if gas prices fall, it will suffer on the long forward position but gain on its short input position. The net effect balances out to zero, meaning ABC Co. is indifferent to the direction of gas prices: it has "locked in" the natural gas price and therefore crystallizes its profit result. This relationship is shown in Figure 7.6.

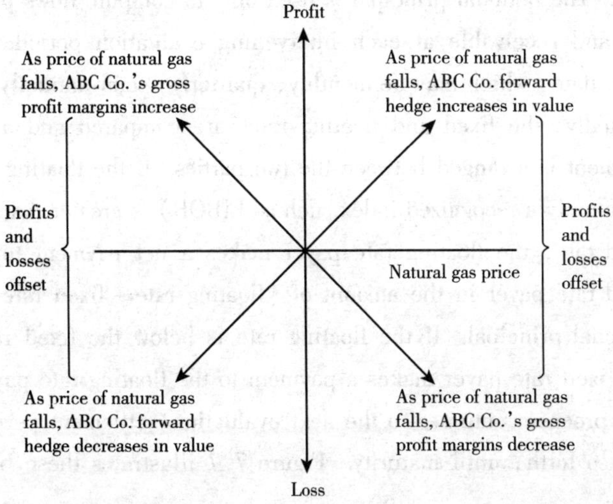

Figure 7.6 Long forward / short asset hedge position

SWAP 掉期交易

The swap, the second major product of the OTC derivatives market, is a package of forward contracts that mature at successive periods in the future, until the stated maturity date. Swaps, like forwards, are bilateral contracts and can be arranged on virtually any asset from any market sector. While interest rate swaps still account for the largest share of the market, active dealing occurs in equity, currency, commodity, and credit swaps. An emerging market has also started to appear in swaps based on inflation, macroeconomic indicators (e. g. gross domestic product), real estate, and weather references (e. g. temperature, precipitation). Maturities in the swap marketplace range from approximately one to ten years.

Let's examine the interest rate swap we introduced earlier in the chapter to illustrate the mechanics of the structure. An interest rate swap is a contract where one party agrees to pay a fixed interest rate and a second party agrees to pay a floating rate. The notional principal is used only to compute flows payable and receivable at each intervening evaluation period. On each date, which may be monthly, quarterly, semi-annually, or annually, the fixed and floating rates are compared and a net payment is arranged between the two parties. If the floating rate (generally a recognized index such as LIBOR) is greater than the fixed rate, the floating rate payer makes a net payment to the fixed rate payer in the amount of (floating rate − fixed rate) × notional principal. If the floating rate is below the fixed rate, the fixed rate payer makes a payment to the floating rate payer. The process continues to the next evaluation/settlement period, and so forth, until maturity. Figure 7.7 illustrates these basic flows.

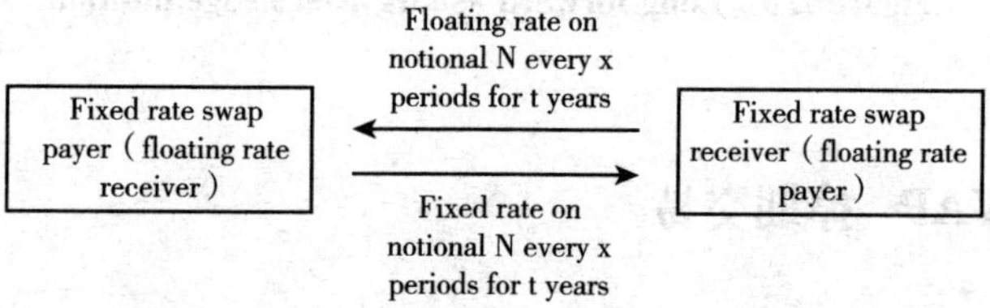

Figure 7.7 Interest rate swap flows

Let's again think about how an interest rate swap can be used to hedge an interest rate exposure. Assume ABC Co. has issued £100 million of five-year floating rate bonds pegged to 6 month £LIBOR, which currently stands at 5 percent. Let's also assume that ABC Co.'s treasurer believes interest rates will rise over the next five years. In order to guard against higher interest expense (which would squeeze profits) the company arranges an interest rate swap hedge with a bank where it pays fixed rates (let's assume 5 percent for simplicity) and receives 6 month £LIBOR over five years; this is illustrated in Figure 7.8. If LIBOR rises, ABC Co. will pay more for its LIBOR-based floating rate debt, but will receive a greater payment from the bank under the swap. So, if LIBOR rises to 6 percent after the first six-month evaluation period, ABC Co. pays 6 percent on its debt, but receives a net 1 percent on the swap (e. g. 6 month £LIBOR – 5 percent fixed); this means its net cost of debt is 5 percent (6 percent – 1 percent), which is precisely equal to the 5 percent fixed rate it is paying on the swap. If the company's forecast is wrong and rates fall, it still faces the same 5 percent fixed cost of borrowing. For instance, if LIBOR declines to 4 percent ABC Co. will pay a lower cost on its floating rate debt but will pay a higher cost on the swap; the two again net out to 5 percent fixed payments. The process then continues for each of the remaining evaluation periods until maturity in five years. We see that, regardless of what happens to interest rates, ABC Co. has hedged itself at a 5 percent fixed rate. These simple scenarios are illustrated in Table 7. 3.

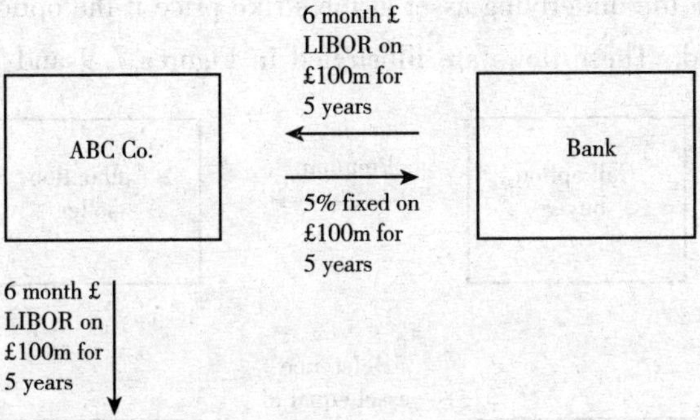

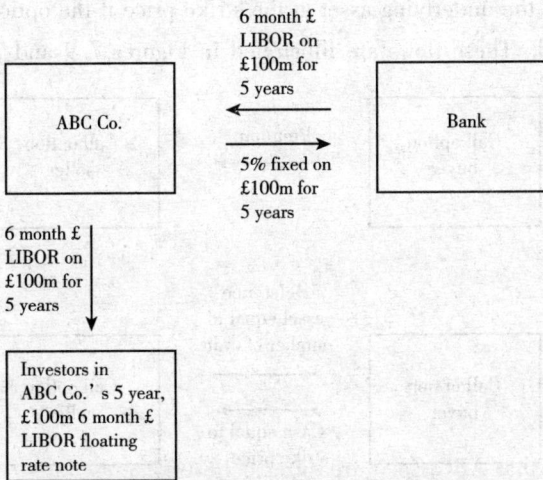

Figure 7. 8 ABC Co.'s fixed/floating swap hedge

Table 7. 3 ABC Co.'s net cost of debt

LIBOR scenario	*(a) Cost of floating rate debt (LIBOR)*	*(b) Gain/loss on swap (LIBOR – 5% fixed)*	*Net cost of debt (a) – (b)*
3%	3%	–2%	5%
4%	4%	–1%	5%
5%	5%	0%	5%
6%	6%	+1%	5%
7%	7%	+2%	5%

OPTION 期权

An option, the third major type of OTC derivative, is a contract that gives the purchaser the right, but not the obligation, to buy (call option) or sell (put option) a reference asset at a particular price (known as the strike price). The option buyer can exercise their rights under the contact at any time until an agreed expiry date (American option), on the expiry date (European option), or on specified dates up to expiry (Bermudan option). In exchange for this right the buyer pays the seller a premium payment. By accepting the premium the option seller has an obligation (rather than a right) to sell (call) or buy (put) the underlying asset at the strike price if the option is exercised. These flows are illustrated in Figures 7. 9 and 7. 10.

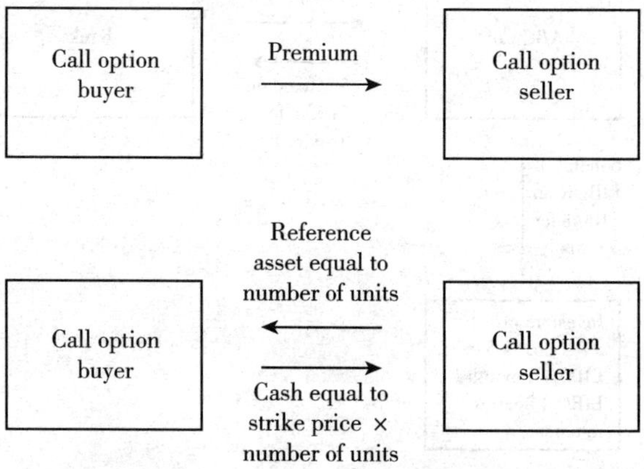

Figure 7. 9 Call option flows: initial and exercise

If the buyer of a call option exercises (e. g. the price of the underlying reference asset is above the strike price), it delivers the required amount of cash, which is defined by the strike price × number of units, and receives the underlying asset.

So, if ABC Co. purchases a call for $1, 000 of premium

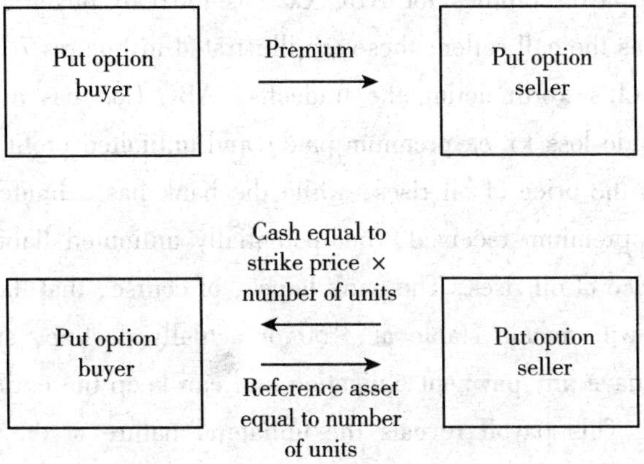

Figure 7.10 Put option flows: initial and exercise

that allows it to buy 1000 barrels of crude oil at a strike price of \$50/ barrel it will be economically advantageous for the firm to exercise whenever the price of oil rises above \$50. Let's assume the price of oil rises to \$55. ABC Co. exercises the call option against the seller, and delivers \$50,000 of cash in exchange for 1000 barrels of oil. Of course, the 1000 barrels of oil are actually worth \$55,000 in today's market (i.e. the market price is \$55/barrel), so ABC Co. has a \$5,000 profit on the position; the net profit is equal to \$4,000 since the \$1,000 premium payment must be deducted. The seller of the option is obliged to supply the 1000 barrels of oil and accept the \$50,000 of cash in exchange. ABC Co. may actually liquidate the asset in the marketplace at the higher prevailing market price, or it may hold the asset for future use. In practice the option is often settled financially, with no physical exchange of the underlying asset (e.g. barrels of oil). Naturally, if the price of oil falls below \$50/barrel, the option has no value to ABC Co. as it can buy oil in the current market for less than the strike price of the option. If this happens, ABC Co. lets the option expire and the seller has no further performance obligation. To help understand the economics of the call position we can examine payoff profiles for ABC Co. as the call buyer and the bank as the call seller; these are illustrated in Figures 7. 11 and 7. 12. It's worth noting the tradeoffs: ABC Co. has a known downside loss (i. e. premium paid) and unlimited profit potential as the price of oil rises, while the bank has a limited gain (i. e. premium received) but potentially unlimited liability as the price of oil rises. The bank hopes, of course, that the price of oil will remain stable at $50 or actually decline, since it won't have any payment obligation and can keep the entire premium. This payoff reveals the unilateral nature of the option contract.

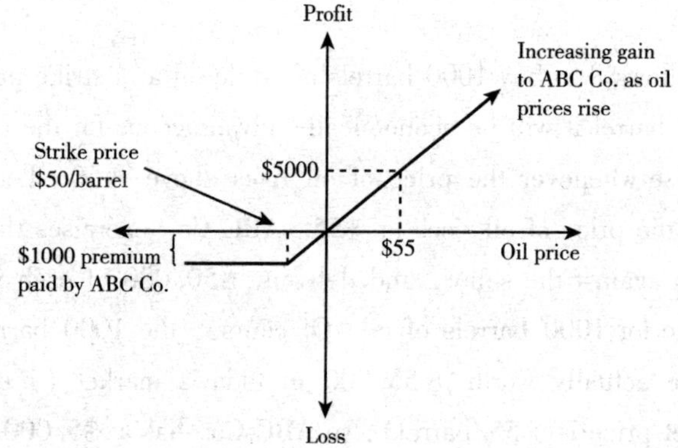

Figure 7. 11　Long call option

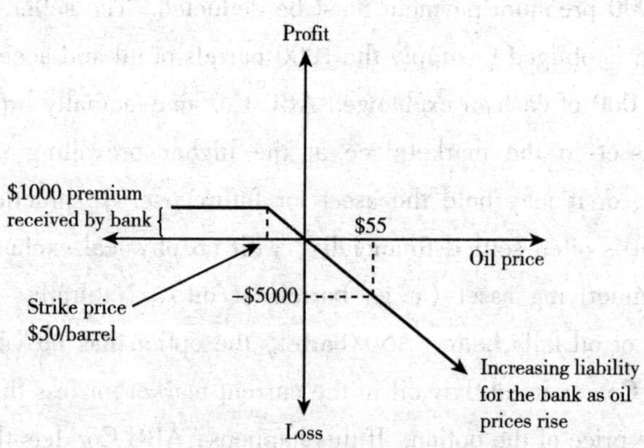

Figure 7. 12　Short call option

A put option gives the buyer the right, but not the obligation, to sell a specified asset at a pre-determined strike price. The buyer will exercise the put option when the market price is below the strike price, delivering the asset to the seller in exchange for the required amount of cash. So, if ABC Co. purchases a put option from a bank for $10, 000 in premium that lets it sell 1, 000 oz of gold at $400/oz it will exercise when the price of gold falls below $400/oz. Let's assume that the price of gold falls to $375/oz. In this case ABC Co. can exercise the put option, delivering 1, 000 oz of gold to the bank in exchange for $400, 000. The bank, as put option seller, is obliged to acquire the gold by delivering cash. If ABC Co. didn't have the put option and needed to sell the gold in the current market, it would only be able to do so for $375, 000; this means that the option has created a $25, 000 gain for the company. Again, if the price of gold remains above the strike of $400/oz, ABC Co. will be better off selling the gold in the current market, meaning it will simply abandon the option; in this case the bank gets to keep the full $10, 000 of premium. We can again summarize these payoff relationships via Figures 7. 13 and 7. 14.

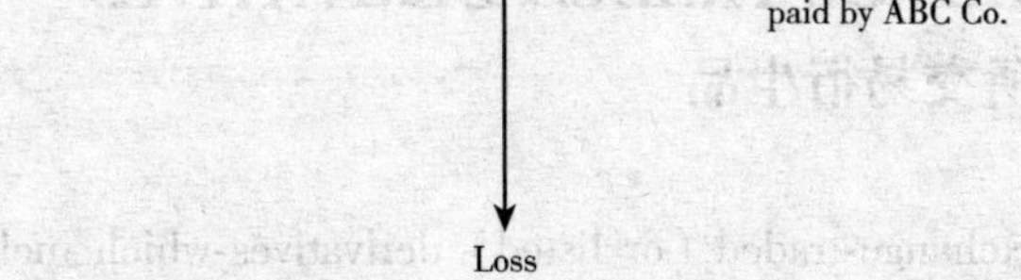

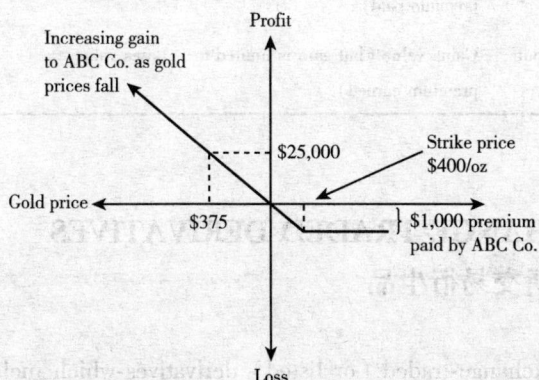

Figure 7. 13 Long put option

Table 7. 4 summarizes the discussion above by describing how the value of long and short calls and puts change as the value of the reference asset increases or decreases.

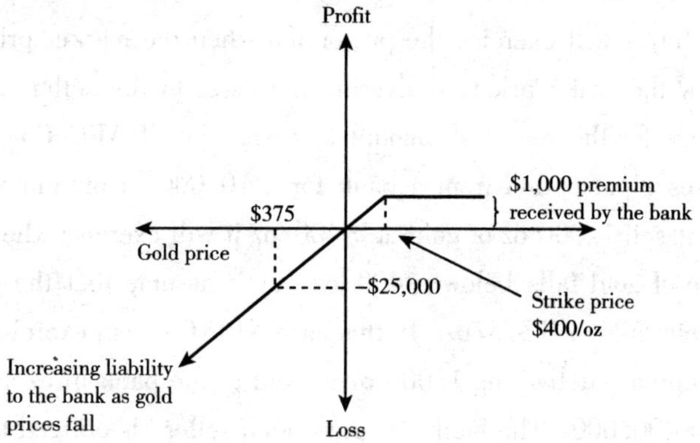

Figure 7. 14 Short put option

Table 7. 4 Long/short options relationships

Position	*Reference asset value* ↑	*Reference asset value* ↓
Long call	Gains value	Loses value (but loss is limited to premium paid)
Short call	Loses value	Gains value (but gain is limited to premium earned)
Long put	Loses value (but loss is limited to premium paid)	Gains value
Short put	Gains value (but gain is limited to premium earned)	Loses value

EXCHANGE-TRADED DERIVATIVES
交易所交易衍生品

Exchange-traded (or listed) derivatives-which include futures, options, and futures options-comprise the second major segment of the derivatives market. Exchange-traded derivatives can be used to achieve many of the same goals as OTC contracts, often at a cheaper cost, but with less structural flexibility. All trading occurs through regulated exchanges (which is distinct from the largely unregulated OTC market), such as the Chicago Mercantile Exchange, the Chicago Board of Trade, the New York Mercantile Exchange, Eurex, Euronext, and the Tokyo Commodity Exchange, among others (indeed, more than 400 registered exchanges exist around the world); some of these exchanges specialize in financial derivatives, others in commodities, and a few in both. An exchange, which may be publicly, privately, or mutually (member-) owned, is counterparty to every trade (either directly or via its clearing house). Trading may be conducted physically (by open outcry), or electronically, through matching systems. Most exchanges have migrated to electronic platforms, and even the remaining physical exchanges feature electronic off-hours capabilities.

The buyer of a listed contract faces the exchange as its selling counterparty, while the seller faces the exchange as its buying counterparty. Each buyer and seller dealing with the exchange is required to post initial margin (or security) with the clearinghouse to protect against possible credit losses. The initial margin is evaluated by the clearinghouse every day based on a client's open positions, and additional calls for margin may be made if a particular maintenance level is breached as a result of losses. Since the exchange serves as counterparty and participants must post margin, the counterparty credit risk that characterizes many OTC derivative contracts is eliminated; this is one of the central advantages of the listed marketplace.

All contracts listed on an exchange are standardized, meaning trade details cannot be customized as in the OTC market. All buyers and sellers deal in the same trading size/units, contract months/maturity, delivery date, deliverable asset, and settlement style. This homogeneity leads to a greater critical mass of liquidity, meaning the cost of arranging a hedge or speculative position can be lower than in the OTC market. Indeed, hedgers and speculators are attracted by the tight dealing spreads that characterize very liquid contracts. Exchange contracts are generally subject to maximum daily price movements, meaning that if buying or selling pressures become too extreme, the exchange can impose price bands lasting for a period of minutes or hours (or even an entire trading session); it may also increase margin requirements to ensure sufficient security. No such price limits exist in the OTC market.

FUTURE 期货

A future is a bilateral contract that allows one party, the seller, to sell a particular reference asset at a forward price for settlement at a future date, and the second party, the buyer, to purchase the reference asset at the forward price on the named date. Based on this description, the futures contract appears to be identical to the forward contract discussed above. In fact, the payoff profiles of the two instruments are precisely the same, so the illustrations in Figures 7.4 and 7.5 are applicable to both futures and forwards. In fact, the example of ABC Co. arranging a forward contract to hedge natural gas exposure can be replicated by substituting a natural gas futures contract in place of the forward; the ultimate economic outcome will be the same. However, as a result of the exchange mechanism, a futures position calls for a daily settlement of cash flows rather than a single settlement of cash flows at maturity: each futures position is revalued by the clearinghouse at the close of each trading day, and a net settlement is made in favor of the party holding the day's gain. So, if the market price at the end of the day is greater than the price at the start of the day, the buyer posts a profit and the seller a loss (and vice-versa if the market price falls). This means that a futures contract does not permit unrealized gains/losses to accumulate, but ensures that they are realized at the end of each trading day. Futures can be settled in physical or financial terms, and the precise settlement mechanism is specified as part of a contract's standardized features. Contract maturities vary, but typically span 1 month to 1 quarter. The most active futures references may be listed concurrently on a monthly or quarterly cycle out to several years (e. g. LIBOR/ Eurodollar futures, S&P 500 futures, Brent crude futures).

OPTION AND FUTURES OPTION 期权和期货期权

The listed market features options that function much like the OTC options described above. In fact, there is no difference between the two contracts, apart from the general characteristics that distinguish listed products from OTC products. Accordingly, ABC Co. can choose to use an exchange-traded crude oil option or gold option rather than the OTC equivalent when crafting its hedging strategy. In fact, exchange options on actively quoted references such as oil and gold are often a cheaper alternative, but may also be less suitable with regard to precise maturity and strike parameters. ABC Co. must therefore weigh the relative costs and benefits of the two classes before deciding which is appropriate. A unique subset of the listed options market centers on futures options, which are options that give the buyer the right to buy or sell an underlying futures contract, and which require the seller to accept or deliver the futures contract upon exercise; this can be viewed as a type of compound derivative (i. e. a derivative on another derivative). The long and short futures options positions are summarized in Table 7. 5.

The key differences between OTC and exchange-traded derivatives are summarized in Table 7. 6.

Table 7.5 Futures options positions

Position	*If exercised…*
Long futures call	Buyer acquires a futures contract at strike price
Long futures put	Buyer sells a futures contract at strike price
Short futures call	Seller obligated to sell a futures contract at strike price
Short futures put	Seller obligated to acquire a futures contract at strike price

Table 7.6 Primary differences between exchange-traded and OTC derivatives

	Exchange-traded	*OTC*
Terms	Standardized	Customized
Trading forum	Central exchange (physical or electronic)	OTC (telephonic or electronic)
Price transparency	Good	Poor/fair
Liquidity	Reasonable/strong	Limited/fair
Credit exposure	Negligible	Possibly significant unless collateralized
Margins	Required	None unless negotiated
Settlement	Generally closed-out	Generally held until maturity
Regulation	Regulated	Largely unregulated

INSTRUMENT CHARACTERISTICS: INSURANCE 工具特征：保险

The insurance sector, like the derivatives sector, features a large number of instruments that can be used to transfer risks from companies (which become "cedants" or "insureds") to insurance companies (insurers). In order to preserve our corporate focus we'll consider the essential contracts that are used to transfer corporate operating risks; we won't consider the very significant life, health, and auto insurance sectors, though many of the same concepts we discuss below are equally applicable to them.

KEY CHARACTERISTICS 主要特征

Before delving into the key characteristics that define any insurance contract, we must first consider several concepts related to insurance contracting. This is important because insurance contracts are intended to cover pure, rather than speculative, risks-a fundamental feature that distinguishes insurance from derivatives.

In order for a contract to be considered insurance, it must usually feature the following:

- The contract must cover an insurable risk with respect to a fortuitous event-an event that is unforeseen, unexpected, or accidental.
- A large number of similar risk exposures must exist so that insurers can measure the exposure with some degree of accuracy.
- The cedant must have an insurable interest and demonstrate proof of actual economic loss if a defined event occurs; this ensures that the cedant receives compensation for losses and cannot create a profit.
- The risk of loss must be specifically transferred under a contract providing indemnity (i. e. financial restitution if a loss occurs) and it must involve the payment of an insurance premium.
- The right of subrogation must exist, meaning that the cedant must agree to transfer to the insurer any loss recovery rights.

A company can transfer any amount of risk it chooses through insurance. A company that is risk-averse can transfer all of its risk, though it may be expensive to do so. Conversely, one that is less risk-averse may choose to transfer only a fractional portion. This is part of the cost-benefit analysis that the financial manager must undertake during the planning process.

Every insurance contract is defined by several key characteristics, including policy size (cap), premium, deductible, coinsurance, coverage and exclusions, and coverage period.

- Policy size (cap): The amount of insurance coverage being arranged, which can range from several million dollars up to $1 billion or more, depending on the specific property being insured and the nature of the risk exposure. The smaller the size of the policy in relation to the amount of exposure, the greater the amount of risk the cedant retains. For instance, ABC Co. may arrange P&C insurance based on a policy size of £300 million to protect against fire damage/destruction at one of its factories. Subject to the deductibles and coinsurance described below, ABC Co. will receive a maximum of £300 million in restitution if a fire occurs and damages or destroys its factory.
- Premium: The amount the ceding company must pay the insurer for the policy. The premium is generally payable annually and is quoted in value terms (e. g. $ or £). Once the premium is paid, the contract is activated and the company is protected by the insurer under the terms defined in the policy. For example, ABC Co. may pay a £500,000 premium for £300 million of fire insurance coverage.
- Deductible: The amount of initial losses the cedant bears before the insurance coverage becomes effective. The deductible can range from a very small amount of the policy size up to 20 percent or more. The greater the deductible, the more risk the cedant retains (and the lower the premium, since the cedant bears more of the first losses); conversely, the smaller the deductible, the less risk the cedant retains (and the higher the premium). Under its £300 million fire insurance policy ABC Co. may be willing to bear a reasonable amount of the initial losses, setting a deductible of £5 mil-

lion. This means that if fire strikes and causes £25 million of damage to the company's plant and equipment, the net restitution to ABC Co. will amount to £20 million (e. g. £25 million of losses minus the £5 million deductible). If ABC Co. were more risk averse, it might set a deductible of £1 million, receiving restitution after bearing only £1 million of losses.

- Coinsurance (copay): The amount of losses that the cedant and insurer agree to share. Coinsurance can range from 0 percent to more than 50 percent, though cedants willing to include coinsurance generally set a range of 10 – 20 percent. The larger the coinsurance, the greater the cedant's retention of risk and the lower the policy premium. Conversely, the lower the coinsurance, the greater the cedant's risk transfer and the higher the premium. ABC Co. may choose a 10 percent coinsurance on its fire policy. Assuming it also has a £5 million deductible, then £25 million of losses will result in net restitution to ABC Co. of £18 million (e. g. £25 million of losses minus £5 million deductible = £20 million × 90 percent = £18 million).
- Coverage and exclusions: The precise terms of risk coverage, including any events or circumstances under which the cedant is not covered. Coverage includes a detailed definition of the perils that can create losses for which the cedant will be indemnified. Exclusions, in contrast, delineate any specific or general circumstances under which losses are not indemnified. The broader the coverage and the narrower the exclusions, the greater the risk transfer and the larger the premium; the narrower the coverage and the broader the exclusions, the lower the risk transfer and the smaller the premium. For instance, ABC Co.'s policy may cover against all damage or destruction caused by an incidence of fire in designated locations (e. g. the company's factories and warehouses). But it may exclude coverage for business interrup-

tion, or the amount of business lost as a result of the company's inability to use its plant and equipment if fire creates damage/destruction.

- Coverage period: The period during which the insurance coverage is effective. In nearly all cases insurance policies are written for a twelve-month period, after which the cedant and insurer can reevaluate terms, conditions, and requirements and decide whether coverage renewal is necessary (and, if it is, at what premium).

The characteristics noted above are usually included as declarations in the insurance policy, which also contains important information on the actual property being insured.

KEY INSTRUMENTS/CONTRACTS 主要工具/合同

Since insurance is a risk transfer mechanism, the actual amount of risk transferred from cedant to insurer depends largely on how the characteristics noted above are defined. Policies may be created so that they transfer very little risk; these are more appropriately described as risk retention policies. Those that transfer some amount of risk are considered partial insurance contracts, while those resulting in a significant transfer are known as full insurance contracts. Several other products, including loss financing contracts and captives, join these contracts.

Figure 7.15 illustrates these instruments/contracts in relation to the amount of risk retained or transferred.

FULL INSURANCE 全面保险

全面保险合同是最大的风险转移合同。

A full insurance contract is a maximum risk transfer contract where the cedant's goal is to shift as much insurable exposure as possible. Following from our discussion above, full insurance is created by crafting a policy with a small (or even no) deductible, a large policy limit, limited (or no) coinsur-

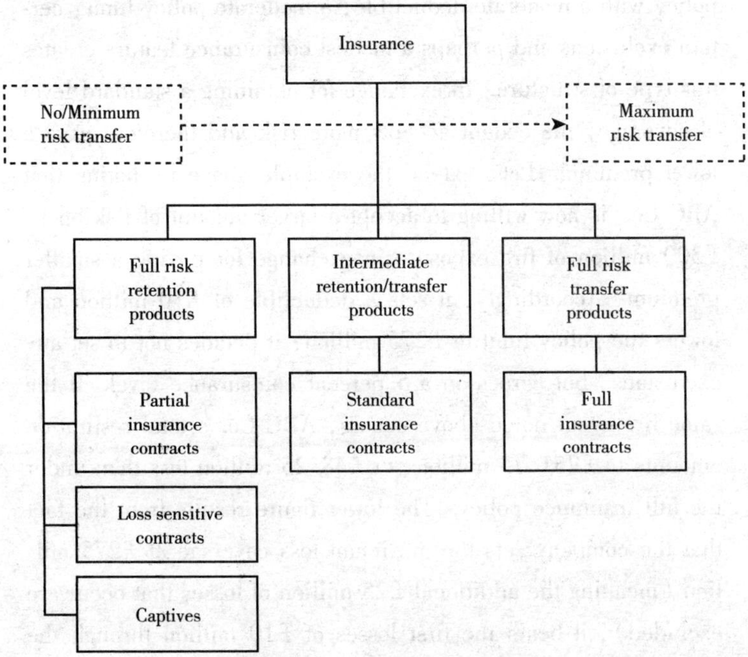

Figure 7.15 Insurance classes

ance, and limited (or no) exclusions. In creating this kind of contract the cedant pays a maximum premium payment (cost) in exchange for what it perceives to be greater risk transfer advantages (benefit). Assume ABC Co. wants full insurance coverage on its £300 million of fire exposure and is willing to pay a high premium if necessary. It can structure a policy with a £300 million limit, no deductible, no exclusions, and no coinsurance. If a fire strikes and causes £150 million of losses from destroyed property and £150 million of losses from business interruption, ABC Co. receives restitution equal to the full £300 million.

STANDARD INSURANCE 标准保险

A standard insurance contract is an intermediate risk transfer mechanism where the cedant retains some amount of exposure and transfers the balance. As we might expect, drafting a

标准保险合同是一个中间的风险转移机制。

policy with a moderate deductible, a moderate policy limit, certain exclusions and perhaps a modest coinsurance feature creates this type of structure. In exchange for obtaining a standard level of coverage, the cedant accepts more risk and therefore pays a lower premium. Let's extend the example above by noting that ABC Co. is now willing to accept a larger amount of risk on its £300 million of fire exposure in exchange for paying a smaller premium. Accordingly, it sets a deductible of £10 million and lowers the policy limit to £275 million; it decides not to set any exclusions, but agrees on a 5 percent coinsurance level. If the same fire event noted above occurs, ABC Co.'s total restitution amounts to £251.75 million, or £48.25 million less than under the full insurance policy. The lower figure results from the fact that the company sets the maximum loss coverage at £275 million (meaning the additional £25 million of losses that occur are excluded), it bears the first losses of £10 million through the deductible, and then receives 95 percent, rather than 100 percent, of the remaining losses as a result of the coinsurance. In estimating, on an ex-ante basis, whether the cost-benefit ratio is acceptable, ABC Co. must weigh the amount of premium saved by moving from full to standard insurance against the potential losses that it might have to fund should an insurable event actually occur.

PARTIAL INSURANCE 部分保险

部分保险合同是从分保人转移最小数额的风险到保险公司。

A partial insurance contract transfers the smallest amount of risk from cedant to insurer. This structure, which is best suited for companies that are not as risk-averse as those purchasing standard or full insurance, features a very large deductible and perhaps moderate policy limit, significant exclusions and high coinsurance. It's relatively easy to see that under the partial insurance structure the ceding company bears the largest amount of first losses, faces limited coverage in the event of very large losses, may have no coverage if certain excluded events come into play, and must share in any losses that arise. In exchange for this relatively small level of coverage, the company pays a much smaller premium. In the most extreme version of our example, let's assume that ABC Co. is interested in accepting even more risk (i. e. transferring less risk) in exchange for paying a relatively small premium. Accordingly, it sets a £250 million policy limit, raises the deductible to £20 million, increases coinsurance to 10 percent, and excludes from the policy losses created by business interruption. Once again, if the event described above occurs, ABC Co. will now receive restitution of only £117 million, or £183 million less than the actual loss sustained. The £150 million of losses attributable to the business interruption component are excluded from coverage, lowering the maximum amount payable to ABC Co. to £150 million. However, the company selected a £20 million deductible (lowering coverage to £130 million) and a coinsurance level of 10 percent (lowering coverage by a further £13 million to £117 million). Again, ABC Co.'s expectation is that the premium savings it expects over time will outweigh any possible losses arising from what should be a relatively rare event.

These simple examples indicate that the optimal amount of insurance that a company like ABC Co. should purchase is a function of the cost of coverage (premium) and the expected benefits (coverage) should an event occur. Preparing different loss scenarios is a key part of the financial planning process, and allows a firm's management to develop strategies that are in line with its cost-benefit estimates and its risk tolerance levels. The process of converting full insurance coverage to partial insurance coverage is summarized in Figure 7.16.

LOSS SENSITIVE CONTRACT 损失敏感合同

A loss sensitive contract is a partial insurance contract with premiums that depend on previous loss experience. Loss sensitive contracts are different from conventional insurance contracts

损失敏感合同是一种保险费依据以前的损失记录的部分保险合同。

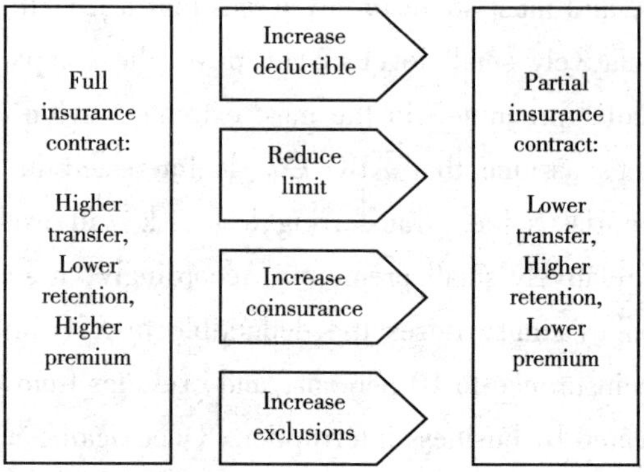

Figure 7.16 Converting full insurance to partial insurance

as premiums are related to losses that occur during a specified period and claims are typically not determined until some period of time has passed. It is common under a loss sensitive contract for the insurer to cover a cedant's entire loss before determining, and then receiving, premium. For instance, ABC Co. may purchase an experienced-rated fire insurance policy where the premium it pays the insurer is a function of its past loss experience: the greater the losses and claims in previous periods, the greater the premium, and vice-versa. Or, ABC Co. may choose a retrospectively rated policy where it pays the insurer an initial premium and, depending on the occurrence/size of any fire-related losses, makes an additional premium payment (if a claim arises) or receives a refund (if no claims arise).

CAPTIVE 自保

A captive is a company-owned (or controlled) insurance subsidiary that is used to facilitate a company's insurance program; it can be thought of as an in-house insurance company. The company (also known as a sponsor) provides capital to commence the operation, receiving interest and/or dividends in exchange. The captive then insures the company directly by accepting premium to absorb particular types of risks. Though the nature and operation of captives varies, the focus is generally on

专属自保公司是一家国有（或控制的）保险附属公司。

high-frequency/low-severity risks-the highly predictable exposures for which this form of "self-insurance" can be a cost-effective alternative. For instance, ABC Co., facing a certain amount of predictable claims from its employee health program, may decide that it is too expensive to purchase conventional insurance coverage. Accordingly, it can create a captive as a "self insurance" fund, paying premium to the captive and receiving coverage on the employee health claims. By doing so it is able to achieve some level of cost savings and retain all cash flows within the corporate structure. Figure 7.17 illustrates the structure of the captive.

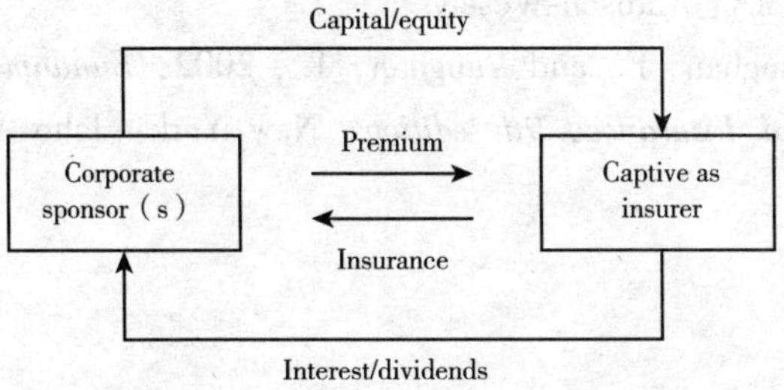

Figure 7.17 Structure of a captive

摘要

衍生品是一种从某些市场或资产中衍生出其价值的合同，比如股票、债券、货币或商品。保险是一种预防一个事件造成损失而提供财务索赔的合同。这两种工具广泛地被公司用于管理财务和经营风险：衍生品而被用于对冲风险，这是通过当标的风险暴露产生损失的时候提供一个盈利实现的；保险通过保险费的支付被用于转移风险给另一方（也就是保险人）。衍生品也可以用于投机或套利；保险不能用于产生利润。衍生品的特征是名义值、标的资产、到期时间、结算、交易机制，而且对于期权还有行权价格。衍生品的主要种类包括通过交易所交易的标准化交易所交易合同（期货、期权、期货期权），以及由交易双方规定的场外交易合同（远期、互换、期权）。保险合同通过保单金额（最高保险金额）、保险费、免赔额、共同保险和保险责任/除外责任来描述。主要的保险类别包括部分、标准和全面保险合同，也包括损失敏感合同和自保。

FURTHER READING 延伸阅读

Cox, J. and Rubinstein, M., 1985, *Options Markets*, New Jersey: Prentice Hall.

Doherty, N., 1985, *Corporate Risk Management*, New York: McGraw-Hill.

Hull, J., 2005, *Options, Futures, and Other Derivatives*, *6th edition*, New Jersey: Prentice Hall.

MacDonald, R., 2005, *Derivatives Markets*, *2nd edition*, Boston MA: Addison-Wesely.

Vaughan, E. and Vaughan, T., 2002, *Fundamentals of Risk and Insurance*, *9th edition*, New York: John Wiley & Sons.

8

CORPORATE FINANCE

公司理财

CHAPTER OVERVIEW 本章概述

In this final chapter of Part Ⅱ we alter our focus from products and instruments designed to directly fulfill funding, investment or risk management goals, to specific financial transactions intended to boost enterprise value and meet other strategic, profit, or market share goals. We shall begin by discussing the uses of corporate finance and then examine the key characteristics of the most common transactions, including mergers, acquisitions, leveraged (management) buyouts, spin-offs, recapitalizations and buybacks. We will then review the general process by which corporate finance deals are valued, and conclude by examining the challenges a company faces in arranging a transaction.

USES OF CORPORATE FINANCE 公司理财的用途

Corporate finance, which includes a broad range of financial engineering deals that can be used to alter the structure and scope of a company's operations, is a central part of long-term financial planning. The decision to acquire, or merge with, another company, sell a piece of the company, or restructure the capital base is achieved only after considerable planning and analysis. Corporate finance finance transactions, which are generally complex to arrange and execute, cannot be done as part of short-term, or tactical, operations. They are part of the long-term planning process, and must often be sanctioned by the board of directors and, in some cases, shareholders.

We'll examine fundamental corporate finance transactions in more detail later in the chapter to gain an understanding of uses and challenges. We begin, however, with some basic definitions:

合并

- Merger: A transaction where one company combines with another company on a relatively equal basis to create a "new" company.

收购

- Acquisition: A transaction where one company buys another company.

杠杆

- Leveraged (management) buyout: A transaction where a publicly listed company takes itself private by borrowing to purchase outstanding shares.

分割

- Spin-off: A transaction where a company sells one or more of its units or divisions to the public (in an IPO) or to a third party (in a private equity transaction).

重组

- Recapitalization: A transaction where a company restructures its capital base, sometimes dramatically.

Each one of these may be driven by slightly different motivations. All, however, are intended ultimately to enhance stakeholder value. Let's consider some of the key reasons why a company like ABC Co. might consider arranging a "generic" corporate finance transaction.

扩大产品/市场份额

- Expanding product/market share: ABC Co., an established company with a full product line, may be reaching a point in its product and market cycle where it can no longer grow simply by adding more workers or equipment. To continue its expansion it may need to look to new geographic areas in the same industry or it may absorb other parts of the production chain. By acquiring or merging with another company, ABC Co. has the potential for increasing its revenue base more rapidly and efficiently. New revenue growth can appear when one of the two companies brings human resource skills, intellectual property, product lines, or physical assets that are so special that they cannot be readily replicated within the other company. In some cases the combination of two companies can produce growth through "synergies" -the creation of new cross-market products or services that can only be done by joining two different firms. Growth through expansion may be the best solution for ABC Co.'s shareholders-particularly if it cannot find any compelling positive NPV projects. If the company can identify the right partner, it may be able to use its capital more efficiently than if it simply pays its shareholders a special one-time dividend; remember, dividends are taxable in many systems, so shareholders may not be receiving the best possible value if ABC Co. returns, rather than externally reinvests, funds.

- Creating earnings stability: We have already noted that the worth of a company can decline when earnings are volatile or unpredictable. Investors don't like surprises, and if the earnings stream cannot be relied on to some degree, the company's stock will trade at a lower price. ABC Co. may be able to dampen its earnings volatility by acquiring, or merging with, a company that has a different pattern of earnings. This goal can only be achieved, however, if ABC Co. and its partner company have different earnings cycles; if they have the same cycle, the earnings volatility effect will be compounded, as illustrated in Figure 8.1. 产生收益稳定性
- Reducing costs: Though ABC Co. may be managing its costs as efficiently as possible, it may find opportunities to create 降低成本

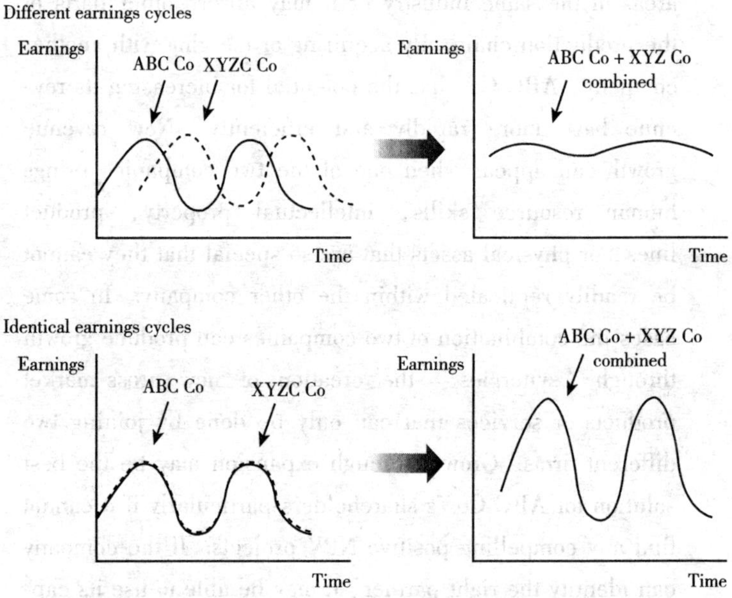

Figure 8.1 Earnings cycles and earnings stability

even greater cost savings by combining with another company. We recall from Chapter 2 that a company can increase its enterprise value by reducing cost of goods sold, SG&A expenses, and other operating expenses. Economies of scale, which arise when large producers negotiate large (and cheaper) input purchases and eliminate duplicative resources (e. g. personnel, real estate, technology), are a key driver of cost savings. Cost savings can also be achieved by divesting inefficient operations. Tax benefits may also factor into the process. For instance, a profitable company that buys an unprofitable company with accumulated tax loss carry forwards can reduce its tax liability. This, however, is a finite benefit, so it should be considered as an ancillary gain rather than a primary driver.

获取知识产权

- Acquiring intellectual property: ABC Co. may want to expand its product line into areas that require a higher degree of technical specialization and knowledge. While it may be able to do so through "organic" development, i. e. adding technical capabilities by hiring individuals with the proper mix of skills, it can also use a corporate finance transaction, such as an acquisition or merger, to obtain the same level of intellectual expertise. The benefit of obtaining intellectual property via a merger or acquisition is speed: rather than waiting for years for the proper base of intellectual property to develop through hiring/ training, ABC Co. can gain the advantage it seeks very rapidly. This can lead to shorter product development times, and quicker revenue and profit results.

- Altering the capital structure: ABC Co. may wish to change its capital structure, either by increasing equity if it believes it has too much debt, or increasing debt if it believes that it is not taking full advantage of the tax shield generated by bonds and loans. In more extreme scenarios it may increase its debt dramatically to purchase outstanding shares and take the company private; this is the initial step in an LBO, which must then be accompanied by radical internal cost restructuring. It can also use other corporate finance techniques to accomplish this goal, such as arranging a buyback of its stock (which increases leverage), acquiring a company with low levels of debt (which decreases leverage), or divesting a portion of the company (which injects cash and allows debt to be reduced). The end result should be a capital structure that is optimized with respect to the firm's overall cost of capital.

调整资本结构

As we've said, each of these factors tells us why companies use corporate finance techniques. Of course the ultimate measure of whether or not a transaction is useful becomes evident in enterprise value: if a company can increase its worth by acquiring intellectual property, altering capital, gaining market share, and so forth, then the financial decision-making process is likely to support a deal. That said, corporate finance transactions can be difficult and complex to arrange; we'll discuss some of the potential pitfalls at the end of the chapter.

TRANSACTION CHARACTERISTICS 交易特征

MERGERS AND ACQUISITIONS 合并和收购

Mergers and acquisitions (M&A) are the most common form of corporate finance transaction. Let's begin with a review of acquisitions. An acquisition, as the name suggests, occurs when one company buys another company outright. In most cases this means a larger and stronger company buys a smaller one, though in some instances the reverse can happen. An acquisition can be arranged within or outside the industry, depending on the specific goal the acquiring firm is attempting to achieve. For instance, if ABC Co. wants to gain market share within its own product line of specialty goods, it may decide to acquire rival company XYZ Co., which makes the same goods; this is known as horizontal integration. The "new" ABC Co. will thus have a larger market share in specialty goods than it did before the acquisition. Alternatively, ABC Co. may be interested in expanding its production chain by acquiring its key raw material supplier, Acme Supply. This is a form of vertical integration. Though ABC Co.'s market share won't immediately increase as a result of the Acme purchase, it will give the company an opportunity to control more parts of its input and production processes, perhaps allowing it to drive down costs. If it wants to continue expanding vertically, it may then acquire a product transportation and distribution company, Transport Co. Again, by combining Transport Co.'s operations into its own, ABC Co. may be able to achieve greater operating efficiencies. Efficiencies can lead to lower operating costs, larger earnings, and greater enterprise value. Since boosting enterprise value is a key corporate goal, ABC Co. 's management must be very certain that it can actually achieve the efficiencies and cost savings proposed through the acquisition before it commits resources.

While many acquisitions are based on horizontal or vertical integration, some are based on conglomeration. This occurs when a company purchases a firm operating in an entirely unrelated industry, and is intended to diversify the firm's revenue base. For instance, ABC Co. may want to expand its revenue base from specialty goods to consulting services in order to protect its earnings should demand for specialty goods decline during the next business cycle. After much analysis of Consult Inc. 's business and earnings, it may conclude that Consult Inc. can provide the proper earnings protection during particular market cycles and proceed to buy the firm. It's worth noting that some conglomerations are successful and others are not. The market may not be convinced of a company's ability to properly manage and integrate an unrelated firm into its overall operations, and may "penalize" the acquiring company's stock by assigning it a lower value (i. e. it may value the ABC Co. + Consult Inc. combination lower than the sum of the individual parts). In extreme situations an acquiring company that cannot generate proper shareholder value may have to divest its unrelated companies. Major types of acquisitions are shown in Figure 8. 2.

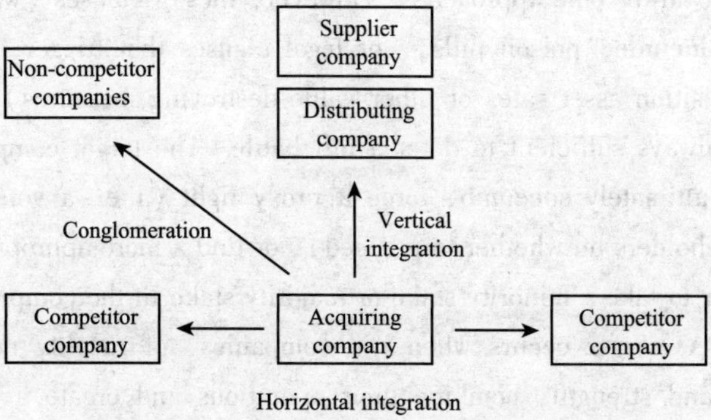

Figure 8. 2 Horizontal and vertical acquisitions

An acquisition can be arranged in various ways. For instance, the acquiring company (e. g. ABC Co.) can buy the shares of the target company (e. g. Acme Supply Co.) for cash. Or, it can use its own shares, or a mix of shares and debt, to acquire the target. Though less common, the acquirer can purchase the majority of the target company's assets (rather than the whole company); this tends to occur primarily when the target is in a financially weakened state but has certain assets with value.

An acquisition can be arranged on friendly or hostile terms. A friendly acquisition, which is the most common deal type, occurs when the executives and directors of the acquiring company and the target company agree to a transaction. In such cases the target company's board of directors recommends to its investors that they accept the deal.

A hostile acquisition (or takeover) occurs when the target company wants to remain independent, doesn't like the terms of the deal, or would prefer to merge with, or be acquired by, another firm. While these transactions are rather more rare, they do occur-and often become the focus of activity by risk arbitrageurs, or speculators who take positions in one or both stocks based on their views on whether or not a deal will occur. The law in many countries provides for certain legal anti-takeover defenses that are designed to provide a modicum of protection again unwelcome approaches. However, these defenses (which may include "poison pills," or legal clauses that trigger post-acquisition asset sales or other value-destroying measures) are not always sufficient to deter a full battle. The target company may ultimately succumb, force a proxy fight (i. e. a vote by shareholders on whether to proceed), or find a more appropriate suitor to take a minority stake or majority stake in the company.

A merger occurs when two companies, of roughly equal size and strength, combine their operations and create a new company. The motivations follow along the lines described above (i. e. vertical or horizontal expansion or conglomeration to boost enterprise value, cost savings from duplicative efforts). For instance, ABC Co. and one of its main rivals, JKL Inc., may decide to join forces in order to create a dominant market position and generate cost savings. If we assume the two companies are of roughly the same size and market share, the transaction may be considered a "merger of equals," yielding an entirely new firm comprised of the consolidated operations of the two.

Government anti-trust regulators scrutinize very large deals to make sure that no unfair competitive advantages appear (i. e. those that might be created by forming a substantial, market-dominating firm). Regulators are very wary of transactions that create monopoly power (i. e. one large seller of goods or services in the market) or oligopoly power (i. e. a few large sellers of goods or services in the market) as these can lead to unfair pricing practices that hurt consumers. They may also scrutinize transactions that yield firms with monopsony or oligopsony power (i. e. one or several large buyers of goods or services); these can, again, create price distortions.

LEVERAGED BUYOUTS 杠杆收购

A leveraged buyout (LBO), sometimes known as a management buyout (MBO), is another common form of corporate finance transaction. An LBO is arranged when a public company, with shares listed on an exchange, is "taken private" -that is, all of the shares held by the public are purchased by a small group of the company's managers and the stock is de-listed from the exchange. Once the company is private it no longer needs to answer to a broad base of shareholders regarding performance and strategy issues. The team taking the company private need only satisfy a small number of stakeholders, primarily those that are financing the deal. This increased operating flexibility is a

管理层收购

key benefit of the LBO deal.

Firms that require significant financial restructuring are good LBO candidates. Companies that have little debt, a relatively high cost base (i. e. they have operating inefficiencies), and a mature and recognized product base generally fit in this category. The strategy behind the LBO is to repurchase outstanding shares from investors by using a great deal of borrowed money (hence the term "leveraged" in LBO) and then begin a multi-year (3 - 5 year) program of reshaping the operating structure of the firm. This centers on reducing the cost of goods sold and operating/SG&A expenses dramatically, introducing new efficiencies, and perhaps realigning or eliminating product lines that no longer produce the desired margins. In some cases entire portions of the company may be sold to generate cash for eventual repayment of debt.

Since the firm's interest expense becomes so much greater, reducing all other costs is an essential part of a successful deal. In addition, a scheduled reduction in debt is typically mandated so that the burden of leverage becomes increasingly manageable. The end goal of the successful LBO is realized after the restructuring program is completed: the newly restructured company, which may still have a reasonably large amount of debt but a leaner cost structure and a more focused operation, is either recapitalized through an IPO or is sold to a third party (e. g. another company). In either case, the equity or cash that is raised is used to pay down the remaining debt, and the new company that ultimately emerges is financially strong. The LBO group sponsoring the deal generates its own profit from the sale proceeds.

So, who provides the initial debt that is needed to buy the shares and take the company private? Many large banks have dedicated lending groups that specialize in financing LBOs, generally by taking some of the company's assets as security. These banks receive interest on the loans that they extend to the management group, and may also receive some upside participation when the company is ultimately sold or publicly listed (i. e. "pre-IPO shares"). Venture capital, private equity, and investment management companies also raise capital from outside investors and use the proceeds to create LBO funds that finance such transactions. Figure 8. 3 illustrates the LBO and post-LBO flows.

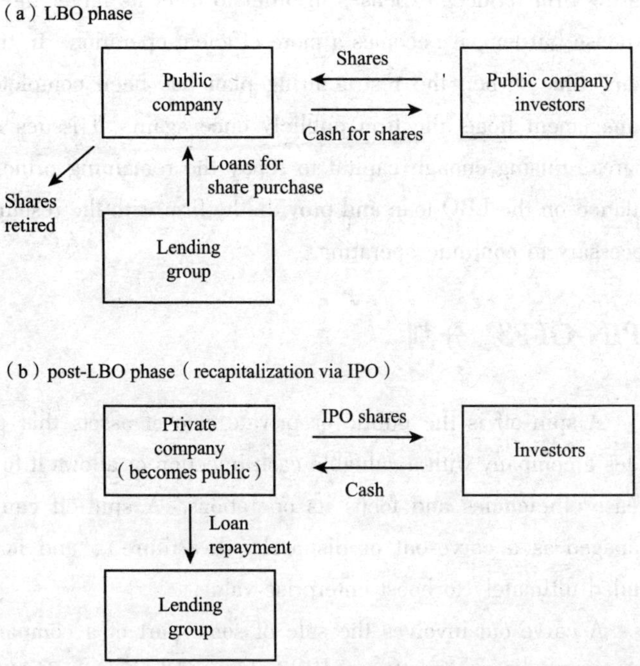

Figure 8. 3 LBO structure

Let's assume that ABC Co., which has been operating for many years, has created a successful line of products. Let's also assume that growth has slowed and operating inefficiencies have set in, but that balance sheet leverage remains reasonable-that is, the company has historically relied more heavily on retained earnings and common stock than debt to fund its business. ABC Co.'s management, working together with LBO financing specialists, believes there is an opportunity to reshape the company by reducing its operations in traditional areas and refocusing the ABC brand in new ventures. Management also wants to dispose of several small, underperforming subsidiaries. Accordingly, the management team arranges an LBO loan to repurchase outstanding shares from investors. The company becomes private once the shares have been repurchased and begins implementing its cost cutting, asset disposal, and product repositioning plan. As the firm reduces expenses in order to meet its larger interest expense burden, it becomes a more efficient operation. In three years' time, when the restructuring plan has been completed, management floats the firm publicly once again. It issues new shares, raising enough capital to repay the remaining principal balance on the LBO loan and provide the firm with the resources necessary to continue operating.

SPIN-OFFS 分割

A spin-off is the public or private sale of assets that provides a company with a valuable cash injection or allows it to increase efficiencies and focus its operations. A spin-off can be managed as a carve-out or disposal (divestiture), and is intended ultimately to boost enterprise value.

分割是对资产进行公开或私下的出售，从而提供给宝贵的现金注资或使其增加效率和集中业务。

A carve-out involves the sale of some part of a company's existing operations, such as a profitable and well regarded subsidiary that is readily divisible from the balance of the firm. By selling one of its units, the company hopes to earn a premium over book value that will increase its own worth. Naturally, such a sale is only contemplated when management believes that the transaction will add value, and will not impair its ability to operate efficiently and profitably. Indeed, there is little point in selling valuable assets if the value of the company will be permanently damaged. Let's assume that ABC Co. has a highly profitable subsidiary, ABC Sub Inc., and that management believes it can create value for ABC Co. shareholders by carving out the subsidiary. It may thus work with a venture capital firm or competitor to structure a private sale of ABC Sub Inc. , or it may decide to float ABC Sub Inc. publicly through an IPO. In either case ABC Co. will receive the financial benefit of the sale, while ABC Sub Inc. will continue its operations as part of another firm or as an independent entity.

Divestiture is another form of spin-off. While the divestiture shares certain similarities with the carve-out-namely, the sale of a portion of a company-the value driver is somewhat different. In the case of a carve-out, a company believes it can create value by selling a valuable asset to the public or a third party, while in a divestiture it seeks primarily to exit a business line that is no longer essential to its operations or which is not performing up to financial expectations. The sale may or may not generate an immediate gain for the company. In fact, the divestiture in some cases may be done at a loss to book value, creating a one-time charge against the income statement. However, if the decision proves to be correct, the value of the firm should rise over time as the operation ceases to hamper the firm's progress or tie up its capital. For instance, if ABC Co. 's management wants to sell ABC Sub Inc. because it feels that the subsidiary is no longer relevant to its new course of operations (or is otherwise dissatisfied with the unit's contribution to overall performance), it can divest the operation through a private sale. Once completed, ABC Sub Inc. will no longer form part of the corporate operation and ABC Co. will be able to focus its efforts on other priorities.

RECAPITALIZATIONS 资本重组

A recapitalization, as the name suggests, is a corporate finance transaction that is used to restructure the form and size of a company's capital base. This generally involves using debt and equity to create a capital base that is more appropriate for a firm's circumstances at a particular stage in its corporate life, or in light of changing market circumstances (including competitive pressures and potential takeover threats).

A recapitalization is often associated with deleveraging of the corporate balance sheet. A firm may become overly dependent on debt over a period of time, causing its financial position to weaken-perhaps to the point where financial pressures from a large interest burden set in and the credit rating is threatened. In such instances a company may implement a recapitalization program to overhaul its funding structure. For example, if ABC Co. finds itself with too much debt and not enough equity, it may arrange for simultaneous issues of common and preferred stock, using the proceeds to repay a variety of medium-and long-term loans and bonds. While this may initially lead to a higher cost of capital-recalling that equity capital is more expensive than debt capital-it will give ABC Co. greater financial strength and flexibility, both of which can boost corporate value.

In some cases a firm may have too little leverage. This means, of course, that it may not be taking full advantage of the tax shield that is generated through the issuance of debt. If we assume that ABC Co. is now underleveraged rather than overleveraged, it can again arrange a recapitalization program where it issues new debt (or borrows from its bankers) and uses the proceeds to buy back some amount of stock. Recalling our discussion from Chapter 4, we know that a stock buyback has the effect of increasing the treasury stock contra account, thereby reducing the overall size of the equity account. Alternatively, ABC Co. may preserve its current level of debt but reduce its equity (retained earnings) account by paying investors a large, one-time, special dividend-the effect on the contra account is the same.

But recapitalization needn't only focus on a pure rebalancing of debt and equity. In some instances these transactions involve restructuring of the voting rights accorded to investors. Again, depending on the specific nature of a company's control structure and its ultimate goals, directors may authorize distribution of voting power by diluting the voting rights of a small block of control investors and expanding those of a larger base of minority shareholders. This places greater legal control in the hands of small investors. Alternatively, directors may propose a dual-class recapitalization that creates two classes of shares: those where minority shareholders are given less (or no) voting power, and those where control shareholders are given virtually complete voting power. These recapitalizations remove from minority shareholders the most fundamental legal rights, leaving them only with rent rights. Not surprisingly, these transactions may not be at all popular, and must generally be ratified by a shareholder vote.

VALUING CORPORATE FINANCE DEALS 估价公司理财交易

A company must only arrange a corporate finance deal when it makes financial sense to do so. In addition to the benefits of increasing market share, expanding into new markets, gaining intellectual property, generating earnings stability, and increasing efficiencies, any transaction-merger, acquisition, LBO, spin-off, or recapitalization-must create value for stakeholders.

The valuation process centers on determining what a company looks like before a deal (ex-ante) and forecasting what it might look like after a deal (ex-post). This involves detailed analysis of operating and financial risks, current and future cash flows, current and anticipated cost of capital, and current and expected earnings per share. However, since the process relates to estimates of future events, it can never be completely accurate. That said, a good valuation process incorporates multiple scenarios (i. e. base case, worst case, and best case), so that the value range of the transaction can be properly considered in the financial planning process.

Let's consider, as an example, the basic steps involved in valuing an acquisition. Consider a deal where ABC Co., expanding horizontally, wants to buy Acme. The first step involves examining the present value of Acme's future (after-tax) income. We know that the value of a firm is based on its after-tax earnings, so this step is fundamental to any plan. The actual process of determining the PV of Acme's future (after-tax) earnings takes us back to our discussion in Chapter 4; we must first compute the PV of future earnings over some reasonable horizon period (e. g. 5 – 10 years) and then estimate the terminal value of the flows for the period extending beyond the horizon. This yields the minimum value that ABC Co. will have to pay for Acme.

The second step is to add in an estimate of the PV of future gains expected from any synergies. This is a critical component as it reflects the perceived benefit management believes can be obtained by joining ABC Co. and Acme. But it is a complicated process that must be approached with a degree of conservatism. The essence of this step is to consider the incremental benefits that will be achieved via the acquisition-those above and beyond the pure "summation" of the two component parts. This can include increased revenues (e. g. from leveraging multiple sales forces), increased cost efficiencies (e. g. from eliminating duplicative efforts), increased depreciation (e. g. from greater asset revaluations), and so forth.

Naturally, Acme's investors are unlikely to sell their shares to ABC Co. without receiving some premium. However, ABC Co.'s directors need to protect their own shareholders by minimizing the size of this premium. In fact, the maximum that ABC Co. should pay Acme's shareholders is the theoretical value of the deal, which we summarize in equation [8.1] as:

theoretical value of acquisition =

PV of future earnings of target [8.1]

+ PV of future earnings from synergies

So, if ABC Co. estimates that the PV of Acme's future earnings amounts to £500 million and conservatively believes that a further £100 million of synergies can be obtained from the purchase, then the maximum it should be willing to pay Acme's shareholders is £600 million.

The process above works well for an "all cash" deal. But what happens if ABC Co. wants to buy Acme using ABC shares? Such stock acquisitions are actually quite common. The same principles apply, but an extra step is needed to determine the number of shares that ABC Co. will have to offer to Acme's shareholders. This is estimated by computing a ratio based on the price offered for the target (Acme) and the price of the acquiring company (ABC Co.). Assume that Acme currently has 100 million shares outstanding, suggesting that the per share purchase price is £6. Assume further that ABC Co.'s current share price is £12. This means that the exchange ratio is 0.50. That is, ABC Co. will give up 0.50 shares of its shares for 1 share of Acme. Let's now assume that ABC Co.'s share price is £20 rather than £12. This yields an exchange ratio of 0.30-meaning that ABC Co. has to give up less shares to acquire Acme. Thus, when the acquiring company has a strong and rising stock price, it will pay "less" in shares than if it has a low and falling stock price. In fact, stock-based acquisitions are very popular when the stock market is strong and the prices of potential acquirers are on the rise.

Valuing corporate finance deals is quite tractable when the parties involved are publicly traded, as the quoted stock prices give an indication of market value. But what happens when one or both companies are private? The process in such cases must turn to the use of a proxy method, such as the constant dividend growth model we discussed in Chapter 4. While this requires assumptions about dividend payout and growth and the cost of capital of the two firms, it provides some estimate of value. We can therefore adapt the constant dividend growth model (assuming that all earnings generated are paid out as dividends):

$$\text{proxy value of shares} = \frac{\text{dividends } (1 + \text{growth rate})}{\text{cost of common} - \text{growth rate}} \qquad [8.2]$$

Assume, therefore, that ABC Co. and Acme are private, rather than public, companies, and that ABC Co.'s finance team has prepared estimates of the data reflected in Table 8.1.

Table 8.1 Company estimates

	ABC Co.	*Acme*
EPS	£2.50	£1.30
Cost of capital	10%	12%
Dividend growth	4%	3%

The fair value of ABC Co. (if it had shares outstanding) would equal £43.33, while the fair value of Acme would amount to £14.88. This would suggest a swap of 0.34 "shares" of ABC Co. for a single "share" of Acme based on a pure exchange ratio. However, since the EPS estimate doesn't include any synergy effects, some additional premium has to be factored in. If we assume that synergies will add a 20 percent premium to the value of the acquisition, we adjust Acme's share value by 20 percent to generate a fair value of £17.85. The new exchange ratio is thus 0.42.

Similar processes can be applied to value other types of corporate finance deals. The essential ingredients remain the same: estimates of future earnings and attendant growth rates, potential synergies, and costs of capital/discount rates.

Proper accounting treatment is vital in corporate finance

deals, especially M&A. Though specific details differ across systems, the essential points center on accounting via the pooling of interest method and the purchase acquisition method. The pooling method is used when two companies involved in a deal exchange stock on a tax-free basis. The resulting "consolidation" is simply an addition of the balance sheets of the two firms. Thus, if ABC Co. and Acme merge by swapping stock, the resulting ABC Co. -Acme balance sheet is a simple summation of the individual parts. If the transaction is an outright acquisition, such as ABC Co. 's purchase of Acme, then the purchase acquisition method must generally be used. If the purchase price is precisely equal to the target company's net worth (i. e. assets – liabilities), then the consolidated balance sheet is again an addition of the two components. However, if the purchase price exceeds the target's net worth, the balance sheet must reflect an upward valuation of assets to reflect the differential. This value is reflected in the goodwill account. The goodwill premium is typically amortized (reduced) over a period of time.

CORPORATE FINANCE CHALLENGES 公司理财面临挑战

We've considered the logic behind corporate finance deals, the nature of key transactions, and how they can be valued to ensure that a company is not over – or under-valuing a deal. If the deal makes sense and is successfully arranged and managed, then shareholders should ultimately reap the benefits of a higher share price. But corporate finance is a challenging discipline. Companies face a number of hurdles in their pursuit of good deals, and must be aware of the potential pitfalls. Some of the most common challenges include:

- Overpaying for an acquisition: The history of mergers suggests that companies acquiring other firms periodically overpay for their targets. We've noted that valuing deals is not an exact science, because much depends on estimates of future earnings-which are unknown and therefore subject to a degree of variability. However, when an acquirer takes an aggressive stance and pays a large premium for a target by assuming overly optimistic future earnings flows and/or synergy effects, it may undermine the financial rationale for the transaction and destroy, rather than create, enterprise value.

- Creating too broad a focus: Managing corporate operations is a difficult task, which can be made more difficult by adding other operations that are only loosely connected with core operations or which are completely unrelated. Many conglomeration-based transactions-created through mergers or acquisitions of very different companies-have proven over the years to be ill-advised; in the extreme, failed attempts at conglomeration have actually reduced, rather than enhanced, enterprise value. Investors may find that it is better to buy a portfolio of shares of individual, well managed and well focused companies than the shares of sprawling conglomerates that may not be able to properly manage disparate operations.
- Failing to capitalize on synergies: We know that the value of certain types of deal lies in the creation of synergies. If the management team of a company that has just merged with, or acquired, another company, cannot crystallize these synergies the premium paid on the deal will be lost. When a firm can't convert "theoretical" synergies into true economic value, the financial decision driving a deal will have been based on bad information.
- Failing to properly integrate operations: Integrating the operations of two (or more) different companies can be a very difficult task-even when they are in the same industry.

Firms often have different corporate cultures, human resource requirements, technology platforms, and business strategies/ approaches. Lack of proper attention to these unique characteristics, and how they need to be handled in order to truly create synergies and add corporate value, can again jeopardize a transaction. This is particularly true of human resources: people ultimately drive a company's operations and define its success, and if they are dissatisfied they may depart.

- Lacking discipline to reduce expenses or sell assets: The financial justification for certain kinds of deals, including acquisitions and LBOs, is very often based on cost reductions and/or asset disposals. If a firm is unable to implement the right regimen of post-deal cost controls or is unable to complete a program of asset sales, it may again undermine the rationale for executing the deal.
- Treating investors unfairly: Investors supply capital and capital drives corporate operations. If directors and executives arrange a deal that is not in the best interests of investors (e. g. significantly overpaying for another company, merging on bad terms, attempting to reallocate voting rights), they risk breaching their fiduciary duties, alienating shareholders and jeopardizing access to future capital. Dissatisfied investors may try to oust directors or sell their shares and put downward pressure on the company's stock.

If these challenges are well understood in advance, then a company's managers can ensure that proper steps are taken to avoid problems.

摘要

公司理财交易被设计为通过扩张、合理化和重组等来最优化一家公司的运营。最一般的交易类别包括合并（一家公司与另一家公司在相对平等的基础上结合在一起组成一家“新的”公司）；收购（一家公司购买另一家公司）；杠杆收购（一家公开发行的公司通过借款购买流通股份使自身私有化）；分割（一家公司卖掉其单位的一个或多个或者在一个IPO中分部公开上市或者私下权益交易）；以及资本重组（一家公司重新构造其资本基础）。交易可以被用来扩大市场份额、创建收益的稳定性、减少成本/产生经营效率、获取知识产权和/或调整资本结构。估值一般集中在研究一项交易对未来收入的影响上；因此这涉及到未知事件，所以它需要对广泛场景的分析。公司理财交易也面临很多在规划阶段必须考虑的挑战。这些包括对另一家公司的过多支付；创建过于宽泛的重点；不能将新获取的业务妥善整合到现有业务中去；不能降低费用或卖出需要的资产以及对待投资者不公平。

FURTHER READING　延伸阅读

Bruner, R. and Perella, J., 2004, *Applied Mergers and Acquisitions*, New York: John Wiley & Sons.

Carey, D., Rappaport, A., Eccles, R., Aiello, R. and Watkins, M., 2001, *Harvard Business Review on Mergers and Acquisitions*, Boston, MA: HBS Publishing.

Gaughan, P., 2002, *Mergers, Acquisitions, and Corporate Restructurings*, 3rd edn, New York: John Wiley & Sons.

第三部分

参与者与市场

9

FINANCIAL PARTICIPANTS

金融参与者

CHAPTER OVERVIEW 本章概述

Chapter 9 begins the first of two chapters focused on macro-finance issues, where we consider how concepts from Parts I and Ⅱ influence, and can be influenced by, a range of individual, institutional, and sovereign parties. We begin by analyzing how key groups of participants-including intermediaries, end-users, and regulators-rely on financial dealings to conduct their daily activities, the role each one plays in supporting the entire cycle of finance, and the motivations that drive activity. We then assemble a complete picture of how the groups interact and conclude by considering forces of disintermediation that can affect financial intermediaries.

THE ROLE OF PARTICIPANTS 参与者的作用

Macro-finance, which involves the study of finance at the systemic level, is concerned with both participants and marketplaces. We'll consider participants in this chapter, and reinforce the discussion with an overview of marketplaces and financial market variables in the next chapter. Both, as we'll discover, are integral to a complete understanding of finance.

The concepts, tools, instruments, and transactions we've discussed in the past chapters form the backbone of micro-based finance. They are the essential ingredients that allow companies to make decisions about how to optimize their operations and to put in motion strategies that lead to the best possible funding, risk management, liquidity, and enterprise value solutions.

Such micro-level financial concepts and instruments exist because of, and on behalf of, a range of participants. If these participants didn't exist, or were uninterested in the overarching corporate goals we've discussed, there would be little point in studying finance. And if they didn't exist there would be no need to develop the tools, products, and transactions we've considered.

Fortunately, these participants exist, and are able to fill the crucial roles required in creating a financial process. Understanding their specific roles is important in gaining a perspective on the macro-financial framework. More specifically, we are interested in understanding how key financial participants rely on financial dealings to conduct their activities, the specific functions they play in supporting the financial "life cycle," and the motivations that drive them to participate. This framework allows us to tie together many of the individual tools, concepts, instruments, and transactions we've already discussed.

KEY PARTICIPANTS AND THEIR OBJECTIVES 主要参与者和目标

To build the macro-finance picture we need to divide our discussion into three broad categories: intermediaries, end-users, and regulators. We can then atomize these classifications to gain greater insight into specific roles and responsibilities.

INTERMEDIARIES 中介机构

Our review begins with intermediaries, or institutions that intermediate (stand between) those providing and those using capital, those acquiring and those purchasing assets, and those transferring and those accepting risks. Though the intermediation function might sound rather simple (i. e. matching up two different parties), it is actually quite complex; the function in its most developed form features product development, risk-taking, and advisory services. To understand the full scope of intermediation we consider the different functions that intermediaries perform and the types of intermediaries that are active in the financial markets.

Let's first consider the functions that intermediaries, as a group, perform. Though the depth and sophistication of these services varies considerably across national systems, intermediaries operating in the world's most advanced financial sectors are able to offer most, if not all, of the services described below.

- Capital raising and lending: While all services provided by intermediaries may be considered important, none is perhaps quite as vital in creating enterprise value as capital raising. We have already discussed the issuance of debt and equity and the granting of loans and other forms of credit in order to finance balance sheet operations. Intermediaries arrange such capital/loan products every day on behalf of clients. In fact, intermediaries are uniquely positioned to provide this essential service: they have access to investors and other banks that are willing to supply capital, they have rosters of corporate clients that need to raise capital, and they have the market knowledge required to properly arrange and execute all manner of fund raisings. If intermediaries did not exist to perform this function, individual companies would be left trying to raise their own funds in an inefficient, and al- 资金筹措

most certainly more expensive, manner.

贸易与流动资金

- Trading and liquidity provision: Intermediaries are often active in trading securities and other assets, either as agent or principal. When an intermediary acts as an agent it simply matches buyers and sellers of securities, taking a small spread as commission (but taking no risk itself). When it acts as a principal it assumes risk by taking one side of the transaction (e. g. purchasing a security) and then retains the risk, hedges the position, or separately arranges an offsetting deal (e. g. selling the security it purchased). When acting as a principal the intermediary provides liquidity to the market at large. If intermediaries did not perform this function the secondary markets for trading of securities and other assets would be far less liquid (if not completely illiquid), meaning investors would be unable to quickly sell or rebalance their portfolios without suffering significant losses.

公司财务咨询

- Corporate finance advice: In Chapter 8 we described the corporate finance framework and the nature of mergers, acquisitions, and LBOs. Intermediaries play a leading role in uncovering and arranging such opportunities. They are again uniquely positioned to serve as an important advisor in such matters, as they have strong market and industry knowledge regarding potential corporate financing opportunities, and they have the expertise to evaluate the fair value of any transaction being contemplated. Furthermore, they are often able to offer clients a "package" that includes corporate finance advice and any associated financing that might be required to conclude a deal (e. g. advice on a takeover and then a stock issue to finance the takeover). If intermediaries did not provide this advice, companies seeking expansion or merger opportunities or some other form of restructuring would again be unable to do so efficiently.

风险管理咨询

- Risk management advice: We have described the importance of risk and the use of derivatives and insurance in managing risk. Not surprisingly, since many intermediaries are in the business of taking and managing risk, they are well placed to provide risk management services to their clients. By analyzing a client's financial risk picture an intermediary can craft a risk management/hedging program that meets stated risk/return and risk transfer goals. In addition, the financial engineering capabilities of major intermediaries permit them to offer clients unique, and sometimes complex, solutions. Again, if intermediaries did not perform this role clients would be forced to analyze, and then manage, their financial and operating risks directly; for many this would be costly, inefficient, and potentially inaccurate.

- Asset management: In Chapter 7 we described the process of creating investment portfolios to give investors an opportunity to allocate their capital in a professionally managed setting. Some intermediaries focus on creating asset management strategies for clients on a customized basis. Others provide similar services to investors at large, allowing a broad base of clients to benefit from the intermediary's research and portfolio risk management expertise. If intermediaries did not provide such asset management functions, client investors would be responsible for identifying potential investment opportunities and creating their own investment portfolios, which would be a difficult, time-consuming, and potentially expensive task for all but the most sophisticated.

资产管理

- Custody: The financial business is founded on trust and reputation, and the safekeeping of financial assets is a cornerstone of the process. Many intermediaries, serving as trusted advisors, provide clients with custody services that include asset safekeeping, valuation and reporting, and principal, interest, and dividend collection. These services are especially important to institutional clients that have very large portfolios of assets and who do not wish to replicate the operational infrastructure needed to ensure integrity. Again, if

金融托管

intermediaries did not supply this service, clients would be forced to create their own processes, which would be costly.

One of the recurring themes in our brief descriptions above relates to costs: though intermediaries charge fees, premiums, or spreads for the services they provide, any attempt by clients to replicate the same services (if even possible) would almost certainly come at a much higher price. Accordingly, by providing economically rational alternatives, intermediaries indirectly help corporate clients achieve their enterprise value maximization goals.

With that background in hand, let's now consider the different types of intermediaries that comprise an advanced financial system.

商业银行

- Commercial banks: Commercial banks are regulated banking institutions that accept deposits from retail and institutional customers and use those funds primarily to grant commercial and industrial loans and residential mortgages. This is, of course, a "traditional" banking model that focuses heavily on the creation of credit. Commercial banks generally feature clients from across the spectrum: individuals seeking mortgage loans or short-term credits, middle-market companies interested in working capital loans, and large companies interested in revolving credit facilities, leases, and medium-to-long-term acquisition loans. Though commercial banks may also be involved with securities and asset management, such business lines comprise a smaller portion of activities.

投资银行/证券公司

- Investment banks/securities firms: Investment banks and securities firms are involved primarily in the capital markets business, including issuance and trading of securities and corporate finance advisory services. These institutions focus heavily on primary issuance of debt and equity securities, along with secondary trading and market-making, and maintain extensive client relationships in both the retail and institutional sectors so that they can distribute/place securities.

Within the advisory sector the most sophisticated investment banks offer corporate finance advice, including M&A and LBO structuring; they may also act as principals in private equity investments in support of such transactions. Some are also active in providing hedging services and derivative-based risk management advice. Many large investment banks also run asset management units that are involved in creating investment funds for retail and institutional investors. Apart from the very largest investment banks, however, most offer little in the way of traditional loan products-leaving that business to commercial and universal banks and thrifts.

- Universal banks: Universal banks can be considered a hybrid of the commercial and investment bank platforms. These institutions, which are usually constituted as very large international financial conglomerates, provide clients with the broadest range of financing and advisory products and services. Most are involved with the issuance and trading of securities, development and execution of risk management, investment management, and corporate finance programs, and extension of short-and long-term credit. Major universal banks tend to offer traditional retail banking services as well as more exclusive, higher margin, private banking services. 普通银行
- Thrifts/building societies: Thrift institutions, also known as savings and loan institutions and building societies, are active primarily in the residential mortgage market. Thrifts accept retail deposits, mainly from individuals, and use the funds to grant residential home mortgages. Though they may provide additional forms of credit to individuals and may even grant commercial mortgages to middle-market enterprises or property developers, most keep quite a strict focus on the residential market. Thrifts can thus be regarded as specialized forms of commercial banks, though they may be governed by different rules and regulations to reflect their 存储机构

unique retail focus.

保险公司

- Insurance companies: Insurance companies provide individual and institutional customers with risk transfer advice and policies/products, including the full range of insurance contracts discussed earlier. The largest insurers operate on a global basis, insuring risks across national boundaries through one or more subsidiaries. National or local insurers, in contrast, concentrate their business within a particular country. Some insurers are focused on life and health coverage, others on property and casualty coverage, and still others on the entire range of insurable risks. Insurers may also offer customers annuities and other savings/investment products.

再保险公司

- Reinsurance companies: Reinsurance companies act as insurers of insurers, providing risk transfer coverage to insurers that are writing primary coverage to their individual and corporate clients. In fact, reinsurers can be regarded as wholesale institutions, as they have no dealings with individual customers on a primary basis; their business focus is strictly on the professional insurance market, where they provide different classes of reinsurance. Since reinsurers deal at the institutional level, they tend to operate with a fairly broad geographic focus, reinsuring risks across borders and exposure classes.

银行保险公司

- Bancassurance companies: Bancassurance companies, which are essentially combinations of universal banks and insurance companies, offer the broadest mix of financial services. Though relatively limited in number, the primary bancassurance firms provide the full range of commercial and investment banking services and insurance services, generally on a global basis. In order to deal with different forms of regulation, bancassurance firms tend to operate through a holding company structure where individual corporate entities provide specific types of products and services. Thus, one unit may be incorporated as a commercial bank, offering deposits and loans, while another unit may be established as a regulated insurer, writing insurance coverage. The intent behind the bancassurance model is to be able to provide individual or institutional clients with "one stop shopping" across all products and services.

There are, of course, various other types of intermediaries, including dedicated asset managers, non-bank financial institutions, and so forth. These players tend to be more specialized, though many are quite large when measured by assets, revenues, or profits.

What motivates financial intermediaries to provide the products and services noted above? We can point to two general objectives: maximization of profits and management of risks. Maximization of profits is simply a reiteration of our familiar theme: financial intermediaries are constituted as corporations and seek to generate as much income for their shareholders as possible, within the confines of their business models and risk-taking abilities. Commercial and investment banks, universal banks, and insurers are in business to generate fees, premiums, spreads, and commissions, and their shareholders will benefit as long as they can offer useful products and services.

Management of risk is a second key objective. By linking diverse pools of clients that have different views and requirements and developing new financial products, intermediaries can manage their own risks more effectively. For instance, if one firm seeks to raise capital through the issuance of bonds, an investment bank can supply the required capital, earning a fee in the process. However, at this stage the investment bank still holds the company's bonds, meaning it is fully exposed to credit risk. By using its investor distribution network or certain derivative contracts it can lower its risk profile dramatically-while still locking in some amount of profitability.

END-USERS 最终用户

If intermediaries symbolize the supply of financial services, then end-users represent the demand for those services. To consider the demand side of the equation, we describe major classes of end-users and the kinds of financial transactions they are most likely to be involved in.

产业和服务公司

- Industrial and service companies: Industrial and service companies represent the key corporate sector that is so vital in defining demand for financial services. Large capitalization and middle-market companies from virtually all sectors (e. g. technology, automotive, energy, pharmaceuticals, consumer goods, and so on) rely on access to financial services to manage their business affairs. These companies regularly borrow funds from commercial/universal banks and issue debt/equity securities via investment banks in order to fund their expansion plans; the significant amount of capital financing companies require is a key source of primary and secondary activity for intermediaries, and also allows the investment demand of investors (noted immediately following) to be met. Large firms are often active users of M&A and risk advisory/hedging services; this allows them to efficiently incorporate acquisition, spin-off, or other corporate restructurings into their strategic plans, and to hedge or transfer financial and operating risks via derivatives and insurance. Companies often "outsource" their retirement benefit programs to intermediaries offering professional asset management capabilities as well. Obviously, if these corporate end-users did not borrow funds or issue securities, the global financial markets would be considerably smaller; similarly, if they didn't avail themselves of M&A services, expansion or restructuring opportunities would be limited.

机构/专业投资者

- Institutional/professional investors: Institutional investors, which we may define to include open and closed-end funds, hedge funds, pension funds, as well as the investment or trust operations of insurance companies and banks, are significant users of specific types of financial services, including primary and secondary investments and risk management services. Institutional investors are the single largest group of capital providers in the financial system. They routinely absorb the greatest amount of debt and equity capital securities issued on a primary basis, and are also active buyers and sellers of securities on a secondary basis. In recent years they have also become important players in the secondary loan market, buying portions of loans originated by banks for their clients. The intent of all of these asset purchases is, of course, to generate returns for their own clients, including other institutional investors, individual investors, and pensioners. If institutional investors didn't provide capital to the financial system, corporate end-users (as well as financial institutions) would be unable to fund their balance sheets appropriately. In addition to acquiring capital instruments institutional investors often use risk management solutions and products developed by intermediaries in order to hedge or augment particular risk exposures.

主权政府和政府机构

- Sovereigns and government agencies: Governments are important borrowers in the debt market and they are periodically active in the corporate finance market through privatization of state-owned assets. Governments and their central banks regularly issue securities to meet various goals. For instance, they may issue short-term securities (e. g. treasury bills) to meet liquidity needs and help manage aspects of monetary policy (which we'll consider in Chapter 10). They may also issue medium-and long-term securities: since nations may have significant expense and investment programs that cannot be adequately funded with tax-based revenues, they may be required to issue medium-or long-term securities. In practice most governments use intermediaries to raise capital; though many could issue directly to investors, the use of intermediaries (socalled primary dealers) is an efficient and effective distribution mechanism. Government agencies are also periodic sellers of state-owned assets that they wish to place into the private sector. Intermediaries may conduct private or public sales of these assets in order to help an agency maximize value.

个人

- Individuals: We have deliberately excluded discussion of individuals in the financial process in order to maintain our corporate focus. It is clear, however, that individuals are an important element of the marketplace, acting as small-scale investors and borrowers. Though each transaction arranged by a single customer may appear small, the collective portfolio of transactions across all individuals can quickly become very significant-meaning that individuals are an influential market force. Individuals invest in debt and equity securities and investment fund shares via their savings and retirement accounts. If individuals didn't participate, capital issuers and borrowers would face periodic capital supply shortages and/or would place excessive demands on the institutional investor base. Individuals are also active in the risk management area, primarily through health, home, auto, and/or life insurance policies that transfer unwanted risks to the insurance sector. They are also frequent borrowers through consumer/credit card debt and home mortgages.

What motivates end-users to participate in the financial marketplace? First, end-users need capital in order to fund public (government) or private (corporate) operations or, at an individual level, to make significant purchases (e. g. homes, automobiles). Access to this supply of capital is essential, and can only be gained by tapping into the financial marketplace. In fact, if end-users were unable to access the capital and loan markets, their ability to grow would be severely curtailed. Second, end-users that have an excess of capital to invest require access to conduits that provide the opportunity of creating real returns. Simply put, it would be impossible for this base of end-users to generate profits on their resources if they were unable to access capital instruments. Third, end-users want to be able to efficiently manage their risks. This, as we have noted, can be accomplished by using a professional risk transfer mechanism, where the benefits of diversification can lead to lower premiums and fees.

REGULATORS 监管机构

Those dealing in the financial marketplace cannot generally do so without some level of guidance and oversight from government-related regulators. Most modern financial systems have some type of regulatory "watchdog" to keep an eye on activities. The intent, in virtually all cases, is to provide end-users with an appropriate level of protection so that they don't become victims of unintentional losses or fraud.

The most effective and efficient way of providing end-user protection is to set minimum standards for those supplying financial services. A regulator has greater confidence that the end-user, whether an individual or an institution, will be properly protected if this can be accomplished successfully. Standards may relate to the minimum required financial position/strength of an institution supplying services, the minimum level of disclosure that must accompany deals or offerings, or the maximum amount that can be charged for specific services.

The national regulatory system can be arranged in different ways, depending on the depth and breadth of the local financial services base. In the most advanced systems, however, we can point to at least three classes of regulatory oversight:

银行监管机构

- Bank regulator: The bank regulator, which may be associated with the country's central bank, is responsible for ensuring that all financial institutions in the local system (either domestic institutions or domestic branches of foreign institutions) operate in a prudent manner by maintaining a minimum level of capital and reserves, minimum standards of asset quality, and maximum amount of leverage. The bank regulator may also require banking institutions to contribute to an insurance fund that provides depositors with protection against losses. Some countries feature regulators for individual segments of the banking sector. Thus, one body may be responsible for regulating commercial banks, another for regulating thrifts/ building societies, and still another for reviewing non-bank financial institutions (e. g. consumer finance companies, leasing companies).

保险监管机构

- Insurance regulator: The insurance regulator may operate at a state/provincial level, a national level, or both. The insurance regulator reviews the skills and capabilities of insurers writing specific classes of insurance and ensures that all participating firms maintain a minimum level of statutory reserves/capital. It also makes certain that insurers conduct their dealings with policyholders in a fair and equitable manner when settling loss claims.

证券/外汇监管者

- Securities/exchange regulator: The securities or exchange regulator, which may again have some relationship to a country's central bank, is typically charged with overseeing the financial soundness and operations of local stock and/or derivative exchanges. The intent is to make sure that market-making, trading, execution, and settlement occur in a transparent and orderly fashion so that investors (especially individuals) are adequately protected. Securities regulators are often responsible for establishing minimum levels of disclosure for stock and bond issues that are to be floated in the public markets, and may also be responsible for the activities of investment banks and securities firms, helping ensure that they remain properly capitalized and keep leverage at prudent levels.

In some countries, such as the UK, bank and securities regulators are combined under a single umbrella. Regardless of the specific structural organization, regulators are critical in ensuring that intermediaries (and marketplaces for intermediation) adhere to minimum standards of financial and professional conduct so that end-users are not prejudiced or financially damaged.

THE COMPLETE PICTURE
完整的场景

We now have the components that allow us to construct the complete picture of financial activities and participants (we'll supplement this discussion with further comments on the financial markets at large in the next chapter). Figure 9. 1 features a simplified, and conceptualized, view of the major groups of participants and the role each plays in the financial process. Note that end-users are separated into two classes to simplify the discussion.

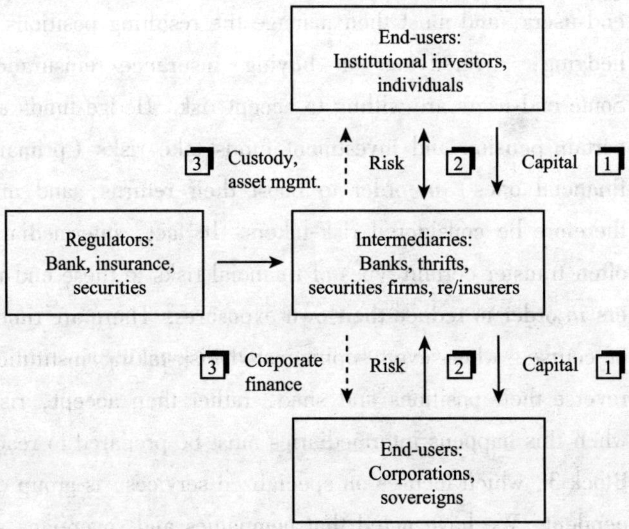

Figure 9. 1 The complete picture of financial participants

Let's briefly summarize the key roles and activities noted in the diagram.

- Block 1 indicates that institutional and individual investors act as suppliers of capital. This capital flows through the group of intermediaries (who may supplement it with their own capital) and on to the group of end-users that demands capital, including companies and sovereigns/agencies. This represents the essential debt and equity capital funding process. Associated with the capital flow function is an implicit trading function. Many investors continue to direct their trading through intermediaries, which execute on exchanges or in the OTC market on behalf of investors.
- Block 2, which centers on risk transfer, is less transparent. Corporate and sovereign end-users often wish to transfer financial and operating risks. This is consistent with our earlier comments where we noted that as long as costs are low enough, companies and government agencies often try to transfer as much risk as possible via derivatives and insurance. The same is true of individuals. Accordingly, intermediaries can expect to receive risk exposures from these end-users, and must then manage the resulting positions by hedging, diversifying or buying insurance/reinsurance. Some end-users are willing to accept risk. Hedge funds and certain pension and investment funds take risks (primarily financial ones) in order to boost their returns, and must therefore be considered risk-takers. In fact, intermediaries often transfer certain types of financial risks to these end-users in order to reduce their own exposures. There are times, of course, when even sophisticated risk-taking institutions reverse their positions and shed, rather than accept, risk; when this happens intermediaries must be prepared to react.
- Block 3, which focuses on specialized services, is group dependent. We have noted that companies and sovereigns are active end-users of corporate finance advisory services, and

would expect to receive the benefit of any such advice from intermediaries. Individual and institutional investors may use custody services (e.g. securities safekeeping) and specific asset management programs and strategies.

The activities supplied by intermediaries are, of course, overseen by the appropriate regulator (s). Naturally, this illustration is simplified, as institutions may be involved in other financial activities or may act in a manner opposite to the ones indicated above. Alternatively, they may perform multiple roles (e.g. a bank may supply capital directly to end-use companies, and may also do so indirectly by financing a private equity fund, which then invests in the capital of an end-use company). Nevertheless, the general structure holds true and allows us to understand the dependencies and relationships.

FORCES OF DISINTERMEDIATION
非居间化的力量

Intermediaries clearly play a vital role in the financial system. They are the key players that stand between demanders and suppliers of capital, and between companies seeking partners and those willing to be acquired; they are adept at creating investment and risk management solutions through their financial engineering expertise and providing the custody services that allow assets to be safely held.

But all of these services come at a price. End-users must therefore address, as part of financial planning activities, the relative cost/benefit tradeoff associated with the financial services provided by intermediaries. If the benefits obtained from efficiently raising capital or completing a corporate finance transaction outweigh the fees/expenses, then the decision rule framework will suggest proceeding. If, however, the costs appear too large, then end-users may seek alternative solutions.

This gives rise to disintermediation, or the process of removing intermediaries from their traditional roles in raising capital and granting advice.

Disintermediation arises when end-users are presented with alternatives or substitutes. For instance, if ABC Co. can issue commercial paper or bonds directly to investors, rather than via an investment bank, it saves on the underwriting fees. Or, if it can trade assets in its portfolio through a self-directed, electronic trading platform rather than via a securities firm, it saves on commissions and asset management fees (institutional and individual investors can, of course, do the same thing). If the firm can identify its own acquisition or merger partners, it can avoid paying advisory fees. Or, if it can detect a predictable pattern of small losses within its employee health or disability benefit portfolio, it can self-insure via a captive and save on insurance premium costs. Whenever ABC Co. can reduce the costs of arranging financial transactions, it boosts its own net income and, by extension, its enterprise value. Figure 9.2 presents a decomposition of the illustration presented earlier to demonstrate how financial institutions can be removed from aspects of the process.

The concept of disintermediation sounds very appealing from the perspective of the end-user. So why not eliminate the "middle man" from all financial transactions? The short answer is inefficiency. It is very difficult, in practice, for most companies to replicate the types of skills, services, relationships, and networks that financial intermediaries have spent decades (and longer) cultivating. Intermediaries have the risk management and financial engineering knowledge that is essential in creating proper hedging, risk transfer, and investment strategies; they can draw on very large networks of clients and contacts to raise and place capital; and they are skilled in identifying corporate finance opportunities-including those that may not be known to end-users. They are also able to operate on a cross-border ba-

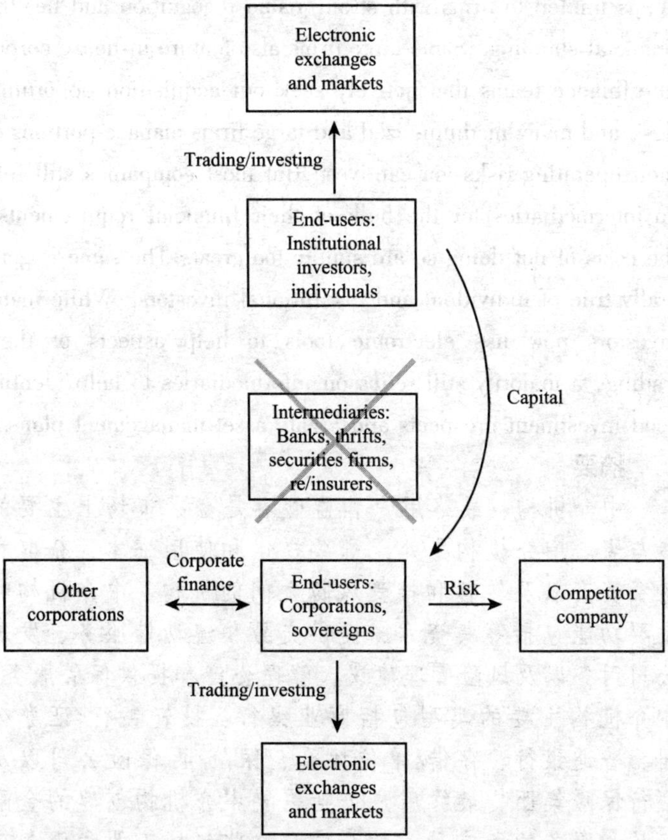

Figure 9.2 Disintermediation of select financial functions

sis, bringing end-users financial opportunities from outside the home market. The process of replicating even a portion of this platform would be an inefficient and expensive exercise for most companies.

Forces of disintermediation are therefore still quite limited. Only the largest multinational companies have the ability to remove financial intermediaries from the process, and even then do so very selectively. This remains true in an era increasingly dominated by electronic communications, information dissemination and execution. In practice some large firms issue short and medium-term liabilities directly to end-users. This, however, is limited to firms with strong name recognition and healthy financial standing. Some large firms also feature in-house corporate finance teams that actively seek out acquisition opportunities, and many medium-sized and large firms manage portions of their operating risks via captives. But most companies still rely on intermediaries for the bulk of their financial requirements; the costs of not doing so are simply too great. The same is generally true of individual and institutional investors. While many investors now use electronic tools to help aspects of their trading, a majority still relies on intermediaries to help identify good investment prospects and create asset management plans.

摘要

中介机构、最终用户和监管者是金融市场上主要的参与者。中介机构是处于那些提供和使用资本、获取和购买资产以及转移和接受风险之间的机构。中介机构的主要功能包括筹集资本、提供交易和流动性服务、发展公司财务以及风险管理建议、管理资产和提供保管服务。中介机构主要的类型包括商业银行、投资银行/证券公司、普通银行、存借/单位协会、保险/再保险公司以及银行保险集团。最终用户包括需要中介机构创建的金融产品和服务的所有种类的公司。这些包括工业和服务公司、机构/专业投资者、主权国家和政府机构以及个人。在金融市场上的那些交易没有政府相关监管机构某种水平的指导和监督，一般不能实现。绝大多数现代金融系统都拥有一个或多个监管者密切注视着那些提供银行、保险和/或证券服务企业的活动。尽管中介机构提供给最终用户的服务是有价值的，但是非居间化的忧虑——或从作为“中间人”的传统角色中去除中介机构——也存在。非居间化理论上有助于为最终用户节省成本，从而导致企业价值的增加。尽管那么说，但是非居间化的程序仍然限于那些能够通过直接将证券分销给投资者获取资本或通过内部的公司理财专业技能就能获取其他公司的大企业。金融服务公司的完全非居间化是不可能发生的，因为它将造成巨大的无效率和附加成本。

FURTHER READING 延伸阅读

Grabbe, O. , 1995, *International Financial Markets*, New Jersey: Prentice Hall.

Kidwell, D. , Peterson, R. L. , Blackwell, D. W. and Whidbee, D. A. , 2002, *Financial Institutions*, *Markets*, *and Money*, 8*th edition*, New York: John Wiley & Sons.

Saunders, A. , 2003, *Financial Institutions and Markets*, 2*nd edition*, New York: McGraw-Hill.

10

THE GLOBAL FINANCIAL MARKETS

全球金融市场

CHAPTER OVERVIEW 本章概述

Chapter 10 continues our discussion of macro-finance issues. In this chapter we consider the macro-structure of the global financial markets and their importance in promoting capital flows and economic growth. We then discuss the impact of key financial variables-including interest rates, inflation, and economic growth-on the markets, and analyze the effect of monetary policy on financial variables. We then consider elements of the financial markets that give rise to its fluidity and dynamism, including deregulation, capital mobility, volatility, and technology. We conclude by considering the practical impact of dynamic forces on the marketplace.

MACRO-STRUCTURE OF THE FINANCIAL MARKETS 金融市场的客观结构

In Parts I and Ⅱ of the book we have considered aspects of finance from a micro perspective; in Chapter 9 we have extended the discussion by examining the macro roles of end-users, intermediaries, and regulators. We now build on that macro picture by considering financial market sectors and how they are impacted by financial variables.

The global financial markets are comprised of broad capital pools and asset classes that are linked by intricate relationships.

货币市场

- Money markets: The money markets, as we've noted in Chapter 5, consist of short-term liabilities issued by banks (e. g. certificates of deposit, bankers' acceptances), companies (e. g. commercial paper), and sovereigns (e. g. treasury bills). In the private sector these instruments are used for liquidity management purposes, while in the sovereign sector they may be used for liquidity management and monetary policy management, which we describe below. Virtually all industrialized and emerging nations feature some type of money market sector.

债务资产市场

- Debt capital markets: The debt capital markets, which include medium and long-term bonds and loans, constitute the single largest element of the global capital markets. Bonds and loans are used for capital investment, acquisitions and expansion, and may be renewed on a regular basis-making the capital appear semi-permanent. The most significant debt capital markets include those of industrialized nations such as the US, UK, Japan and various European Union countries; the offshore market, which crosses national borders, is also significant.

股票市场

- Stock markets: The stock markets include common and preferred stock issued by corporations to fund productive operations/permanent investments, and ensure balance sheet leverage remains reasonable. All market-based economies feature companies that are capitalized via equity instruments, making the overall market deep and broad.

外汇市场

- Foreign exchange markets: The foreign exchange market represents the single most actively traded element of the financial markets, with intermediaries and end-users dealing very large amounts of spot (or current market) and forward transactions every business day. Market activity is centered primarily on the major exchange rates, including dollars, euros, yen, Swiss francs, sterling, Canadian dollars, and Australian dollars. Additional activity occurs in secondary currencies (e. g. non-EU currencies, New Zealand dollars) and emerging market currencies (e. g. Latin America, Southeast Asia).

商品市场

- Commodity markets: The global commodity markets are broad and deep, and feature a significant amount of spot and forward dealing. Hedgers (commodity producers and commodity users) and speculators actively use the market, which adds significantly to market flows. Key traded commodities include precious metals (gold, silver, platinum, palladium), industrial metals (iron, copper, aluminum, zinc), energy (oil/products, natural gas, electricity), agricultural products (corn, wheat, soybeans), and softs (cocoa, coffee, sugar).

衍生品市场

- Derivative markets: The derivative markets, as noted in Chapter 7, are based on financial contracts linked to specific asset classes, including all of those mentioned above. Hedgers and speculators use the markets to achieve specific goals, injecting liquidity in the process. In fact, derivatives can serve as substitutes for, or complements to, other financial instruments.

Each of the broad sectors noted above is linked to the other sectors directly or indirectly. The relationships between different sectors are complex and sometimes unstable. Changes in one market can impact capital flowing in to, or out of, another market. While such relationships may hold true under most market conditions, they may change during times of market stress; this causes previously held notions of "normal behavior" to be brought into question. Let us review several simplified examples of what happens to financial markets as key macro variables-including interest rates, inflation rates, and economic growth rates-change.

For example, consider that when a country's short-term interest rates rise, the general cost of public and private borrowing rises in tandem. Rising interest rates tend to attract a greater amount of investment capital-investors in other assets classes, including equities, sell their existing investments and redeploy capital in the higher earning asset. This puts downward pressure on stock prices (and the prices of other financial assets), making money market and debt capital market investments look that much more attractive at least for a time.

Several "ripple effects" are then likely to appear. First, higher interest costs can lead to greater corporate profit pressures, which can cause stock prices to fall. Reinvestment in productive ventures may also slow, as the internal hurdle rate a company must achieve becomes higher as a result of the increased cost of capital. Second, higher domestic interest rates will prove attractive to foreign investors, for the same reasons cited above. Accordingly, they will convert (sell) their home currencies and buy the domestic currency, causing it to appreciate in value. We may also note that a strong currency has important implications on a country's trade balance, causing goods exported abroad to appear expensive in foreign markets; this can lead to a decline in demand, which can also negatively impact corporate earnings. There is, of course, a limit to this process. As more domestic and offshore investors acquire fixed income assets they force prices up and yields down. This will eventually cause investors to stop allocating additional capital to fixed income assets and may generate a temporary equilibrium.

The opposite scenario can also appear: when interest rates fall, fixed income investments appear less attractive, causing capital to flow into other asset classes, including stocks and diversified investment funds. Corporate interest expense declines, allowing companies to boost their earnings and reinvestment, which helps increase their stock prices. Under this scenario the domestic currency may appear less attractive in foreign eyes, and will lose value as offshore investors liquidate their fixed income holdings and repatriate capital (the amount repatriated depends, of course, on their perception of domestic stock market opportunities). Separately, a weaker domestic currency makes export goods appear more competitive on the global stage, meaning global demand for products can rise and earnings can grow. This can also lead to higher stock prices. There is, of course, an equilibrium under this scenario as well: at some point stock prices may trade at unsustainable earnings multiples, causing investors to pull back and search for other opportunities. This slows, and may even halt, the rise in stock prices, perhaps to the point where fixed income investments begin to appear attractive once again.

The general impact of interest rates on financial markets is summarized in Table 10. 1.

Table 10. 1 Interest rates and financial market impact

Scenario	*Key financial market impact*
Rates ↑	• Capital is attracted to fixed income assets, causing stock (and other asset) prices to fall. • Borrowing costs rise, causing corporate profits to decline and reinvestment to slow. • Domestic currency strengthens, causing export goods to become less competitive.
Rates ↓	• Capital is diverted from fixed income assets to stocks and other alternatives, causing their prices to rise. • Borrowing costs decline, causing corporate profits to rise and reinvestment to increase. • Domestic currency weakens, causing export goods to become more competitive.

Let us also consider an example based on inflationary forces. Inflation measures the price of goods and services at the wholesale level (via indexes such as the producer price index) and at the consumer level (through the consumer price index or the retail price index). Rising inflation can result from excess demand for goods/services during a strong phase of economic expansion. Higher commodity prices can be a benefit to commodity producers (e. g. oil and natural gas companies, resources/mineral companies), who may see their stock prices trade at strong earnings multiples, but can be detrimental to commodity users (e. g. every company that relies on commodity inputs to produce finished goods), who may suffer from weaker earnings and/or be forced to hedge their input exposures. During a period of growing inflation the national central bank may be forced to deal with the problem by raising interest rates; in fact, this is an important tool of monetary policy, as we shall discuss below. Higher interest rates create two "antiinflation" effects: they make corporate borrowing more expensive, which causes investment in production to slow, and they make debt-financed purchases of goods more expensive, again causing them to slow. Rising rates are thus used to cool an overheated economy and bring prices back down. There is, of course, a balancing act involved: we've noted in the example immediately above that rising rates lead to greater corporate profit pressures and lower stock market prices, which can reinforce negative signals about an economic slowdown. Naturally, the opposite scenario occurs when inflation is under control.

The general effects of inflation on financial markets are summarized in Table 10. 2.

Let's analyze a third scenario where economic growth, as measured by gross domestic product-GDP, or the total output of goods and services in an economy-weakens. When a national economy is contracting, corporate profits decline and stock prices fall. In order to help restart economic activity, monetary authorities may lower interest rates, which causes the prices of fixed income securities to rise. Lowering rates also weakens the domestic currency, making export goods appear more attractive on the world markets, which ultimately helps boost earnings, and

Table 10. 2 Inflation and financial market impact

Scenario	*Key financial market impact*
Inflation ↑	• Prices of core commodities increase, causing corporate earnings and stock prices of non-resource companies to decline. • Short-term interest rates begin to rise as the central bank combats the price pressures, causing capital to be diverted to fixed income assets. • Borrowing costs rise, causing corporate profits to decline and reinvestment to slow. • Domestic currency strengthens, causing export goods to become less competitive.
Inflation ↓	• Prices of core commodities decrease, causing corporate earnings and stock prices of non-resource companies to rise. • Short-term interest rate hikes will cease, causing capital to flow from fixed income assets to stocks and other financial assets. • Borrowing costs decline, causing corporate profits to rise and reinvestment to increase. • Domestic currency weakens, causing export goods to become more competitive.

stock prices, of companies active in the export sector. Inflation is unlikely to be much of a problem when the economy is weak: companies and customers will curtail demand for goods, easing price pressures. In addition, the prices of many commodities are likely to decline. Easing of price pressures allows the central bank to lower interest rates without fear of a rise in inflation. The cycle of lowering rates will continue until there is some evidence that spending and capital investment are building once again. When the economy begins its upturn-as evidenced by growing sales, consumer debt, and corporate inventories-the central bank will become more vigilant about inflation. Again, the opposite scenario plays out when the economy is expanding.

Table 10. 3 summarizes the financial market impact of GDP scenarios.

Table 10.3　　GDP and financial market impact

Scenario	*Key financial market impact*
GDP ↑	• Corporate profits rise, causing stock prices to rise. • Short-term rates are increased (gradually), causing fixed income asset prices to fall. • Domestic currency strengthens, causing export goods to become less competitive. • Inflation pressures build, causing commodity prices to rise.
GDP ↓	• Corporate profits fall, causing stock prices to decline. • Short-term interest rates are lowered, causing fixed income asset prices to rise. • Domestic currency weakens, causing export goods to become competitive. • Inflation pressures abate, causing commodity prices to fall.

We must, of course, be careful in generalizing these relationships, because exceptions appear during specific market-driven cycles. In fact, there is no concrete rule indicating the scenarios we have discussed will always hold true. Nevertheless, there is sufficient empirical evidence to suggest that these basic relationships tend to occur under "normal" market conditions; they can therefore be regarded as a useful guide.

MONETARY POLICY AND FINANCIAL VARIABLES 货币政策和金融变量

Monetary policy is the set of actions implemented by a government that allows it to manage inflation and economic growth. Most countries try to promote steady economic growth while keeping inflation under control. The latter point is very important, as an economy that is growing rapidly, but which also features high inflation rates, is in an unsustainable position: as noted above, the purchasing power of consumers and companies will eventually decline, leading to an economic slowdown (and an associated rise in unemployment as workers are dismissed). Conversely, an economy that is expanding at a steady pace with inflation held in check represents a far more balanced system.

Implementing monetary policy is a delicate task. Those responsible, generally a group of officials within a country's central bank, must analyze and interpret a great deal of economic information, some of which may offer conflicting signals on the health of the economy. A sampling of the key data that officials use to gauge the state of economic affairs is summarized in Table 10.4. Proper interpretation of this data is vital, as any misreading may cause officials to take the wrong actions. Unfortunately, some of these measures are subject to "after the fact" revisions, which makes the job even more challenging.

Table 10.4 Sample of key economic measures

Measure	*Indication*
Gross domestic product	Amount of goods and services produced, overall size and pace of economic growth
Employment	The level of the employment pool and the amount of workers that are unemployed
Producer price index	Level of retail prices/inflation in the wholesale sector
Consumer price index	Level of retail prices/inflation in the consumer sector
Industrial production	Level of production in the wholesale sector and the degree to which productive processes are utilized
Durable goods orders	The amount of durable goods, plant, and equipment processed
Merchandise inventory	The level of inventory on hand
Merchandise trade	The balance of trade (exports minus imports)
Housing starts	The amount of new home construction started
New home sales	The amount of new homes sold
Construction spending	The amount spent on commercial and residential construction
Retail sales	The amount of sales conducted at the consumer level

In order to actually manage policy to stated goals, central banks rely on several different tools, including changes in the discount rate, open market operations, and changes in bank reserve requirements.

改变贴现率

- Changes in the discount rate: The most visible, and frequently used, tool of monetary policy involves changing official short-term interest rates. For instance, the central bank may raise interest rates to slow an overheating economy that is showing signs of inflation. When the central bank raises its short-term rates all other risky short-term rates rise as well. As we've already noted, higher rates cause firms and individuals to borrow less. Less borrowing, in turn, means less investment/ expansion in productive endeavors, a slowdown in production, and less debt-financed purchases by consumers and companies. A smaller amount of purchases translates into less price pressure, which leads to a gradual slowing of the economy and a decline in inflation. The opposite scenario holds true: if the economy is sluggish and free of inflationary pressures, the central bank can lower rates to stimulate borrowing, spending, and investment in productive processes; these lead ultimately to an expansion in economic growth.

公开市场操作

- Open market operations: A subtle, but effective, tool that central banks frequently employ involves open market operations, or management of liquidity in the financial system. For instance, when the financial system at large is awash with liquidity (e.g. an excess of cash) banks continue making loans, spurring economic activity and placing upward pressure on prices. To keep inflation in check the central bank's dealing desk may issue government securities to financial institutions. Since banks and dealers must pay cash for the securities, the central bank draws liquidity out of the system, giving banks less cash by which to make loans; this flows through the system and leads to some curtailment of economic activity. The opposite is also true: the central bank can offer to buy holdings of government securities from financial institutions, reinjecting liquidity into the system; banks can then use the additional liquidity to make loans, thereby stimulating economic activity. A central bank can also balance the requirements through repurchase and reverse repurchase agreements; as noted earlier, a repurchase agreement is simply a collateralized borrowing, while a reverse repurchase agreement is a collateralized lending.

改变银行存款准备金需求

- Changes in bank reserve requirements: Central banks can also implement monetary policy through a third tool, though they tend to do so infrequently. Specifically, they can influence the level of interest rates, inflation, and economic growth by altering the reserve requirements applied to banks operating in the national system. In most financial systems a bank must set aside in non-interest bearing assets a particular percentage of its balance sheet. For instance, if the current reserve requirement is 10 percent, a bank is able to create €90 of new loans with €100 in new deposits; the remaining €10 of reserve requirements must be held in the form of non-interest bearing assets. If the central bank is concerned about an overheated economy, it will try to slow the amount of new credit being extended by banks to individuals and companies. Rather than increase short-term rates, it may raise the reserve requirement (e. g. from 10 percent to 15 percent); this means that a bank that previously granted €90 in new loans for every €100 of new deposits taken in, can now only make €85 in new loans. The credit phase is thus less expansionary and should lead to a slowdown in the purchasing and investing activities of borrowers. While the example above is simplified, we can easily imagine the same requirement applied to all banks throughout the system: if the entire banking system has €1 billion in deposits and the reserve requirement changes by 5 percentage points, loan capacity declines by €50 million; if the deposit base is €10 billion, loan capacity declines by a rather significant €500 million; and so forth. We can see, then, how this might be a useful macro-economic management tool. The opposite can also occur, of course: if the central bank wants to stimulate economic growth it can reduce the reserve requirement, enabling banks to lend more to individuals and companies that are ready to consume and invest.

These elements of monetary policy are summarized in Figures 10. 1a and 10. 1b.

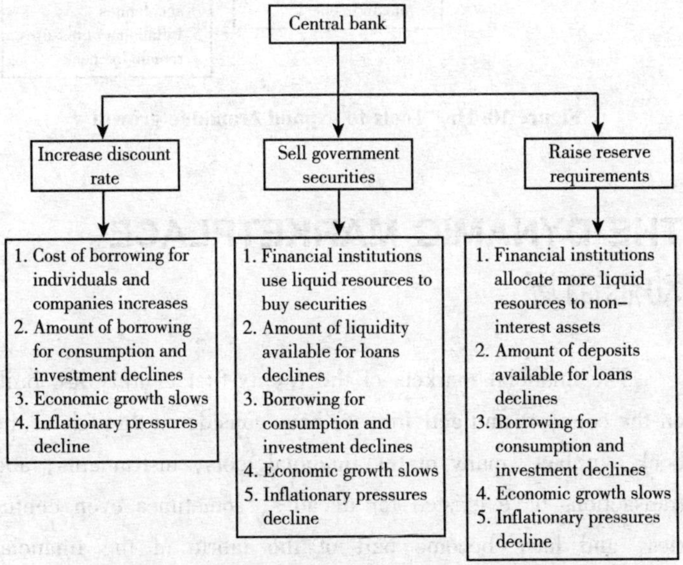
Central bank
Increase discount rate
Sell government securities
Raise reserve requirements
1. Cost of borrowing for individuals and companies increases
2. Amount of borrowing for consumption and investment declines
3. Economic growth slows
4. Inflationary pressures decline
1. Financial institutions use liquid resources to buy securities
2. Amount of liquidity available for loans declines
3. Borrowing for consumption and investment declines
4. Economic growth slows
5. Inflationary pressures decline
1. Financial institutions allocate more liquid resources to non-interest assets
2. Amount of deposits available for loans declines
3. Borrowing for consumption and investment declines
4. Economic growth slows
5. Inflationary pressures decline

Figure 10. 1a Tools to slow economic growth/inflation

We must also be aware that, in addition to monetary policy, nations rely on adjustments to fiscal policy to influence economic growth. However fiscal policy, which attempts to influence inflation and economic growth through changes in taxes and government spending, is generally agreed to be a medium- to long-term process.

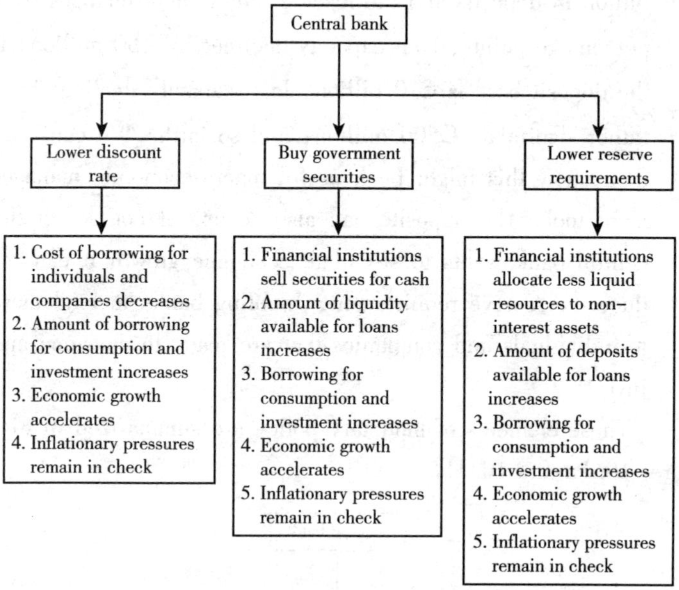
Central bank
Lower discount rate
Buy government securities
Lower reserve requirements
1. Cost of borrowing for individuals and companies decreases
2. Amount of borrowing for consumption and investment increases
3. Economic growth accelerates
4. Inflationary pressures remain in check
1. Financial institutions sell securities for cash
2. Amount of liquidity available for loans increases
3. Borrowing for consumption and investment increases
4. Economic growth accelerates
5. Inflationary pressures remain in check
1. Financial institutions allocate less liquid resources to non-interest assets
2. Amount of deposits available for loans increases
3. Borrowing for consumption and investment increases
4. Economic growth accelerates
5. Inflationary pressures remain in check

Figure 10.1b Tools to expand economic growth

THE DYNAMIC MARKETPLACE
动态市场

The financial markets of the twenty-first century are built on the concepts and activities we have considered throughout the book. In fact, many of the financial tools, instruments, and transactions have existed for decades, sometimes even centuries, and have become part of the fabric of the financial process. But events of the past two decades, in particular, have altered fundamentally certain aspects of the marketplace. Specifically, the marketplace has become more dynamic, flexible, and innovative, primarily as a result of forces of deregulation, capital mobility, volatility, and technology.

放松管制

- Deregulation: As we've observed in Chapter 9, financial regulations exist to help protect end-users and/or to control the behaviors of intermediaries. While regulations are designed to provide proper control, they can create inefficiencies, particularly in free market economies that operate on the basis of market forces. Industrialized and emerging economies have historically featured some amount of financial regulation. While many rules have been useful in protecting end-users (e. g. mandatory deposit insurance offered by banks), others have actually led to the development of competitive barriers (e. g. forbidding commercial banks from offering investment banking services, prohibiting offshore insurance companies from offering insurance in the local marketplace, requiring all stock trading to flow through a certain exchange, placing interest rate ceilings on deposit accounts). Regulatory barriers have the effect of stifling competition and creating inefficiencies-which can hurt end-users through higher costs and fewer options. There has, however, been a greater turn toward deregulation in many markets over the past few decades. Rules that no longer fill the function originally intended have been dismantled (e. g. commercial banks can now offer investment banking services, interest rate ceilings on deposits have been eliminated, offshore insurers can participate in the local marketplace). The operating environment has, in many cases, become more competitive and innovative as a result.

- Capital mobility: We have seen at various points that capital is the essential ingredient in corporate expansion and economic progress. When capital can be raised at reasonable rates, companies (and sovereigns) are likely to borrow or issue stock/ bonds in order to fund their investment and expansion plans; this, in turn, helps boost production, consumption, and economic growth. When capital is mobile, it is able to freely search for the best possible return opportunities. In many cases pools of capital are no longer trapped within national or regional borders but can circulate throughout the international financial system.

资金流动性

波动性

- Volatility: Financial market volatility drives investment, funding, and risk management decisions. If the financial markets were perfectly stable, there would be no risk and little need to make complicated financial decisions. The very forces of deregulation and capital mobility mentioned above have led to steady increases in the volatility of asset prices and market indicators over the past few decades, meaning that the marketplace at large has become much more dynamic. The seminal event contributing to the rise in financial volatility was the dismantling, in 1972, of the fixed exchange rate regime that had pegged the value of major currencies for nearly three decades. Once the major global economies moved to a floating exchange rate regime, financial asset volatility began to rise. Various subsequent events have compounded the volatility effect, e. g. elimination of interest rate ceilings, removal of commodity price controls, dismantling of fixed stock commissions, and deregulation of energy distribution systems, to name but a few.

技术

- Technology: Advanced computing, communications, and networking technologies have been instrumental in changing the shape of the financial landscape and there is certainly no indication that the pace of change will slow. The creation of new technology allows intermediaries, end-users, and regulators to conduct their business and duties more efficiently and accurately, generating cost savings in the process. We must, of course, remember that recurring cost savings and incremental revenues generated by new technologies represents only the cash flow portion of the NPV framework; the initial investment in technologies, which is often quite substantial, has to be factored into the equation. Nevertheless, it is clear that long-term investment in technology is often a positive NPV decision.

The dynamism created by these forces has changed the face of finance over the past few decades, and there is little to suggest that things will slow. The effects of market impact are widespread, and include:

- Greater competition: Deregulation and the race for new business in various international financial markets has intensified the level of competition amongst traditional intermediaries (banks, insurers) as well as "new" intermediaries (e. g. non-bank financial institutions, captive finance companies). What are the implications of this competition? Margin and profit compression within the group of intermediaries as they try to gain or preserve market share, and greater economic advantages for end-users, who become the beneficiaries of cut-rate pricing.

更大的竞争

- More innovation: The financial markets have long provided participants with innovative ways of solving financial problems. Intermediaries are likely to develop increasingly innovative solutions as technology advances permit more precise pricing of risks, the capital bases and risk-taking abilities of intermediaries continue to expand, and competitive pressures threaten profits. In fact, there is already substantial evidence that this is occurring: many new derivative instruments and corporate financing techniques have been created in recent years, and electronic trading conduits (e. g. electronic communications networks, or ECNs, which allow for virtually instantaneous online trading) have become commonplace, supplementing more traditional trading forums.

更多的创新

- Greater transparency: We have stressed the importance of financial statements in the analysis and decision-making process, and we've noted some of the efforts that have occurred in recent years to inject a greater level of transparency into the corporate accounts (e. g. moving off balance sheet items back on the balance sheet, disclosing more information about risks, and so on). As the major accounting approaches of the world begin to harmonize, and as investors and analysts continue to demand more information as part of the

更大的透明度

governance and accountability process, financial statement transparency should continue to improve. Competitive pressures should also play a role: as one company begins to publish increasingly detailed accounting information, peer companies may be "forced" to do the same-again, to the benefit of investors, creditors and other stakeholders.

提高效率

- Increased efficiencies: Enterprise value can be enhanced through improved efficiencies. We know that companies that are able to reduce SG&A or operating expenses and manage their working capital and risks more efficiently can boost value. Technology is, of course, central to enhanced efficiencies. We cite just a few of many examples: workplaces are increasingly automated, meaning firms spend less time and expense on manually intensive work processes; computer-based real-time inventory management is also increasingly common, allowing firms to keep a minimal amount of raw materials on hand-this leads to smaller inventories and lower inventory financing costs; e-commerce distribution/sales solutions, an important channel of revenue generation for small and large firms, are increasingly used to shrink or eliminate aspects of the physical distribution system; and so forth. Deregulation can also generate efficiencies. Since forces of deregulation lead to the opening of markets to new competitors, price competition often results. Those operating in a previously regulated market may be beneficiaries of such price competition through lower input prices. Naturally, firms that must generate revenues in a deregulating market will feel the same price pressures; to preserve profit margins they will be forced to find new ways of cutting costs or, in more extreme scenarios, merge or acquire in order to achieve economies of scale.

深化全球渗透

- Deeper global penetration: The concept of the global corporation has been mooted for many decades and appears now to be a reality. Firms with a national focus have long sought to expand their geographic presence by creating operations in other countries or acquiring/partnering with foreign entities. Deregulation and mobile capital, coupled with increasingly simple and efficient forms of technological communication across borders, means that companies choosing to establish a global footprint can do so with greater ease. This has important implications for various aspects of finance: greater opportunities to source raw materials in offshore locations; larger currency exposures that need to be managed actively; more chances to distribute goods and services to a wider audience, accompanied by faster inventory and receivables turnover; and so on.

Forces of change and market impact are summarized in Figure 10. 2.

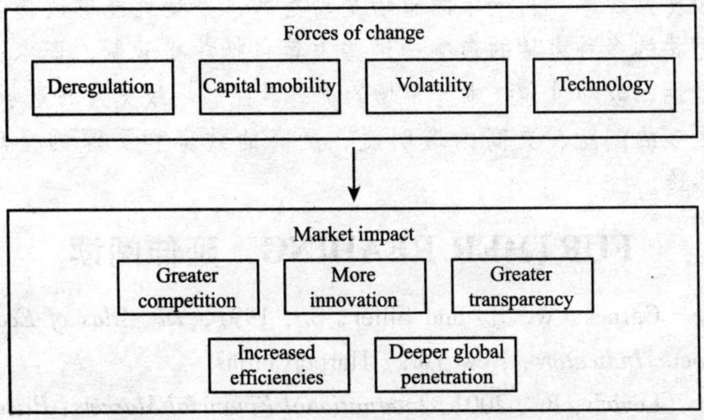

Figure 10. 2 Forces of change and market impact

Our list here is not, of course, all-inclusive. Other benefits will invariably accrue to companies that use the latest financial techniques, products and instruments to manage their daily operations. And others as yet unknown will appear over time as the landscape continues to evolve. However, many of the core financial operating principles we have discussed in this book will continue to remain a relevant, and important, cornerstone of prudent management.

摘要

全球金融体系包括的主要市场有货币、债券和贷款、股票、外汇、商品以及金融衍生品市场。金融市场这些不同部分之间的关系是复杂而且多变的：一个市场上的改变能够影响资本流入或流出另一个市场。尽管这些关系在绝大多数市场条件下是适用的，但是它们也可能在市场压力时期不同，导致以前持有的“正常行为”的观念受到质疑。提高和降低利率、通货膨胀率和经济增长率能够影响不同资产类别的表现。为了帮助管理金融市场和国民经济的各个方面，国家能够采用财政和货币政策技术。财政政策主要是与税收和支出的变化相关，它是一种中期到长期的方法。一般由国家中央银行实施的货币政策是一种管理通货膨胀和利率以及由此扩展到经济增长的短期机制。货币政策主要的工具包括银行准备金需求、公开市场操作和改变贴现率。新千年的市场是动态的，并受到能够改变其结构的多种力量的影响；这些力量包括放松管制、资本流动性、波动性和技术。市场的动态性能够导致更大的竞争、更多的创新、更高的透明度、更高的效率和更深的全球渗透。

FURTHER READING 延伸阅读

Carnes, W. S. and Slifer, S., 1991, *The Atlas of Economic Indicators*, New York: HarperCollins.

Levich, R., 2001, *International Financial Markets: Prices and Policies*, *2nd edition*, New York: McGraw-Hill.

O'Brien, T., 2005, *International Financial Economics*, *2nd edition*, Oxford: Oxford University Press.

Ross, S., Leroy, S. and Werner, J., 2000, *Principles of Financial Economics*, Cambridge: Cambridge University Press.

参考文献

Banks, E., 2005, *The Financial Lexicon*, London: Palgrave Macmillan.

—— 2004, *Alternative Risk Transfer*, Chichester, John Wiley & Sons.

—— 2002, *The Simple Rules of Risk*, Chichester: John Wiley & Sons.

Bodie, Z. and Merton, R., 1999, *Finance*, New Jersey: Prentice Hall.

Brealey, R. and Myers, S., 2002, *Principles of Corporate Finance*, New York: McGraw-Hill.

Bruner, R. and Perella, J., 2004, *Applied Mergers and Acquisitions*, New York: John Wiley & Sons.

Carey, D., Rappaport, A., Eccles, R., Aiello, R. and Watkins, M., 2001, *Harvard Business Review on Mergers and Acquisitions*, Boston: HBS Publishing.

Carnes, W. S. and Slifer, S., 1991, *The Atlas of Economic Indicators*, New York: HarperCollins.

Cox, J. and Rubinstein, M., 1985, *Options Markets*, New Jersey: Prentice Hall.

Damodaran, A., 1994, *Damodaran on Valuation*, New York: John Wiley & Sons.

Doherty, N., 1985, Corporate *Risk Management*, New York: McGraw-Hill.

Donaldson, J., 1982, *The Medium-term Loan Market*, London: Palgrave Macmillan.

Einzig, P., 1969, *The Eurobond Market*, *2nd edition*, London: St Martin's Press.

Fabozzi, F. (ed.) 2003, *Bond Markets*, 5*th edition*, New Jersey: Prentice Hall.

—— 2005, *Handbook of Fixed Income Instruments*, 7*th edition*, New York: McGraw-Hill.

Fama, E., 1972, *The Theory of Finance*, New York: Holt, Rinehart and Winston.

Fridson, M., 1995, *Financial Statement Analysis*, 2*nd edition*, New York: John Wiley & Sons.

Gaughan, P., 2002, *Mergers, Acquisitions, and Corporate Restructurings*, 3*rd edition*, New York: John Wiley & Sons.

Grabbe, O., 1995, *International Financial Markets*, New Jersey: Prentice Hall.

Hale, R., 1989, *Credit Analysis*, Singapore: John Wiley Pte.

Haugen, R., 2000, *Modern Investment Theory*, 5*th edition*, New Jersey: Prentice Hall.

Hull, J., 2005, *Options, Futures, and Other Derivatives*, 6*th edition*, New Jersey: Prentice Hall.

Kidwell, D., Peterson, R. L., Blackwell, D. W. and Whidbee, D. A., 2002, *Financial Institutions, Markets, and Money*, 8*th edition*, New York: John Wiley & Sons.

Koller, T., Goedhart, M. and Wessels, D., 2005, *Valuation*, 4*th edition*, New York: John Wiley & Sons.

Lake, R., 2003, *Evaluating and Implementing Hedge Funds Strategies*, 3*rd edition*, London: Euromoney.

Levich, R., 2001, *International Financial Markets: Prices and Policies*, 2*nd edition*, New York: McGraw-Hill.

MacDonald, R., 2005, *Derivatives Markets*, 2*nd edition*, Boston, MA: Addison-Wesely.

Maness, T. and Zietlow, J., 2004, *Short-Term Financial Management*, Mason OH: Southwestern College Publishers.

Melicher, R. and Norton, E., 2005, *Finance*, 12*th edition*, New York: John Wiley & Sons.

O'Brien, T., 2005, *International Financial Economics*, *2nd edition*, *Oxford*: *Oxford University Press*.

Oxford University Press, 1998, Dictionary *of Finance and Banking*, *2nd edition*, Oxford: Oxford University Press.

Pozen, R., 2002, *The Mutual Fund Business*, *2nd edition*, New York: Houghton Mifflin.

Ross, S., Leroy, S. and Werner, J., 2000, *Principles of Financial Economics*, Cambridge: Cambridge University Press.

Saunders, A., 2003, *Financial Institutions and Markets*, *2nd edition*, New York: McGraw-Hill.

Schwartz, R. and Francioni, R., 2004, *Equity Markets in Action*, New York: John Wiley & Sons.

Seitz, N. and Ellison, M., 2004, *Capital Budgeting and Long-Term Financial Decisions*, *4th edition*, Mason OH: Southwestern College Publishers.

Stigum, M., 1989, *Money Market Instruments*, *3rd edition*, New York: McGraw-Hill.

Vaughan, E. and Vaughan, T., 2002, *Fundamentals of Risk and Insurance*, *9th edition*, New York: John Wiley & Sons.

White, G., Sondhi, A. and Fried, D., 1994, *The Analysis and Use of Financial Statements*, New York: John Wiley & Sons.

主题词索引

A

会计　accounting
应付账款　accounts payable
应收账款　accounts receivable
收购　acquisition
资产　asset

B

资产负债表　balance sheet
银行监管机构　bank regulator

C

资本　capital
资本性账户　capital accounts
资本结构　capital structure
自保　captive
现金　cash
封闭式基金　closed-end fund
商业银行　commercial bank
商业票据　commercial paper
商品市场　commodity market
普通股　common stock
公司　company
公司理财　corporate finance
成本　cost
金融托管　custody

D

债务资产市场　debt capital market
衍生品　derivative
衍生品市场　derivative market
递延税款　deferred taxes

E

环境风险　environmental risk
交易所交易基金　exchange traded fund

F

金融　finance
筹资性现金流量　financing cash flow
财务杠杆　financial leverage
财务管理　financial management
金融参与者　financial participant
财务规划　financial planning
财务流程　financial process
财务比率　financial ratio
财务报表　financial reporting
financial statement
财务风险　financial risk
外汇市场　foreign exchange market
远期　forward

全面保险　full insurance
期货　future
期货期权　future option

G

毛利润　gross profit
总收入　gross revenues

H

对冲基金　hedge fund

I

收益表　income statement
保险　insurance
保险监管机构　insurance regulator
无形资产　intangible asset
知识产权　intellectual property
利息费用　interest income
中介机构　intermediary
保险公司　insurance company
存货　inventory
投资性现金流量　investing cash flow
投资银行　investment bank
投资基金　investment fund

L

租赁　lease
杠杆收购　leveraged buyouts（LBO）
法律风险　legal risk
流动性　liquidity
流动性比率　liquidity ratio
贷款　loan
损失敏感合同　loss sensitive contract

M

管理层收购　management buyout（MBO）
市场　market
市场份额　market share
中期和长期负债　medium and long-term debt
合并　merger
货币　money
货币市场　money market
货币政策　monetary policy

N

净收益　net income

O

经营性现金流量　operating cash flow
经营（税前）收入　operating/pre-tax income
经营风险　operating risk
期权性　optionality
开放式基金　open-end fund

P

部分保险　partial insurance
优先股　preferred stock
预付款　prepayment
盈利比率　profitability ratio
房地产/财产　property

R

利率　rate
资本重组　recapitalization

再保险公司　reinsurance company
留存收益　retained earnings
收益　return
资产收益率　return on asset
权益收益率　return on equity
风险　risk
风险管理　risk management
风险参照　risk reference

S

规模　scale
二级市场交易　secondary trading
结算　settlement
短期负债　short-term debt
短期贷款　short-term loan
短期证券　short-term security
偿付能力　solvency
投机　speculation
标准保险　standard insurance
股票市场　stock market
掉期交易　swap

U

普通银行　universal bank

V

价值　value

金融学基础——原理篇

Finance：the Basics　　by Erik Banks

图字：01－2009－4720

策　　划：龚　勋
责任编辑：龚　勋　孙　偲